Criminal Agreements and Negotiated Justice

Vinicius Gomes de Vasconcellos

Criminal Agreements and Negotiated Justice

An Analysis of the Expansion Trends Towards Consensus in Brazilian Criminal Procedure

Springer

Vinicius Gomes de Vasconcellos
Criminal Procedure Law
University of São Paulo (USP)
São Paulo, São Paulo, Brazil

ISBN 978-3-032-16961-7 ISBN 978-3-032-16962-4 (eBook)
https://doi.org/10.1007/978-3-032-16962-4

The original submitted manuscript has been translated into English. The translation was done using artificial intelligence. A subsequent revision was performed by the author(s) to further refine the work and to ensure that the translation is appropriate concerning content and scientific correctness. It may, however, read stylistically different from a conventional translation.

This Springer imprint is published by the registered company Springer Nature Switzerland AG
The registered company address is: Gewerbestrasse 11, 6330 Cham, Switzerland

Preface

This work is the result of a dissertation submitted as a partial requirement for obtaining a Master's degree in Criminal Sciences at the Pontifical Catholic University of Rio Grande do Sul, in Brazil. It was presented in November 2014 before a panel composed by Professors Nereu Giacomolli (advisor—PUC-RS), Aury Lopes Jr. (PUC-RS) and Gustavo Badaró (University of São Paulo), obtaining approval with the highest grade and commendation.

I must acknowledge, with gratitude, the institutions that contributed to the development of this dissertation: the Pontifical Catholic University of Rio Grande do Sul; the Coordination for the Improvement of Higher Education Personnel (Capes), for the full scholarship granted during the period of study; the Brazilian Institute of Criminal Sciences and the Max Planck Institute for Foreign and International Criminal Law, for the opportunity to access their libraries, which provided essential materials for the literature review on the topic addressed herein.

Ten years after the publication of the book, originally as the winning monograph of the 19th IBCCRIM Contest, the opportunity arose to prepare an English translation and publication with a foreign publisher, which prompted an update of the work. Since then, much has happened and changed regarding negotiated justice in Brazil and worldwide.

In addition to the mechanisms of the Small Claims Courts (JEC), there was an expansion of cooperation agreement and its subsequent retraction due to jurisprudential and legal limitations, reinforced by Law 13.964/19. This legislation also introduced Article 28-A into the Code of Criminal Procedure (CPP), regulating the non-prosecution agreement, which is certainly an important step towards the expansion of negotiated criminal justice.

I have dealt with such mechanisms in a detailed and systematic manner in specific works, to which I refer for further study.[1] However, without doubt, the foundation of my analysis was and continues to be the critical perspective developed in

---

[1] Vasconcellos (2023, 2024).

Barganha e Justiça Criminal Negocial, which has become a fundamental reference on the subject.

It is undeniable that the perspective defended here, in opposition to the expansion of agreements in criminal procedure, is being displaced by reality, which, as had long been anticipated, fosters the advance of negotiated justice. Undoubtedly, some of the criticisms raised are thought-provoking questions that should, at the very least, raise a red flag for legal practitioners.

On the other hand, it is also undeniable that, in limited cases and with clear boundaries, a more legitimate system of criminal agreements can be established in accordance with fundamental rights. The foundations laid out in *Barganha e Justiça Criminal Negocial* served to establish a critical and opposing view against the generalisation of plea negotiations, based on the perception that their interpretation should seek to reduce harm, through the strengthening of judicial review, the provision of adequate legal assistance, among other examples.

Thus, it was decided to essentially maintain the content already established, while adding relevant updates and expansions, especially regarding the non-prosecution agreement. Moreover, aiming to foster international debate, a section about the perception of the Brazilian model in comparison with mechanisms of conviction without trial, which are generally common in foreign legal systems, has been included.

Finally, I would like to highlight that the update and translation of this book were carried out within the scope of research funded by the Foundation for Research Support of the Federal District (FAPDF, Brazil), under call 05/2024 (Spontaneous Demand), by the University of São Paulo (USP, Brazil), through the Support Program for New Faculty Members (Ordinance PRPI n° 1032/2025) and by the Instituto Brasileiro de Ensino, Desenvolvimento e Pesquisa (IDP/DF). I therefore express my gratitude to those institutions for promoting scientific research.

São Paulo, Brazil Vinicius Gomes de Vasconcellos

Acknowledgments

The English text has been revised by Regina Fleck Bergmüller and Aline Lampert.

Contents

Chapter 1
Introduction

Amid the contemporary scenario of intense questioning regarding widespread judicial delay, numerous proposals seek to transform criminal procedure into an effective tool for the enforcement of State punitive power, essentially through the relativisation of fundamental rights and guarantees that underpin the aim of protecting public freedoms. One of the main concepts put forward in this regard concerns the ideas of procedural acceleration and simplification, which aim to shorten the path necessary for the imposition of a punitive sanction, the foremost example of which being negotiated justice,[1] essentially characterised by the mechanism of bargaining.[2] This phenomenon reflects a contemporary trend towards State recognition of the need for the accused's cooperation with the criminal prosecution, through their admission of guilt[3] and/or the incrimination of third parties, aiming to facilitate

[1] In this work, the terms negotiated, consensual, settled, pact-based, transactional, bargained, and agreed will be used interchangeably to refer to the model of criminal justice that is characterised by agreements between the prosecutor and the accused, aiming to accelerate the imposition of a conviction. For a more detailed discussion of terminological issues, see Sect. 2.1.3. Although some authors distinguish consensual justice from negotiated justice based on the presence of actual negotiation between the parties (Leite 2013, pp. 22–23), it is thought that such a criterion is not relevant for the analysis of the mechanism of bargaining, because, even in the absence of express negotiation, the core element of the phenomenon is still present: the acceptance by the accused, stepping away from a position of resistance due to expected benefit.

[2] Introductory remarks: it is worth mentioning here that, in this research, bargaining will be defined as "the procedural instrument that results in the waiver of defence through the acceptance (and possible cooperation) of the accused with the prosecution, generally presupposing their confession in exchange for some benefit (usually a sentence reduction), negotiated and agreed between the parties or only expected by the accused". For a more detailed conceptual analysis and terminological justifications, see Sect. 2.2.1.

[3] Although aware of the complexities that involve the concept of culpability in criminal dogmatics, the term "guilty plea" was chosen to broadly represent the submission of the accused to the imposition of a punishment without the proof of the crime and its authorship through due criminal process, which, albeit implicitly in certain cases, entails the acknowledgement of the accused's

V. G. de. Vasconcellos, *Criminal Agreements and Negotiated Justice*,
https://doi.org/10.1007/978-3-032-16962-4_1

accusatory activity by removing the imperative of full proof of incriminating facts—based on lawfully produced evidence by the public prosecutor—and to nullify the defensive stance of resistance to the indictment.

Given this panorama, this work aims to develop a critical analysis of the trends towards the expansion of spaces for consensus in the Brazilian criminal procedure, fundamentally guided by influences from foreign examples, as well as recurring legislative proposals and national Brazilian scholarship constructions, which seek to introduce mechanisms of broader applicability to authorise the imposition of provisional criminal sanctions in abbreviated procedures based on a limited (or non--existent) scope for defensive action, due to an alleged consent with the terms of the prosecutorial claim. In other words, the following issues are outlined: (1) What are the characteristics of negotiated justice and, specifically, of bargaining?; (2) What is its relationship with the trends towards procedural simplification and diversification, such as the provision of the principle of opportunity?; (3) What are the consequences of expanding spaces for consensus for the premises of criminal procedure?; (4) A reagreements between prosecution and defence for the imposition of criminal sanctions based on guilty pleas in exchange for benefits legitimate options within the criminal justice system of the Rule of Law?

Thus, it is important to point out that this work departs from the hypothesis that bargaining and negotiation-based mechanisms in a broader sense inevitably entail violations of fundamental premises of criminal procedure—which must necessarily be conceived as an instrument for establishing the facts in order to limit the State's punitive power[4]—by rendering the exercise of the defence unfeasible, distorting the roles of the actors within the legal-criminal field, exponentially increasing the risk of convicting innocent individuals, leading to illegitimate punishments for the exercise of the right to trial, undermining the presumption of innocence and the adversarial principle, among other criticisms. Moreover, their justifications reveal questionable legitimacy by grounding themselves in an alleged systemic need for negotiation between prosecution and defence, which conceals a symbiotic functional instrumentalisation that enables the undue expansion of State control through punitive power within a broader context of penal expansionism, in which the use of bargaining is supposedly limited and legitimised by admissibility requirements that are illusorily constructed, yet invariably inoperative in settlement practice.

liability for the alleged fact. It is thought that the term "fault" would cause confusion in the Brazilian context, as it is normally used in opposition to "intent". Furthermore, by using the term "guilty", it is assumed that the other elements of the analytical concept of crime are characterised, thus encompassing the entire criminal phenomenon. For a detailed discussion on the complex issues surrounding the category of guilty in Criminal Law, see: Buonicore (2014). Using the terminology "guilty plea": Grinover et al. (2005), pp. 42 and 164; Ferrajoli (2014), p. 691.

[4]According to Cunha Martins (2011), p. 95, "according to scholars, the constitutional framework serves as a limit to authoritarian procedural deviations, imposing a procedural system that can itself be considered a limiting apparatus to punitive power". In the same vein, Melchior (2013), p. 146, states that "the core of democracy in criminal procedure lies in the elements of the system designed to contain and restrict the exercise of punitive power, as the exercise of power itself is the unbreakable core of any democratic concern".

Bargaining is, therefore, situated within a broader framework of debate regarding certain premises of contemporary criminal procedure, where, for example, the paradigm of the compulsoriness of public criminal action is questioned with the introduction of spaces for opportunity, based on the argument that the aim of modern penal systems to provide a State punitive response to every criminal case is unfeasible in the practical implementation of the procedural model. However, procedural acceleration has not proven sufficient to meet social demands for swift sanctions, so that the very notion of due process has become an obstacle for certain legal actors.

Thus, an emblematic moment of tension in the legal-criminal field arises, as the broad characterisation of a model of negotiated criminal justice—already recurrent in various legal systems worldwide and allegedly inevitable in Brazil—exposes the doubt as to whether the "the Rule of Law" comes to an end or a "new principle" emerges.[5] In other words, jurists' discourse regarding the adoption of negotiation mechanisms ranges from the extreme characterisation of a "revolution", or "the new panacea of criminal procedure",[6] to the unveiling of a resulting "crisis of continental criminal procedure" and a "mortal blow to the liberal Rule of Law".[7] Regardless, the description of the state of affairs is undeniable: "full trial is in decline everywhere"[8]; which highlights the importance of a critical study of the topic herein proposed.

Despite this notable trend, the bargaining mechanism and the resulting negotiations in criminal justice is subject to intense criticism in the legal literature, even in countries where its practical use is indisputable, such as in the United States.[9] It is pointed out, in fact, that US courts initially rejected plea bargaining. However, through a process of gradual acceptance, various theoretical constructs were developed to justify the negotiation-based mechanism, especially due to an alleged unavoidable necessity for the functioning of contemporary criminal justice, which, latently, serves perfectly the interests of the actors in the legal-criminal field.

The statistical data on the percentage of criminal convictions obtained through bargains (with the accused's guilty plea) are both disturbing and alarming. In the US system, plea bargaining is the absolute rule, meaning that its acclaimed pure jury--based adversarial model is, in practical terms, a myth, even though it is theoretically

---

[5] "The question I wish to pose, in its straightforwardness, is the following: should conversations and agreements regarding sentencing—intended to facilitate, simplify, and consequently shorten the procedure and outcome of the trial—be considered admissible under our criminal procedural constitution (notably detailed, as is widely acknowledged) and our ordinary criminal procedural system?, Is the functionally oriented efficiency, which undoubtedly results from this, still compatible with the respect due to the principles of the Rule of Law? Does it represent—as it has been called—the 'farewell to the Rule of Law'? Or, on the contrary, could it constitute 'a new principle' for it?" (Dias 2011, p. 28).

[6] Teixeira (2000), p. 25.

[7] Schünemann (2004), p. 188; Anitua (2005), p. 142.

[8] Damaška (2010), p. 82.

[9] Turner (2009), p. 01.

guaranteed as a right to all citizens prosecuted in criminal proceedings.[10] On average, it is estimated that 90% of conviction sentences are based on guilty pleas, obtained through agreements between prosecution and defence and therefore without the need for solid and lawful incriminatory evidence, beyond reasonable doubt.[11] In this regard, 2002 data showed that in the US federal criminal system 73% of investigations resulted in indictments (that is, they are not dismissed), of which 89% led to convictions, and 96% of those were reached through agreements between the prosecution and the defence.[12] In 2013, Dervan and Edkins reported that almost 97% of convictions in the federal justice system were due to guilty plea agreements.[13]

Globally, although numerous and relevant objections are widely recognised, especially in relation to their compatibility with systems of continental origin,[14] bargaining mechanisms are being, or have been, implemented in various legal systems internationally. Some even venture the hypothesis of a "triumphant march of the North American criminal procedural model across the world",[15] given the expansion of mechanisms similar to plea bargaining throughout Europe and Latin America.

In order to systematically address this intriguing topic and its related issues, this work will be divided into three parts. Initially, the first chapter will define the fundamental premises necessary for a consistent engagement with the proposed object. For this purpose, it is essential to clarify the definitions of the principles involved in the debate about negotiated criminal justice (opportunity, legality, compulsoriness, and consensus), which are generally used in a confusing manner by both Brazilian and foreign jurists. Thus, in Sect. 2.1, the issues surrounding these concepts that hinder consistent scholarship approach will be outlined, leading to the proposal of new interpretations for these principles. Finally, the study will focus specifically on the mechanism of bargaining (Sect. 2.2), beginning with the US example, which is undoubtedly the international reference model. Its scholar and jurisprudential

---

[10] Langbein (1992), pp. 119–123. According to Milton Heumann (1981) p. 1, the well-known US "trial courts" are, in fact, "plea bargaining courts".

[11] Alschuler (1968), p. 50; Rodríguez García (1997), p. 82. Some have pointed out that such statistics reach as high as 95% (Lippke 2011, p. 1). John Langbein (1978), p. 9 states that the US criminal justice virtually solves all serious crime cases through plea bargaining noting that in certain jurisdictions this procedure accounts for 99% of trials. Candace McCoy (2005), p. 8, reported a figure of 96%. George Fisher (2003), p. 223, describes that, between 1984 and 2001, the percentage of plea bargaining in the US federal justice system rose from 84% to 94%.

[12] Turner (2009), p. 7.

[13] Dervan and Edkins (2013), p. 7.

[14] Regarding the differences between bargaining systems in legal systems of Anglo-American origin (common law) and continental (European and Latin), see: Damaška (2010), pp. 88–91; Armenta Deu (2012), pp. 133–139.

[15] Schünemann (2002), pp. 288–302.

development will allow for the proper establishment of its fundamental contours. Its concept, justifications (legitimising theories) and admissibility requirements will be analysed. In a critical fashion, the aporias of such constructions will be unveiled, especially through the depletion of justificatory arguments and the demonstration of the limiting inadequacy of the aforementioned assumptions, artificially constructed by US caselaw.

Next, the current Brazilian panorama will be addressed by describing examples of spaces for consensus in the national criminal procedure, namely the mechanisms regulated within the scope of the Small Claims Courts—"composição civil" (civil composition), "transação penal" (criminal settlement), and "suspensão condicional do processo" (conditional suspension of the criminal prosecution) (Sect. 3.1)—, "delação premiada" (turn state's evidence) (Sect. 3.2) and the "acordo de não persecução penal" (non-prosecution agreement) (Sect. 3.3). Without intending to be exhaustive, the aim is to outline an analysis of the contours of such mechanisms in their points of intersection with the characteristics of negotiated justice and the principle of opportunity, prioritising useful insights for the subsequent study of their expansion trends. Then (Sect. 3.4), an investigation into the legislative proposals for expanding spaces for consensus in Brazilian criminal justice will be developed, fundamentally based on criticism of the provisions on fast track and bargaining, regulated respectively, in Senate Bills 156/2009 (comprehensive reform of the Penal Code)[16] and 236/2012 (comprehensive reform of the Penal Code). Finally (Sect. 3.5), a comparative analysis of the Brazilian model in relation to the international scenario of expanding mechanisms for conviction without trial, similar to plea bargaining, will be presented.

In the fourth and final chapter of this work, a systematic theoretical foundation of criticisms against negotiated justice will be constructed, pointing out its insoluble aporias that violate the precepts of a democratic criminal procedure grounded in respect for the rules of due criminal process. These notes are directed at the conception of bargaining in broad terms, characterised by the accused's compliance (typically involving a confession) and the waiver of defence, which allows its applicability (with possible variations in degree) to the current Brazilian scenario and, in particular, to the previously analysed proposals for expansion.

To that end, six study topics will be addressed: (1) *Expansion of Criminal Law and the obstacle of due process of law*, which will examine the procedural commodification caused by the authorisation of agreements between the parties and the resulting relativisation of fundamental guarantees, both phenomena intrinsically related to the instrumentalisation of criminal procedure as a swift means of anticipating the exercise of punitive power in response to the demands arising from an uncontrolled expansion of State criminal intervention; (2) *Bargains, relationships and concessions,* which will unveil the distortion of the roles of the actors in the criminal system due to the primacy of their personal interests through the power of

[16] The Senate Bill 156/2009 was approved in its originating house (Senate) and referred to the Chamber of Deputies, where it was assigned the number 8045/2010. So far, there has been no final approval.

bargaining, ultimately corrupting the foundations of the procedure; (3) *The issue of the innocent and the coercibility of the proposal,* whose purpose will be to clarify the pressure inherent in the possibility of bargaining, which potentially leads to innocent people confessing out of fear of more severe punishments if they exercise the right to trial; (4) *The authoritarian procedural setback,* in which the violation of fundamental procedural principles will be exposed, such as the return of a tariffed evidence system prioritising confession and the consequent complete obstruction of the exercise of defence and adversarial rights; (5) *The imbalance of the scales between the procedural actors,* in which one of the fundamental premises of bargaining—the equality between the negotiating parties—will be weakened, in addition to exposing the undue usurpation of decision-making functions by the prosecutor, given their crucial role in determining the charged individual's guilt and punishment; and, (6) *The disappearance of the trial and the defence*, in which the possibility of waiving the right to defence and the supposed autonomy of will for the execution of the agreement will be critically examined.

Finally (Sect. 4.2), based on an empirical description of the implementation of negotiated justice within the contemporary Brazilian legal-criminal field through the mechanisms of the Small Claims Courts and the non-prosecution agreement, this section will outline some features of the practical materialisation of the criticisms previously set thereby exposing the fundamental issues inherent in agreements between prosecution and defence within the Brazilian context. Therefore, it will be assessed whether, given the characteristics of the Brazilian scenario (such as the striking selectivity and inequality reproduced by the State's punitive power), the implementation of any expansions of spaces for consensus will result in intensified aporias and, consequently, serious violations of rights and fundamental guarantees of the criminal procedure of the Rule of Law.

References

Alschuler AW (1968) The prosecutor's role in plea bargaining. Univ Chic Law Rev 36:50–112

Anitua GI (2005) El juicio penal abreviado como una de las reformas penales de inspiración estadunidense que posibilitan la expansión punitiva. In: Maier JBJ, Bovino A (comps) El procedimiento abreviado. Del Puerto, Buenos Aires

Armenta Deu T (2012) Sistemas procesales penales. La justicia penal en Europa y América. Marcial Pons, Madrid

Buonicore BT (2014) O fundamento onto-antropológico da culpa: contributo para o estudo do conteúdo material da culpabilidade na dogmática penal contemporânea. Dissertation, Pontifícia Universidade Católica do Rio Grande do Sul, Porto Alegre

Damaška M (2010) Negotiated justice in international criminal courts. In: Thaman S (ed) World plea bargaining. Consensual procedures and the avoidance of the Full Criminal Trial. Carolina Academic Press, Durham

Dervan LE, Edkins V (2013) The innocent defendant's dilemma: an innovative empirical study of plea bargaining's innocence problem. J Crim Law Criminol 103(1):1–48

Dias JF (2011) Acordos sobre a sentença em processo penal. O "fim" do Estado de Direito ou um novo "princípio"? Conselho Distrital do Porto, Porto

Ferrajoli L (2014) Direito e razão. Teoria do garantismo penal. 4 ed. RT, São Paulo
Fisher G (2003) Plea bargaining's triumph. A history of plea bargaining in America. Stanford University Press, Stanford
Grinover AP, Fernandes AS, Gomes Filho AM, Gomes LF (2005) Juizados Especiais Criminais. Comentários à Lei 9.099, de 26.09.1995. 5 ed. RT, São Paulo
Heumann M (1981) Plea bargaining. The experiences of prosecutors, judges, and defense attorneys. The University of Chicago Press, Chicago
Langbein JH (1978) Torture and plea bargaining. Univ Chicago Law Rev 46(1):3–22
Langbein JH (1992) On the myth of written Constitutions: the disappearance of criminal jury trial. Harv J Law Public Policy 15(1):119–127
Leite RV (2013) Justiça consensual e efetividade do processo penal. Del Rey, Belo Horizonte
Lippke RL (2011) The ethics of plea bargaining. Oxford University Press, Oxford
Martins RC (2011) O ponto cego do direito: The Brazilian Lessons. 2nd ed. Lumen Juris, Rio de Janeiro.
McCoy C (2005) Plea bargaining as coercion: the trial penalty and plea bargaining reform. Crim Law Q 50:1–41
Melchior AP (2013) O juiz e a prova: o sinthoma político do processo penal. Juruá, Curitiba
Rodríguez García N (1997) La justicia penal negociada. Experiencias de derecho comparado. Ediciones Universidad de Salamanca, Salamanca
Schünemann B (2002) ¿Crisis del procedimiento penal? ¿Marcha triunfal del procedimiento penal americano en el mundo? In: Schünemann B (ed) Temas actuales y permanentes del derecho penal después del milenio. Tecnos, Madrid
Schünemann B (2004) Cuestiones básicas de la estructura y reforma del procedimiento penal bajo una perspectiva global. Revista de Derecho Penal y Criminología 25(76):175–197
Teixeira CA (2000) Princípio da oportunidade. Manifestações em sede processual penal
Turner JI (2009) Plea barganing across borders. Aspen, New York

Chapter 2
Legality or Opportunity: Defining Variables and Delimiting the Boundaries of Bargaining in the Consensual Justice System

The plea bargaining mechanism is intrinsically related to underlying issues of Criminal Procedural Law, as its existence and occurrence entail unique consequences for the structuring of the founding principles of a given legal system. Therefore, before attempting a conceptual delimitation of its contours, certain preliminary clarifications are required. Firstly, in Sect. 2.1, the principles of legality, opportunity, and consensus shall be examined. We begin by highlighting the need for a revision of the definitions commonly outlined by the legal scholarship, as they result in interpretative difficulties, especially when the analytical framework is that of a Democratic Rule of Law.

Finally, Sect. 2.2 will specifically address bargaining, especially through the lens of the American example, due to its academic and jurisprudential development, as well as its perception as a source of inspiration for the introduction of similar mechanisms in foreign legal systems. In addition, input from continental models will also enrich this study, aiming to establish comprehensive concepts. Thus, adopting a critical stance intended to problematise the study of the theme of this work by exploring the concept, justifications, and requirements of bargaining. Thereby, a theoretical foundation capable of supporting the subsequent critical debates to be addressed later will be constructed.

V. G. de. Vasconcellos, *Criminal Agreements and Negotiated Justice*,
https://doi.org/10.1007/978-3-032-16962-4_2

2.1 Legality, Opportunity, and Consensus: Initial Delimitations and Problematisations

Before delimiting the contours of the plea bargaining mechanism, it is necessary to clarify preliminary issues—principles[1] that permeate the theme of negotiated justice in criminal procedure. As it will be seen, the agreement on the sentence belongs to a broader scenario of debates concerning the compulsory nature of State criminal prosecution and the spaces for discretion afforded to the prosecutorial authority to choose between refraining from indicting or pursuing an accusation in court until its final sentence. Therefore, in this first subtopic, an analysis of the figures of legality, opportunity, and consensus in criminal procedure will be developed in order to clarify the scope from characterising bargaining. However, this task proves difficult due to the disorder of meanings established by the general legal literature, which results in dissonances in the study of the theme.[2] By unveiling the dysfunctionality of the term "legality", even when confined to "procedural legality", this analysis seeks to open the way for the need to outline new parameters, or rather, to impose a rational choice between the terms "compulsoriness" and "non-compulsoriness /opportunity", which may materialise in a scenario of respect for legality or of broad discretion. Finally, the notion of "consensual justice" will be addressed, tracing the characteristics of the negotiation model between prosecution and defence aimed at imposing a penalty without trial.[3]

2.1.1 Legality and Opportunity in Criminal Procedure: An Example of Scholarly Confusion Arising from Inoperative Definitions

Based on a dichotomy structured through the opposition between two legal scenarios, scholars commonly distinguish the terms "legality" and "opportunity" with regard to the exercise of prosecutorial activity in criminal proceedings by the Public

[1] For an analysis on the characterisation of opportunity as a principle, see: Teixeira (2000), pp. 24–27; Antonucci (2021); Le et al. (2025).

[2] For a historical analysis of these definitions and their applications (and resulting distortions), see: Divan (2014), p. 205–217.

[3] It is important to highlight the scholarly disagreement regarding the characterisation of the measure imposed through a criminal settlement as a penalty. This issue will be analysed in Sect. 3.1 of this work. However, one can affirm that the imposition of an obligation other than a custodial sentence, as a consequence of the commission of an alleged minor offence, even without the full course of a trial, attests to the intrinsic nature of criminal penalty imposed by the State. The designation of such an imposition by a name other than "penalty" occurs under the unjustified and unsuccessful pretense of warding off criticism against punishment without due process. On this subject, see: Karam (2004), pp. 100–106.

Prosecutor's Office.[4] Starting from the conception of legality characteristic of Public Law, according to which public authorities are subject to the Law in their action,[5] it passes through its manifestation in the substantive criminal sphere. Such a construction entails various consequences for the study of criminal law,[6] its main expression being the *nullum crimen, nulla poene sine lege*, which limits the possibility of arbitrariness "by subjecting criminal intervention to a strict principle of legality, whose essential content consists in the notion that there can be no crime or penalty that does not result from a prior, written, strict and certain law".[7]

The *principle of legality* extends into the procedural domain, generally identified as a consequence of the substantive manifestation previously described, because, according to Santiago Martínez, "the *nullum crimen* is the limit that the person in charge of exercising the criminal action has in the prosecution of crimes. In other words, if there is no conduct "criminalised by law, the Public Prosecutor's Office cannot proceed with the criminal charge against the person".[8] Based on such a negative finding, scholars usually conclude that there is a mandatory criminal proceeding with a charge whenever an offence is detected.[9]

Therefore, according to most scholars, the principle of legality within criminal procedure corresponds to the compulsoriness to prosecute,[10] or, in the words of Jacinto Coutinho, "it is common practice to treat (the principle of compulsoriness) as the principle of legality, as it establishes a duty on the official prosecution authority".[11] He thus characterises "the idea that the Public Prosecutor's Office is obliged to proceed and bring charges in relation to all offences of which it has become aware and for which it has managed to gather sufficient evidence during the investigation".[12] Therefore, there is a duty to charge arising from the law that is imposed when there are sufficient indications of the existence and perpetration of a criminal offence,[13] which cannot be influenced or waived by discretionary

[4] As pointed out by Carlos Adérito Teixeira (2000), p. 48, "the legal-constitutional framework of the opportunity is outlined, as its background, around the principle of legality, essentially directed, in this text, towards the Public Prosecutor's Office".

[5] Armenta Deu (1991), p. 184. On the principle of legality in administrative law, according to Hely Lopes Meirelles (2006), p. 87, "legality, as a principle of public administration (CF, art. 37, caput), means that the public administrator is, in all of their official activity, subject to the mandates of the law and the demands of the common good, from which they may not depart or deviate, under penalty of committing an invalid act and incurring disciplinary, civil and criminal liability, as the case may be". On the contours of legality in contemporary legal thought, see: Bergalli (1998), pp. 58–63.

[6] Roxin (1997), pp. 177–206.

[7] Dias (2011), p. 177.

[8] Martínez (2002), p. 524.

[9] Costa (2001), p. 39.

[10] Teixeira (2000), p. 35.

[11] Coutinho (2001), p. 41.

[12] Dias (2004), p. 126.

[13] Anitua (2010), p. 37.

considerations or by motives unrelated to the mere assessment of the existence of the offence based on the evidence obtained.[14]

In such a scenario, the principle of legality[15] entails several consequences for Criminal Procedural Law,[16] since, in view of the obligation to initiate the criminal prosecution of all offences, there is also the prohibition of withdrawal, retraction and pardon of the accused by the Public Prosecutor's Office.[17] In light of the identification of such effects in the national context, the majority of national legal literature points to the adoption of the principle of legality by the Brazilian criminal procedural framework.[18] According to Scarance Fernandes, although not backed by the constitution, the compulsoriness was adopted by the Code of Criminal Procedure of 1941, as articles 42 and 576 attest that, once the charge is made or the appeal is lodged, the prosecutor cannot withdraw from the case.[19]

In contrast to the principle of legality,[20] "another side of the same coin",[21] arises the *principle of opportunity*. According to Armenta Deu, "any conception of the principle of opportunity that is adopted must inevitably derive from the principle of legality in its procedural aspect".[22] Adérito Teixeira even argues for the non-existence of such a definition, since this conceptualisation is based exclusively on a reference to the principle of legality.[23] However, it is both relevant and possible to delimit an acceptable concept of opportunity,[24] even if diluted amidst the controversial issues that will be pointed out later. According to Montero Aroca, one can say, in general terms, that opportunity implies the "recognition of the power granted to

---

[14] "The principle of compulsoriness, then, consists in the requirement that every fact with a delinquent appearance must necessarily result in the development of a criminal investigation, under conditions of equality and without resorting to discretionary criteria to define the exercise of criminal action", Rivera and Araque (2010), pp. 22–23.

[15] In view of the description of most scholars' stance, in this section the terms "legality" and "compulsoriness" will be used interchangeably, in opposition to "opportunity" and "discretion", since this reflects the practice of the aforementioned scholar current. As it will be seen, such thinking is criticised in this work, so that later (Sect. 2.1.2) different meanings will be assigned to these terms.

[16] On the effects of legality in criminal proceedings, also see: Hassemer (1988), pp. 8–9.

[17] Cafferata (1998), pp. 26–27.

[18] In this regard: Tovo and Tovo (2008), pp. 72–74; Silva (2000), p. 32; Jardim (1998), pp. 92–99. Describing the dominant position of Brazilian legal literature in favour of adopting the principle of compulsoriness: Prado (2014), p. 22.

[19] Fernandes (2005), p. 263.

[20] Contrast here is understood as directly related, but not always opposite, since, as it will be seen, the principle of opportunity "positions itself as either opposed to legality or as a correlate or, simply, a corrective or a means of flexibilising it" (Armenta Deu 1991, p. 185).

[21] Anitua, Borinsky (1999), p. 450.

[22] Armenta Deu (1999), p. 187. Although the view is widely held, Alberto Binder (2005), pp. 205–209, criticises this premise, fostering a debate that will be resumed in Sect. 2.1.2 of this work.

[23] Teixeira (2000), pp. 34–35.

[24] "In contrast to this paradigm, the principle of opportunity does not present a single model. It is fundamentally characterised by an idea of malleability, pragmatism and utilitarianism [...]" Costa 2001, p. 39.

the holder of the criminal action of the faculty to dispose of its exercises in accordance with certain circumstances, regardless of whether the existence of a punishable act committed by a determined perpetrator has been established".[25]

Although commonly defined as the inverse of the principle of legality, such a simplification masks the complexity of the issue, as the study of opportunity reveals numerous meanings and characterisations attributed to it. Some scholars identify this principle with discretion,[26] that is, a decision guided by the prosecutor's subjective criteria.[27] Therefore, in this conception, opportunity would be identified precisely by the absence of requirements set out in law. On the other hand, it is argued that such discretion can never mean arbitrariness, but rather "a power of choice of paths, solutions and measures allowed by law",[28] always tending towards substantial binding, whose use must be grounded in law.[29]

Thus, the main point of questioning is revealed here: does the legal definition of criteria for refraining from prosecution characterise a scenario of adopting the principle of legality or opportunity? Moreover, this legal provision, even if objectively described, will inevitably involve margins of interpretation.[30] Here arises the attempt to differentiate between discretion and indeterminate legal concepts, the latter being characterised by the possibility of control.[31] In any case, the difficulty of delimiting and applying the concepts presented here is evident.

Furthermore, the definition of opportunity can be broad or narrow. In the former, it manifests itself in both the criminal procedural and substantive spheres,[32] for instance, in cases of private or public conditional criminal action and victim forgiveness.[33] Also, in broad terms, one might consider the inclusion of "all modes of implementing dispute resolution pathways, available to a wide range of entities

[25] Montero Aroca (2008), p. 302. Similarly: Caeiro (2000), p. 32.

[26] Silva (2000), p. 55.

[27] Dias (1997), p. 478.

[28] Teixeira (2000), p. 33.

[29] Andrés Ibañez (1997), p. 24.

[30] "In the factual and legal assessment of the offence, various conceptions are naturally possible, so that in the decision of the Public Prosecutor's Office there is—as in every genuinely legal decision—an unavoidable margin of discretion" (Dias, 2011, p.132). On this space for interpretation and the criteria for applying the Brazilian penal transaction, see: Prado (2006c), pp. 155–156.

[31] "Indeed, discretion implies a plurality of equally fair solutions, which is the same as a plurality of legally indifferent solutions. Precisely because they are indifferent to the law, it does not impose a concrete solution. On the other hand, in indeterminate legal concepts there is a single just solution. Sometimes it is difficult to delimit it, but, in any case, there is a single just solution" (Delgado Barrio 1990, p. 151). See also: Armenta Deu (1991), pp. 181–183. Perfecto Ibañez (1997), p.191, criticises the use of the distinction between discretion and indeterminate legal concepts (a characteristic institution of Administrative Law), since "in a penal system governed by the principle of legality, forms of action of the first type would always have to be excluded, leaving only the possibility of occurrence of those of the second kind".

[32] Armenta Deu (1991), p. 191.

[33] Giacomolli (2006), p. 65.

(Government, Providers, Schools, Churches, etc.)",[34] that is, the diversified treatment of the social conflict generated by the criminal act, thus encompassing means of diversification.[35] On the other hand, in a narrow sense, attention is paid to the activity of the Public Prosecutor's Office as a State prosecution authority,[36] whereas opportunity would pertain to the "procedural and processual forms, expedited and simplified, of dispute resolution",[37] at its initiative. Armenta Deu outlines the characteristics that attest to the manifestation of the principle of opportunity, in an also narrow view[38]: subjectively, it is directed at public actors (prosecutor and judicial body)[39]; objectively, it refers to the essential content of the obligations of such actors in the criminal case, "ranging from the obligation to prosecute upon knowledge of all crime reports to its finalisation through a resolution, as provided for in the criminal procedural law".[40]

In an effort to ease such aporias,[41] especially aiming at reconciling the particularities of the principle of opportunity with the rules of legal systems historically based on legality,[42] a new concept was developed: *regulated discretion*.[43] This refers to the situation in which the principle of compulsoriness is softened in a limited way, only in cases explicitly provided for by law and according to criteria set therein. In other words, "within the general framework of formally recognising the principle of legality, limitations—whether broader or narrower—are introduced to its application by granting the Public Prosecutor's Office the possibility of waiving the

[34] Teixeira (2000), p. 18.

[35] "In this sense, one possibility to 'diversify' the treatment of the social conflict represented by the punishable act consists in avoiding the traditional penal solution and, at the same time, allowing the victim to obtain their reparation" (Bovino 2005, p. 32).

[36] "In a stricter conception, we are facing a system that admits opportunity when it is lawful for the Public Prosecutor's Office not to pursue all the criminal facts submitted to it, or when it can address them by dispensing with relevant factual circumstances, from the criminal-legal perspective, according to objective norms, or when it is allowed not to adhere to legality to legally assess these facts" (Giacomolli 2006, p. 68).

[37] Teixeira (2000), p. 18.

[38] Armenta Deu (1991), p. 208.

[39] Arguing that opportunity only applies to the acts of public actors, Armenta Deu's concept excludes various manifestations commonly highlighted by scholars, such as private and public prosecutions dependent on the victim's representation. This issue will be further addressed later, in Sect. 2.1.2 of this work.

[40] Armenta Deu (2012), p. 130.

[41] "With this term, the aim is to avoid the criticisms directed at the principle of opportunity, which stem from the principle of legality being the guiding principle of our legal system" (Armenta Deu 1991, pp. 210–211).

[42] The issue of reconciling mechanisms based on the principle of opportunity, such as conditional suspension of the criminal prosecution, began to gain traction especially in Germany starting in 1965, when these mechanisms were introduced without abandoning legality as the general rule. For more on this, see: Jardim (1998), pp. 76–79; Armenta Deu (1991), pp. 43–85.

[43] Regulated opportunity, which can also be referred to as mitigated, conditioned, limited or attenuated compulsoriness (Silva 2000, p. 59).

exercise of criminal prosecution".[44] According to Armenta Deu, "the term 'regulated' implies that the law itself will set the conditions for applying the principle of opportunity and, thus, it would not constitute an exception, but rather a variety of legality itself".[45] However, such term has been criticised by legal scholars, who argue that its use does not fully resolve the issued mentioned above.[46] According to Silva Jardim, mitigated compulsoriness "cannot really exist, because, either we have strict compulsoriness, or it comes paired with opportunity in the cases enumerated by law, or, rarely, discretion becomes the general rule".[47] Furthermore, Armenta Deu points out that the expression "regulated opportunity" is, on one hand, contradictory in itself[48] and, on the other, an inappropriate borrowing of concepts typical of administrative law.[49]

Given the above, the supposed simplicity of the definitions presented prove s to be illusory. In short, criminal proceedings would be governed by the principle of legality when the prosecuting authority is required to file charges and thereby initiate judicial prosecution whenever there are sufficient indications of the existence and perpetration of an offence. Conversely, the principle of opportunity would apply in a scenario where, faced with such a situation, the Public Prosecutor is authorised to act at their discretion, deciding whether or not to prosecute.[50] However, such a straightforward distinction cannot be upheld, as relying on this dichotomy without deeper analysis inevitably leads to confusion when addressing the issue. The main difficulty lies in defining the criteria for making such a decision: if the law were to establish certain criminal-policy-based requirements for authorising the initiation of criminal proceedings, going beyond the mere verification of sufficient indications of the existence and perpetration of an offence, would that amount to adopting the principle of opportunity?[51] In other words, is it possible to conceive of an opportunity model that still respects legality (here understood as the subordination of the

[44] Andrés Ibañez (1997), p. 27.

[45] Armenta Deu (1991), p. 211.

[46] "In my view, the use of the qualifier 'regulated' does not have—as it seems to be intended—a healing effect in the sense that the simple use of it would result in alleviating possible violations of the principle of legality that could occur" (Armenta Deu 1991, p. 211). See also: Giacomolli (2014), p. 278.

[47] Jardim (1998), p. 93.

[48] In this sense, also: Montero Aroca (2008), p. 313.

[49] Armenta Deu (1991), p. 211. Also, Nereu Giacomolli (2006), p. 70, clarifies that "the expression 'regulated opportunity' is not correct because it is not the opportunity, in itself, that is subject to a rule: the judgement of opportunity always consists in saying what is considered opportune, even if it does not coincide with what, in principle, is inferred from the legal norm".

[50] In summary, Goldschmidt (2010), p. 782, points out that, according to the principle of legality, "in all cases where there is a punishable act, prosecution must be mandatory" and, on the other hand, according to the principle of opportunity, "considerations of opportunity, especially public interest, must also be taken into account".

[51] As it will be further explored, Alberto Binder (2005), p. 206, defines legality as "the obligation that weighs on public officials to exercise criminal action in all cases provided for by law as offences, other than the exceptions also established"; in other words, he argues that the principle

State actor to the law)? Moreover, given the space for discretion inherent in any interpretation of legal texts when determining the prosecutor's stance, does that entail a weakening of legality? It becomes clear that the earlier conceptual framework is not capable of adequately answering such questions. Therefore, it is necessary to seek new ways of outlining the distinction between opportunity and legality.

2.1.2 *Mandatory Prosecution and Opportunity in a Scenario of Legality or Discretion: Shedding Light in the Search for Conceptual Precision and Proposing Definitions*

Based on the considerations outlined in the previous section, the aim was to expose the insufficiency of the opposition between opportunity and legality in the terms commonly proposed by legal scholarship. By dichotomising such conceptions and equating the latter with compulsoriness, a critical analysis of the issue, grounded in the pursuit of alignment with the premises of the Rule of Law, is rendered unfeasible.[52] Therefore, this section will delve deeper into the theoretical constructions that attempt to draw distinctions within the topic under study—but which, in our view, fail to satisfactorily overcome the previously identified issues—before outlining a new perspective on such definitions. A framework will be developed to distinguish between the principles of legality and compulsoriness in the field of criminal procedure, thereby enabling a better understanding of opportunity (and consensual) mechanisms in a democratic criminal justice system—one that necessarily limits and conditions the exercise of punitive power to the legally defined rules of the game.

Initially, it is important to stress the need to recognise that, on the one hand, there is legality, which legally defines (and thereby limits) the scope of action of the actors in the criminal field—especially those who seek to impose the State's punitive power. The compulsoriness of the prosecution, by contrast, is of a different nature: in our view, it may admit exceptions within the framework of legality, that is, as long as such exceptions are provided for by law. To a certain extent, Alberto Binder develops this line of reasoning when criticising the denomination ("principle of legality") commonly used to represent the obligation of public officials to initiate criminal proceedings in all cases that fall within the legal definition of an offence,

of compulsoriness (legality) can still be upheld even when charges are not filed, as long as such an exception is provided for by law.

52 Criticising the use of the term "legality" as a synonym to compulsoriness, Gabriel Divan (2014), p. 293, points out that "one could argue for the abandonment of the term 'legality' in the discussion now highlighted, as it thus approaches a view that suggests confronting 'illegality' through a ('compulsory') State proposal for action—which may evoke traces of the ill-fated procedural configuration of punitive claim (the process as conformation/endorsement of a *ius puniendi* demanded by the prosecutor)".

except for the exceptions also established by law.[53] In other words, the author clarifies that there is indeed a distinction between legality and compulsoriness. Ventura Leite also seeks to distinguish these criteria, pointing out that "the compulsoriness of criminal action can coexist with criteria of opportunity", and that, in such a scenario, the Public Prosecutor's Office must act within the limit s dictated by legality.[54]

Furthermore, Jacinto Coutinho questions the immediate relationship between compulsoriness and legality by suggesting the impossibility of directly linking both notions, stating that "it is necessary to consider that such a principle of compulsoriness, even if it could be thought of as tied to the principle of legality, must be relativised [...]".[55] Finally, Silva Jardim expressly points out the distinction between these concepts, stating that they are mistakenly used interchangeably by most scholars, while the use of the term "compulsoriness" makes it clearer "that the legal duty of the Public Prosecutor's Office to initiate criminal proceedings is, in fact, a consequence of the principle of legality itself, which, from a broader perspective, guides the conduct of public authorities in the so-called Rule of Law".[56]

It can be said that the use of the term "legality" to refer to the obligatoriness of prosecution of criminal action causes difficulties in interpreting legal literature and thus hinders an objective debate on the topic at hand. Adérito Teixeira, for example, defines the principle of legality as compulsoriness, pointing out that "such a principle means that the Public Prosecutor's Office must conduct an inquiry and bring charges whenever the legal-factual assumptions of the crime and the requirements for the admissibility of criminal action are met".[57] However, he then points out that the principle of legality is the hallmark of the Portuguese system, since "the Public Prosecutor's Office must act under the sign of the law and not according to criteria of opportunity, whether they are of public order, financial, statistical or other".[58] In other words, the same term is used to characterise different legal phenomena, as "legality" is often employed indiscriminately by various authors to represent both submission to the law and the compulsoriness of public criminal prosecution.

Perhaps in an attempt to resolve such a discrepancy, some authors distinguish criminal and procedural legality,[59] the latter being identified with compulsoriness.[60]

---

[53] "Indeed, the very name of the principle of legality in procedural matters is a confusing name that causes problems and should be abandoned" (Binder 2005, p. 206). However, the author develops his in-depth critique while still employing such terminology, so that, in our view, his critique is in fact targeted at the compulsory nature of public criminal prosecution rather than at the principle of legality itself.

[54] Leite (2013), pp. 40–41.

[55] Coutinho (2001), p. 42.

[56] Jardim (1998), p. 48.

[57] Teixeira (2000), p. 48.

[58] Teixeira (2000), p. 49.

[59] Martínez (2002), p. 518.

[60] "[...] the principle of procedural legality imposes on the competent State authorities the duty to initiate criminal prosecution in all cases where there is knowledge of a report concerning the possible commission of a punishable act subject to public prosecution" (Bovino 2005, p. 15).

Furthermore, Pedro Caeiro puts forward an even more artificial construction, attempting to distinguish "respect for legality" and the "principle of legality".[61] Certainly, none of the proposals adequately overcomes the previously highlighted aporias, and both end up fostering similar interpretative uncertainties. As Lopes Jr. points out when analysing the inappropriateness of transplanting the conditions of civil action into criminal action, each word carries a semantic load that limits its range of possible meaning; when one engages in "conceptual gymnastics ", the original conceptual framework is distorted, making it impossible to provide an adequate response to the issue under study.[62] This view is also applicable to the aforementioned proposals, which do not distort the critical weight of the term "legality", but also fail to successfully represent the notion of compulsoriness.

Given the above, it becomes essential to adopt a new perspective on the principles addressed here. The *principle of legality* is understood to require that State actors within the criminal justice system ground their conduct and decisions in accordance with and, therefore, based on legal provisions, constraints and limitations provided for by law.[63] In other words, both in the substantive and procedural criminal spheres, albeit with different implications, such a principle is essentially about linking the exercise of punitive power, and thus the conduct of criminal justice actors, to the legal norms defined by law.[64]

Conversely,[65] the *compulsory nature of public prosecution* requires the pursuit of all facts that come to the attention of public authorities and qualify as punishable

[61] "Indeed, there is a tendency to, on the one hand, confuse the *principle* of legality with *respect* for (or the *defence* of) legality [...]" (Caeiro 2000, pp. 31–32).

[62] Lopes Jr. (2012), pp. 369–372.

[63] In this sense, although without refining the distinctions proposed here, Armenta Deu (1991), p. 189, appears to take a stand: "By governing such a principle (legality), any discretion regarding the convenience or opportunity of prosecution in the specific case is excluded. The sole criterion for the prosecuting authority must be the Law". Similarly, Nereu Giacomolli (2006), p. 50, states that "legality, in a stricter sense, is the principle which establishes that criminal prosecution, the assertion of an accusatory claim, and the support of the accusation cannot depend on the subjective will of those authorities that have the legal duty to act in accordance to the existing legal order".

[64] "From the substantial perspective, the principle of legality is conceived with the precept of: 'nullum crimen, nulla poena sine lege scripta, stricta, certa et praevia', meaning that 'there is no criminal offence, penalty, or security measure without written, strict, certain and prior criminal law. From the procedural perspective, the principle of legality is expressed by the axiom: 'nemo damnetur nisi per legale iudicium; nemo iudex sine lege', meaning that 'no one may be punished except in accordance with a lawful trial, and that criminal law may only be applied by authorities and judges established by law for that purpose '"(Rivera, Araque. 2010, p. 22).

[65] "It is true that the principle of opportunity has been traditionally regarded as the opposite of the principle of legality. However, it is necessary to emphasise that the connection between the principle of opportunity and the exercise of criminal prosecution should not be regarded as conflicting issues, but rather that what truly stands in opposition to the Public Prosecutor's exercise of opportunity is the principle of compulsory prosecution (the necessity to prosecute)" (Ortiz Pradillo, 2014, p. 387).

under the current legal framework.[66] In other words, in such a scenario, no utilitarian rationale or consideration of the minor seriousness of the criminal offence may be used to justify refraining from filing charges or initiating criminal proceedings,[67] even if such discretion is provided for by law.

However, as Geraldo Prado points out, "it is a matter of bringing an accusatory claim, but this does not oblige the Public Prosecutor's Office to relentlessly pursue the conviction of the accused", as there is no legal duty to appeal an acquittal or to unconditionally request a conviction in final arguments.[68] Thus, it is important to note that the exclusion of facts that lack good cause[69] for the filing of a criminal action[70]—such as petty[71] or insignificant offences—, or the lack of sufficient evidence to support a charge,[72] does not contradict the principle of compulsoriness. This is because its insignificance leads to a typicality and, therefore, to the non--existence of an offence,[73] making prosecution illegitimate (and prosecution is only compulsory in situations that legally qualify as criminal offences). In other words, as Silva Jardim points out, one can only speak of compulsoriness when the duty of the Public Prosecutor to act is effectively triggered.[74] Therefore, even though criteria of opportunity are excluded in cases of public prosecution, the bringing charges "is not placed absolute, as judicial protection is only granted when, in exercising the

---

[66] It is worth pointing out the scholarly debates concerning the minimum requirements for establishing the duty to prosecute: these include "legal-factual prerequisites of incrimination and requirements for the admissibility of the action" (Teixeira, 2000, p. 48); the "punishable act" (Lynch, 1998, p. 314); the presence of "all elements of the crime" (Paschoal, 2001, p. 115); as well as the need to consider unlawfulness and guilt (Jardim, 1998, p. 43).

[67] Bovino (2005), p. 16.

[68] Prado (2006c), p. 154.

[69] On the good cause in the Brazilian criminal procedure, see: Moura (2001); Divan (2014); Jardim (1998), pp. 42–43.

[70] Thus, one may question the conclusion of Scarance Fernandes (2006), p. 263,—according to which the Brazilian Code of Criminal Procedure (CPP) adopts the principle of compulsoriness except when one of the circumstances of art. 43 (now art. 395 following the 2008 reform), such as the absence of good cause, is present. Given the above, there can be no exception to compulsoriness in cases where the duty to prosecute does not arise.

[71] It is worth noting that Armenta Deu (1991), p. 23, appears to use a broader concept of petty crimes (not only insignificant and atypical), defining them as of a "patrimonial and economic nature, one of their most characteristic features being their minor relevance—hence the term 'petty crimes'—as well as the frequency of their commission" and as "conducts covered by in criminal laws whose reproach worthiness is scarce and whose protected legal interest is considered of lesser relevance". However, in Brazil, petty crimes are generally regarded as those of insignificant nature (Zaffaroni, Pierangeli 2008, pp. 484–485).

[72] Jardim (1998), p. 55.

[73] On the discussion regarding the basis of the non-punishability of petty (insignificant) crimes, see: Dias (2004), pp. 676–667; Zaffaroni, Pierangeli (2008), pp. 484–485. On the instrumentalisation of procedural control over the fragmentariness of punitive power through the mechanism of good cause, see: Lopes Jr. (2012), pp. 380–383.

[74] Jardim (1998), p. 54. According to the author, in cases where one of the grounds for summary rejection is present, what in fact exists is the opposite—a duty not to act.

action, the so-called preliminary issues are fulfilled, including the conditions for action and the procedural prerequisites that can be assessed in the admissibility judgment".[75]

Opportunity (or non-compulsoriness) is defined in opposition to compulsoriness, as it allows for the non-filing of charges or the suspension of the criminal prosecution at the discretion of the State prosecuting authority (usually with the defences's consent) based on utilitarian, criminal-political, economic criteria, among others,[76] even when the evidentiary basis is sufficient to establish the existence and perpetration of an offence. Such decision-making parameters may be strictly defined by law, thus respecting the principle of legality,[77] or left to the wide discretion of the prosecutor.[78] Clearly, only the former is acceptable in a democratic criminal system.

The principle of opportunity, therefore, does not necessarily conflict with the requirement to uphold legality, which is intrinsic to the Rule of Law, but rather qualifies it and creates exceptions (legally regulated and limited) to its compulsory nature.[79] Thus, even when spaces for opportunity are recognised, according to Geraldo Prado, "the freedom of the Public Prosecutor's Office will always be guided by the principle of legality, protecting the community from the personal decisions of each member of that institution".[80]

It is important to mention the existence of scholars, such as Silva Jardim in the passage cited,[81] who maintain the necessary correlation between the principles of legality and compulsoriness, the latter being not accidental but inherent to the former.[82] In this regard, Andrés Ibañez criticises the claim that criteria of opportunity

[75] Coutinho (2001), p. 42.

[76] "Given the recognition of the empirical impossibility of prosecuting all offenses that presuppose the validity of the principle of procedural legality, the principle of opportunity arises, according to which, when punishable acts become known, one may not initiate or suspend criminal prosecution, for reasons of convenience, utility or a more efficient organisation of resource allocation" (Bovino 2005, p. 25).

[77] "Therefore, the introduction of the principle of opportunity is not opposed to the principle of legality, as it does not breach legality when it is the law itself that determines the criteria under which a criminal proceeding should be initiated or maintained" (Ortiz Pradillo 2014, p. 387–388).

[78] Similarly, Alberto Bovino (2005), pp. 25–28, identifies two models for the application of the principle of opportunity: one in which it constitutes the rule and is commonly characterised as virtually unrestricted; and another in which it is the exception to the rule of compulsoriness, usually having its criteria defined by law. Also in: Anitua, Borinsky (1999), p. 451.

[79] In the same vein, Perfecto Ibañez (1997), pp. 27–28, observes that "it is no longer a matter of legality *versus* opportunity, but rather of accepting this second criterion as informing certain procedural instruments available to the Public Prosecutor's Office, affecting only the compulsory nature of prosecution".

[80] Prado (2006b), p. 113.

[81] "The legal duty of the Public Prosecutor's Office to initiate criminal proceedings is, in fact, a direct corollary of the principle of legality itself, which, from a broader perspective, governs the actions of public authorities in the so-called Rule of Law" (Jardim 1998, p. 48).

[82] Andrés Ibañez (1997), p. 26. "The application of the law cannot be subordinated to extra or meta-normative determinations, hence the principle of criminal legality necessarily implies the obligation to prosecute, provided that certain sufficiently defined assumptions are met" (Andrés Ibañez

challenge legality less than they challenge the compulsoriness, emphasising that "one must not forget that the latter is an essential and inseparable consequence of the former".[83] However, under the framework proposed here, it becomes clear that such a necessary implication is broken, whereas respect for legality is not violated in cases of non-prosecution based on criteria of opportunity expressly provided for by law.

The proposal for a new perspective on the concepts examined here, although sharing the common goal of reconciling the introduction of opportunity criteria within legal systems governed by the principle of legality, does not align with the construction of *regulated opportunity* previously analysed and criticised. On one hand, this term proves inadequate to overcome the identified aporias, as it is usually employed within definitions fraught with the aforementioned confusions.[84]

Furthermore, it is important to make a caveat to justify the terminology employed here. As Montero Aroca points out, "it makes no sense to say that a decision based on opportunity, that is, founded on what is considered most appropriate in a specific case, can amount to subjection to the provisions of a norm".[85] It is undeniable that, by adopting the term "opportunity" in the sense proposed by the author, the introduction of opportunity criteria becomes irreconcilable with respect for legality. Thus, the term *non-obligation,* as opposed to *obligation*, would be more appropriate[86] when authorising the non-filing of an indictment or the suspension of criminal proceedings based, for example, on utilitarian, criminal-political, or economic criteria. This would be the ideal approach. However, given the near-universal jurists' adherence to the term "opportunity", the present proposal is structured around its use, thereby enabling reconciliation with compliance to criteria established by law.

Given the foregoing, it is concluded that a distinction exists between the meanings of the principles of legality and compulsoriness, and that there is no necessary connection between them. Accordingly, it becomes possible to envisage the characterisation of spaces for opportunity/non- obligation[87] within a framework of legality, where compulsoriness retains its structuring and general role as the rule.[88] Such a framework would arise from the objective and exhaustive definition, by law, of the

---

1997, pp. 22–23). Although the first part of this assertion is accepted, it is thought that there is no necessary implication between legality and compulsoriness.

[83] Andrés Ibañez (2001), p. 27.

[84] Particularly notable is the conflation of the concepts of legality and compulsoriness, thereby presenting opportunity as opposed to legality, which hinders a proper analysis of opportunity as opposed to legality, which hinders a proper analysis of the subject under consideration.

[85] Montero Aroca (2008), p. 313.

[86] On this: Gazoto (2003), pp. 93–112.

[87] Opportunity would therefore be defined as the "faculty vested in the holder of the criminal action to decide, under certain conditions, whether to exercise it, irrespective of the belief in the existence of a punishable fact committed by a specific perpetrator" (Gimeno Sendra 1987, p. 7).

[88] "In this regard, the principle of opportunity merits recognition, along with its limitation by law, within a system that adopts compulsoriness as a rule" (Pereira 2002, p. 30).

circumstances in which, although there is a minimum necessary grounds of existence and perpetration of a punishable act, the State prosecutor may justifiably refrain from initiating criminal proceedings in accordance with legally specified criteria of a utilitarian, criminal-political, economic etc.; in other words, criteria that extend beyond the mere verification of a fact punishable under criminal law and of minimal evidence to support an indictment.[89]

Therefore, the possibility of a scenario of *legally regulated opportunity* arises.[90] In this regard, Nereu Giacomolli notes that "when the legal system itself permits and regulates a certain discretionary power, it may be said that one is faced with a regulation of a judgement of opportunity, albeit subject to judicial review".[91]

Such differentiation aids in understanding[92] the classification of criminal proceedings whose initiation depends on the victim (private prosecution or conditional public prosecution).[93] At this juncture, employing the prevailing concepts of opportunity and legality, divergences amongst scholars persist: on the one hand, it is argued that such cases constitutes expressions of opportunity.[94]

Conversely, Armenta Deu notes that these principles pertain to the powers and limits of public authorities, such that the option granted by the legal system for the victim to decide whether or not to initiate criminal proceedings does not constitute a manifestation of the principle of opportunity, as it involves a private decision.[95] This exposes yet another problematic aspect arising from the commonly employed

[89] "The discretionary powers of the Public Prosecutor's Office are confined to the possibility of renouncing criminal prosecution, either by not initiating the corresponding lawsuit or by withdrawing from its exercise, when permitted after initiation; in any event, the conditions for applying the principle of opportunity will be exhaustively enumerated in law, whether procedural or substantive, and, as a general rule, its exercise will be subject to judicial approval" (Guariglia 1993, p. 92).

[90] "Thus, the criteria of opportunity would stand opposed to the principle of compulsoriness, but would in no way affect legality, since the public prosecutor would act out of convenience by refraining from pursuing certain lawsuits, yet supported by the legal framework that governs the principle of legality, and always provided that judicial review is contemplated—as in the Colombian case, where the judge responsible for guarantees ensures the rationality and legality of such acts" (Rivera 2010, p. 23).

[91] Giacomolli (2006), p. 72. The author, however, continues: "In these cases, one is not acting according to the principle of opportunity—understood purely and solely as a principle—but rather under the principle of legality, which authorises and guides conduct imbued with a certain degree of opportunity". At this juncture, our analysis diverges, as the author's reasoning remained anchored in the opposition between legality and opportunity, a dichotomy already critically examined at various points in this work.

[92] Regarding the characterisation of other penal or criminal procedural mechanisms as expressions of opportunity, and given the thematic limitations of the present work, reference is made to: Armenta Deu (1991), pp. 202–207.

[93] On this, see: Lopes Jr. (2012), pp. 385–418.

[94] Tovo and Tovo (2008), p. 75; Pereira (2002), p. 11.

[95] "Ultimately, it is appropriate to speak of the principle of legality within the framework of Public L aw, where its concept originates and develops, as well as it fulfils a specific guarantee function for individuals. In a strict sense, therefore, the principle of opportunity—irrespective of the conception that is maintained about it—should pertain to the prosecutor and the judicial authority, and

terminological limitations. When applying the proposed concepts of compulsoriness and non- compulsoriness, it becomes evident that offenses whose initiation depends on the affected individual cannot be characterised as expressions of non-compulsoriness, since, in such cases, there is no imposition of a duty on the public authority responsible—namely, the Public Prosecutor's Office—to indict.[96] Similarly, situations involving the civil settlement of damages in minor offences fall outside the scope of the notion of opportunity proposed here, since these generally occur in proceedings whose continuation depends on the victim's will and—in cases of unconditional public prosecution where the duty to prosecute is imposed—do not prevent the submission of an indictment.[97]

2.1.3 Consensual Justice in Terms of Opportunity

With the preliminary definitions relevant to the study of negotiation mechanisms now established—according to the proposed new perspective on the principles of legality, compulsoriness and opportunity—a theoretical basis has been laid for analysing and characterising the legal phenomenon known as "consensual justice". Consensus is closely linked to the principle of opportunity,[98] in that the former arises in connection with the latter.[99] As Nereu Giacomolli observes, "to the legal permission of opportunity, forms of consensus must be added",[100] which can be either unlimited or limited based on legal regulation. Consensual mechanisms can be said to operate in the procedural sphere on the basis of opportunity criteria[101];

not to offences themselves, according to the example cited, whose prosecution initially attributed to those harmed by the offence" (Armenta Deu 1991, p. 185).

[96] Caeiro (200, p. 37) identifies a different situation in cases where the victim files a representation in a public prosecution subject to condition, and a minimal evidentiary basis exists to support the accusation. In such instances, the duty to prosecute (compulsoriness) indeed arises, although it may be excepted in cases such as criminal settlement or conditional suspension of the criminal prosecution, in which, despite the existence of such a duty, the public authority opts not to fulfil it, favouring the early resolution of the criminal case through consensual mechanisms. However, it is essential to highlight that, when the concrete case presents the conditions for offering a criminal settlement or a conditional suspension of the criminal prosecution, one could speak of a duty not to prosecute and a duty to offer such a proposal (Caeiro 2000, pp. 41–42), since in these situations the accused holds a right to such treatment (an issue that will be analysed later in this work). This does not weaken previous conclusions, as in these cases the duty to prosecute is established initially, given the minimal conditions necessary to prosecute a punishable act, and only thereafter would opportunity criteria justify its waiver.

[97] In the sense of not constituting spaces for opportunity: Pereira (2002), p. 75.

[98] Diego Diez (1999), p. 191.

[99] Teixeira (2000), p. 38.

[100] Giacomolli (2006), p. 72.

[101] "Naturally, there is an intimate relationship between opportunity and consensus, since the way to implement consensual solutions regarding the penal treatment of the accused is none other than the use of opportunity [...]" (Diego Diez 1999, p. 191).

that is, for the agreed decision to take effect, the prosecuting authority must refrain from pursuing the criminal case to its ordinary conclusion. Furthermore, these mechanisms differ from those based solely on opportunity in that both parties in the criminal proceedings—prosecution and defence—are involved. In such cases, "there is a volitional manifestation with the same meaning and purpose from both procedural poles", whereas opportunity may be exercised through decisions taken exclusively by the prosecuting authority.[102]

The origins of the consensus model, or more precisely its introduction into criminal procedural law, are subject to controversy. Some authors argue for the influence of civil law thoughts, particularly the contractual theory, as it would represent "a common point toward which opposing interests converge, enabling the conclusion of a legal transaction".[103] More broadly, Geraldo Prado observes that this discourse involves more than a mere shift in legal culture; it reflects the "way in which Brazilian society as a whole conceives of this form of justice".[104]

Ventura Leite defines *consensual justice* based on a supposed distinction from the negotiated model, since, according to the author, in the former, "certain measures are submitted to the prior consent of the accused person, instead of being unilaterally determined"[105]—that is, an acceptance (or non-refusal) of a proposal already fixed in its terms—[106] whereas in the latter there is the accused's effective participation in decision-making, in which influences the content of the determinations made.[107] Such a distinction, however, proves dysfunctional to the conceptualisation proposed here for two reasons: first, it departs from, and thereby obscures, the essence of the subject at hand, namely, the suppression or abbreviation of the proceeding; second, it seems to focus on an aspect that, in fact, reflects a dysfunction in the practical implementation of consensual justice—the characteristic coercion of negotiation mechanisms in which the accused's will, although presumably free,[108] becomes circumstantially imposed,[109] so that the vast majority, if not all of the agreements, would be consensual rather than negotiated.

[102] Giacomolli (2006), p. 74.

[103] Leite (2013), pp. 21–22. The indiscriminate importation of civil law ideas into criminal procedure is the subject of pertinent and well-founded criticism; on this, see: Lopes Jr. (2012), pp. 91–94; Moreira (2013), pp. 11–18; Armenta Deu (2013).

[104] Prado (2006a), p. 67.

[105] Leite (2013), p. 22.

[106] According to Scarance Fernandes (2005), p. 263, "consensual justice may take two forms: positive and negative. The former is based on acceptance, and the latter on the abstention from refusal".

[107] "In comparative terms, consensual justice would resemble an adhesion contract, while negotiated justice would resemble a synallagmatic contract" (Leite, 2013, p. 23).

[108] "Negotiated justice, theoretically, implies freedom of choice for the parties" (Tulkens 2005, p. 707).

[109] On the coercibility of the consensual agreement proposal and the fallacy of freedom in the accused's decision-making, see Sect. 4.1.3 of this work and, in particular: Langbein (1978); Dervan and Edkins (2012).

Therefore, *consensual (or negotiated) justice*[110] is understood as a model based on the acceptance (consensus) of both parties—prosecution and defence—[111] of a procedural collaboration agreement, in which the accused withdraws from a position of resistance, generally leading to the early termination, abbreviation, or suppression of one of the proceeding's phases or even the proceeding as a whole. Its fundamental aim is facilitate the imposition of a criminal sanction with some percentage of reduction,[112] which constitutes a benefit to the accused in exchange for waiving the full course of the criminal proceeding with all its inherent guarantees. This category includes, for example: bargaining,[113] criminal settlement,[114] and conditional suspension of criminal prosecution in Brazil and Portugal[115]; *abbreviated procedures* in Latin America[116]; *plea bargaining* in the United States[117]; *absprachen* in Germany[118]; *patteggiamento* in Italy[119]; proceedings by decree or monitory proceedings[120]; among many others.

Accordingly, this model is characterised by the encouragement of participation by the procedural actors in the pursuit of a convergence of wills. It should be noted that, at first glance, when dealing with consensus, one might assume that those involved would invariably be the offender and the victim.[121] However, it becomes evident that, in the vast majority of the mechanisms examined, the victim does not

---

[110] According to Françoise Tulkens (2005), p. 674, negotiated justice, in a broad sense, refers to "different situations, in fact or in law, where the criminal matters intersect with the theme of 'negotiation', that is, a debate between the parties with the aim of reaching an agreement".

[111] "The phenomenon under discussion encompasses a model of criminal procedure that gives greater relevance to the expression of will of the parties involved—the prosecuting authority, the accused, and, possibly, the victim—so that the convergence of purposes amongst them plays a decisive role in the judicial pronouncement that marks the conclusion of the proceeding or procedure" (Leite 2013, p. 23).

[112] "There are settlement solutions that affect the content of the criminal proceeding. They may influence it by determining, as a result of an agreement between the parties to the criminal proceeding, the amount of the penalty that the accused agrees to bear, or even the conditions they are willing to accept to so that the request for conviction is not adjudicated, extending even to the definition of the legal classification of the fact *sub judice*" (Prado, 2002, p. 90).

[113] As proposed in the draft of the new Brazilian Penal Code PLS 236/2012.

[114] Among others, see: Giacomolli (2006), pp. 326–356.

[115] See, for example: Rodríguez García (1997), pp. 267–287; Giacomolli (2006), pp. 283–286 and 357–386.

[116] In general, see: Maier and Bovino (2005).

[117] Rodríguez García (1997), pp. 27–118; Ross (2010), pp. 107–124; Alschuler (1981), pp. 652–730.

[118] For an introduction, see: Rauxloh (2011), pp. 296–331; Schünemann (2013), pp. 240–261.

[119] Among others, see: Vasconcellos and Capparelli (2015), pp. 435–453; Rodríguez García (1997), pp. 119–210; Formmann (2009), p. 197–220.

[120] Fernandes (2005), pp. 210–212.

[121] Leite (2013), p. 23.

play a decisive role in the formation of the agreement, which is generally shaped by dialogue between the prosecuting authority and the defence—the accused and their legal counsel.[122]

In this vein, the widely cited notion is that consensual justice develops a participatory model for resolving criminal conflicts,[123] to the point of sustaining that it "is the ideological heart of a system that treats the accused as an active participant, rather than as a passive object".[124] The illusory nature of such an assertion is evident: without delving into further (and numerous) theoretical objections, it is sufficient to refer to empirical research carried out within the Special Criminal Courts, established by the Law 9.099/1995 and representing the Brazilian expression of consensual justice in the current legal framework.[125] These studies highlight the inoperability of settlement mechanisms in resolving conflict, thereby reinforcing the fallacy of belief in a participatory model.[126]

Revisiting the initial considerations on this topic, despite the widespread, largely unquestioned acceptance of the relationship between the principle of opportunity and the consensual mechanisms described above, a pertinent problematisation arises. Given that in cases of criminal settlements (and, more broadly, bargaining and consensual justice), the prosecutor achieves their objective—the imposition of a penalty—one may ask: are these truly spaces for opportunity?[127] Geraldo Prado, for instance, seems to answer negatively, maintaining the persistence of the principle of compulsoriness, arguing that its operation occurs in "a dimension distinct from the traditional one", since the option of offering a criminal settlement is added to the set of possible courses of action available to the prosecutor.[128] Silva Jardim similarly contends that, by making such an offer, the prosecutor is in fact exercising criminal action.[129]

Aware of the solidity of such a position, it is nonetheless argued that non-compulsoriness/opportunity is characterised in situations where the course of criminal prosecution does not follow its legally prescribed trajectory, due to the prosecutor's choice or an agreement between the parties. Such cases may arise through the non-fiing of the indictment, the suspension of proceedings or the imposition of a penalty without completing the evidentiary stage.[130] In this regard, Anitua and Borinsky note

---

[122] Giacomolli (2006), p. 73; Leite (2013), p. 25.

[123] "In summary, consensual criminal justice aims to be an alternative model, less conflictual and more participatory. The interested parties themselves are called upon to find the solution" (Leite 2013, p. 28).

[124] Vogler (2002), p. 306.

[125] Fernandes (2006).

[126] On this, see: Azevedo (2000), p. 195; Anziliero (2008); Almeida (2014), p. 225.

[127] Given that, in various conceptualisations, "opportunity" represents the abstention from criminal prosecution and, consequently, the non-application of a penalty. On this, see the discussions in Sects. 2.1.1 and 2.1.2 for ementioned.

[128] Prado (2006c), p. 154.

[129] Jardim (1998), p. 100. In this regard, also see: Gerber and Dornelles (2006), pp. 148–155.

[130] Martínez (2002), p. 524.

that the compulsoriness of criminal prosecution occurs in two steps—"to promote" and "to maintain"[131]—so that bargaining clearly disregards the latter duty. Nereu Giacomolli similarly asserts that legality (compulsoriness) prohibits the Public Prosecutor's Office from requesting suspension of the proceeding or consenting to its early termination.[132] Opportunity, according to Montero Aroca manifests both at the moment of exercising criminal action and at the conclusion of proceedings without a judgement, even when a criminally typified fact exists.[133] Moreover, in the context of a bargain, it may be observed that the prosecutor relinquishes part of their accusatory claim, since, as a general rule, the penalty is reduced in exchange for the accused's consent—constituting a form of partial renunciation.

2.1.4 *Consensual Justice Among the Mechanisms of Diversification and Procedural Acceleration*

Building on the previously established delimitations regarding the principles relevant to this study, it becomes necessary to situate consensual justice among the various mechanisms of procedural acceleration currently being introduced in legal systems worldwide. As noted earlier, bargaining and other consensual mechanisms do not constitute the only means of reducing the time spent on criminal trials,[134] yet they stand at the forefront for numerous efficient-related reasons.[135] In a context of ongoing scrutiny regarding the speed of criminal justice, some scholars argue that these mechanisms seek to "transform the proceeding into an effective instrument for the delivery of criminal justice".[136]

---

[131] Anitua, Borinsky (1999), p. 450. According to the authors, "the principle of legality can be understood as the duty that certain State representatives (the Public Prosecutor's Office, but also, to a limited extent, the police) have to promote and maintain the investigation of any fact with a sufficient appearance of criminality, in pursuit of a jurisdictional resolution that concludes the investigation and, if applicable, assigns responsibilities" (Anitua and Borinsky 1999, pp. 449–450).

[132] Giacomolli (2006), p. 54.

[133] Aroca (2008), p. 305.

[134] "Speed, simplification and consensual justice are closely interconnected themes, but they should not be conflated. As a rule, the simplification of procedures and the introduction of agreements that prematurely terminate the proceeding are tools made available to achieve a more expeditious justice. However, speed and simplification are broader concepts, which manifest through various techniques, with or without requiring consensus." (Leite 2013, p. 61).

[135] The influence of utilitarian and efficiency-oriented approaches will be examined in detail in Sect. 4.1.1 of this work.

[136] Rodríguez García (1997), p. 23. However, this position should be critically assessed. For this purpose, refer to Sect. 4.1.1 of this work, where the presumed functionalisation of the criminal procedure is questioned.

The pursuit of attention and respect for a reasonable time for criminal trials is legitimate and commendable,[137] but it does not justify an ideological inversion of the discourse to the point of legitimising the imposition of penalties without trial,[138] through the unrestricted introduction of consensual mechanisms, such as bargaining.[139] Therefore, consensual justice represents one variant amongst those that seek to accelerate and simplify procedures, with a view to enhancing the effectiveness of the criminal procedure.[140]

According to Armenta Deu, the reforms of procedural codes that occurred contemporaneously in Europe and Latin America shared a common feature: the establishment of a set of special procedures that streamline certain phases of the procedural rite, eliminating them when deemed unnecessary, for instance, in cases of flagrancy or when the evidentiary basis in less complex crimes is easily established.[141]

Furthermore, an international overview is presented regarding the adoption of a broad set of measures, termed *diversification*.[142] In essence, this involves "diversion before reaching the legal-penal solution",[143] encompassing everything from dejudicialisation measures to the use of fast track.[144] Accordingly, Alberto Bovino describes the principle of opportunity, in broad terms, as a means to diversify the treatment of social conflict, aiming to avoid the traditional penal solution while simultaneously allowing for victim reparation.[145]

---

[137] On the reasonable duration of criminal proceedings, see: Lopes and Badaró (2006).

[138] It is noted that the Italian reform introducing consensual mechanisms ostensibly aimed to adapt the procedural model to address the multiple convictions imposed on Italy in the European Court of Human Rights for violating the right to a reasonable time, as set forth in Art. 6th, §1st of the European Convention on Human Rights and Fundamental Freedoms (Rodrigues, 1998, p. 237).

[139] "This is because the unreasonable duration of a proceeding can occur either due to sluggishness or excessive speed. Indeed, the set of rights and guarantees of the accused requires an adequate time span for their effective exercise. Just as arbitrary and illegitimate is a proceeding that lasts longer than necessary, so is one that, within the framework of the Rule of Law, despite the swift delivery of judicial services, does not allow for the development of the basic faculties of the accused (right to defense, right to adversarial proceedings, etc.)." (Casara 2011, p. 154, free translation).

[140] Leite (2013), p. 63.

[141] Armenta Deu (2012), p. 142.

[142] According to Costa Andrade, the concept and the criminal policy programme of diversion emerged in the United States at the end of the 1960s and quickly influenced various European countries (Costa Andrade 1977, pp. 321–322).

[143] Jakobs (1997), p. 17. The author cites the German example of juvenile criminal law, in which procedural forms and faster response mechanisms are developed, ranging from police inactivity in trivial cases to intensive education programmes.

[144] "As a mitigation of this type of more absolute diversion, there are other alternative mechanisms within the scope of Criminal Justice that, without excluding all formality, seek to provide greater flexibility in resolving conflicts of a criminal nature." (Fernandes, 2001, p. 134).

[145] Bovino (2005), p. 32. See also Leite (2013), p. 20. For alternative models in criminal justice, see Achutti (2009), pp. 55–60.

Certainly, there is also a link with initiatives aimed at developing alternative methods of conflict resolution (AMCRs).[146] According to Françoise Tulkens, "negotiated justice is, at a procedural level, part of what is known in Quebec as *solutions de rechange* (alternative solutions)", and it is "also represented in the Alternative Conflict Resolution movement that developed in the 1970s in the United States".[147] This model exerted significant influence across various branches of law,[148] particularly civil and labour law, spreading its principles to proposals for its applicability in the criminal field.[149] At this point, brief considerations on criminal mediation are appropriate.[150] Generally, analysis of the topic cites the French example, which promotes the practice before the start of the criminal proceedding.[151] It is important to note a fundamental distinction between this mechanisms and the bargaining ones: in criminal mediation, consensus occurs between the victim and the offender, whereas in bargaining, the agreement is reached between the accused and the public prosecutor.[152]

In addition, the contemporaneously debated proposal of Restorative Justice is highlighted.[153] It is an open and constantly evolving model, so no single comprehensive definition exists. However, its contours are shaped by the central role of the parties directly involved in the offence (offender and victim), who collaboratively determine the best way to address its consequences and how to prevent or manage similar issues in the future.[154] Gradually incorporated into various foreign legal systems[155] and in notable examples in Brazil,[156] it represents an important shift in the

[146] On the contours and limitations of such linkage, see Leite (2013), pp. 47–53; Armenta Deu (2012), pp. 152–156.

[147] Tulkens (2005), p. 682.

[148] "The use of ADRs seems to be a growing phenomenon with which society must coexist and the law must contemplate and regulate. In this sense, the Committee of Ministers of the Council of Europe, in Recommendation 12/1986, addresses measures to prevent and reduce court overload and urges governments to adopt the appropriate provisions." (Armenta Deu (2013), p. 155).

[149] Leite (2013), p. 50.

[150] "For purely educational purposes, mediation involves the intervention of a mediator—an arbitrator—who is completely disinterested in the relevant outcome of the agreement between the parties. The mediator intervenes solely so as to facilitate a consensual resolution to the conflict opposing parties' dilemma. In this context, the functions of the State, linked to the enforcement of criminal law through the punishment, or considerations of substantive justice, yield to the full autonomy of the parties." (Prado, 2002, p. 89). For a critique of definitions of criminal mediation based on the instrumentalist theory of procedure, see: Barros Pellegrini et al. (2005), pp. 151–153.

[151] Tulkens (2005), p. 691; Guinchard and Buisson (2013), pp. 971–983. For a legal model guided by mediation, see: Salas (2010), pp. 48–59. See also: Sica (2009), pp. 289–319.

[152] Borges (2013), p. 169; Leite (2013), p. 119.

[153] For further discussion, see primarily: Pallamolla (2009); Achutti (2009), pp. 71–77; Moraes (2022).

[154] Achutti (2013), pp. 156–158.

[155] Armenta Deu (2012), p. 156.

[156] On the possibility of implementing Restorative Justice principles through Special Criminal Courts mechanisms, see: Paulo (2013), p. 15.

understanding of criminal conflicts, particularly in terms of diversifying approaches to their resolution.[157]

Returning to the initial reasoning of this topic, and to shed light on the complexity and variety of options for mechanisms aimed at accelerating or bypassing the proceeding, it is necessary to introduce some relevant models. It is important to emphasise that each example has its essential characteristics as well as numerous specifications, which certainly go beyond the objectives outlined here. Therefore, it should be noted that these delimitations, particularly in a comparative sense, are illustrative, aiming to foster interest in exploring alternatives to the consensual model, while also contributing to its own conceptual delineation.

According to Scarance Fernandes, mechanisms for simplifying proceedings can be divided into three groups: (1) those that conclude the proceeding prematurely; (2) those that eliminate certain stages of the procedures; and (3) those that reorganise the ordinary procedure.[158] It is noteworthy that consensual justice is particularly instrumental in the first two situations, in which an agreement between the parties results in either the early judgement of the case or the elimination of a procedural stage. Furthermore, Anabela Rodrigues maintains that the concept of expediency can permeate the proceedingin two ways: horizontally, through negotiation mechanisms in which the conflict is returned to the parties, and vertically, where response times are shortened by eliminating procedural stages.[159]

Citing alternatives that do not fundamentally depend on the accused's consent, one may identify mechanisms that eliminate certain stages of the procedure, whether it is the preliminary investigation or the production of evidence during the evidentiary stage.

Another striking and controversial example amongst scholars is the model of judgement by decree, also called the penal monitory procedure.[160] Although it can be considered consensual, since the accused accepts the punishment by choosing not to

---

[157] In comparison to the consensual justice model, Ventura Leite (2013), p. 60, notes similarities and distinctions, concluding that "in consensual justice, even though significant space is given to dialogue, the focus remains on the legal treatment of the act considered delinquent. In this sense, effective attention is not always given to the repercussion of the infringing behaviour on relationships, feelings, and social bonds of the perpetrator and the victim alike. Therefore, consensual justice has less ambitious objectives than the restorative model, and its pedagogical character is also diminished". However, this distinction is thought to be even more pronounced and significant when considering the main form of consensual justice: negotiation mechanisms such as bargaining. As this study will demonstrate, the idea that consensual justice fosters dialogue and conflict resolution aiming at the direct participation of the parties is misleading, since agreements on penalties are instrumentalised primarily as a means of enforcement. In other words, equating consensual justice, as commonly presented in legal literature, with Restorative Justice is unsustainable due to their fundamentally distinct premises and objectives.

[158] Fernandes (2005), p. 263.

[159] Rodrigues (1998), p. 234.

[160] "In the monitoring procedure, once the preliminary investigation phase is concluded, the judge, based on the available evidence, may convict the accused and apply the penalty, after which the citation is carried out. If the accused contests the conviction, the ordinary procedure for minor offences follows. Benefits are provided to encourage acceptance of the penalty without a trial." (Fernandes 2005, p. 211).

contest the accusation,[161] there are significant differences compared to negotiation mechanisms, such as bargaining. On the one hand, Langbein considers this procedure as similar to bargaining; on the other,[162] Figueiredo Dias and Costa Andrade criticise this comparison, arguing that "beyond the complete absence of formal negotiation, the accused has no bargaining power over the nature or extent of the penalty, being left only with the option of accepting or rejecting it in full and *ex post*".[163]

Finally, it is worth highlighting examples of acceleration through alternatives that provide differentiated treatment of criminal matters, based on the belief that the criminal proceeding (with its intrinsic guarantees) can be replaced by a swifter branch of law, such as Administrative Sanctions Law.[164] The adoption of a Law of Offences,[165] for instance, is part of "the broad movement aimed at simplifying the criminal system".[166] Two problematic points, particularly illustrated by the Portuguese example, are worth mentioning: on the one hand, the definition of criteria differentiating crimes from offences is complex and nebulous, ultimately becoming a mere legislative choice[167]; on the other hand, there are strong criticisms regarding the neglect of fundamental guarantees in administrative proceedings compared to criminal proceedings, highlighting a trend toward convergence between the two.[168]

Therefore, this topic aimed to reveal the various ways in which the pursuit of swiftness in criminal justice can be operationalised. Indeed, beyond these avenues, it is necessary to discuss the scope of punitive power itself, particularly in contexts of its inexorable expansion (as observed in Brazilian society and across various international legal systems).[169] In this regard, it is crucial to emphasise that the debate on consensual justice and the overburdening of the judiciary power cannot overshadow more complex debates about the legitimacy of criminal intervention in social relations. Furthermore, it is important to expose the reductionism of narratives that present bargaining and the imposition of penalties without due process as the only sole answer to such scenarios.

---

[161] Rauxloh (2011), p. 304.

[162] Langbein (1974).

[163] Dias and Andrade (1997), p. 496. It should be noted, however, that in practice bargaining is generally instrumentalised without genuine negotiation.

[164] Armenta Deu (1991), pp. 31–33.

[165] "In general terms, several characteristics mark the new procedural ordinances: a) broader adoption of the principle of opportunity; b) no requirement for the involvement of the Public Prosecutor's Office; c) absence of a preliminary evidentiary stage; d) waiver of the accused's presence; e) simplification of the interrogation formalities; and f) reduction of procedural acts to the minimum necessary." (Fernandes 2005, p. 297).

[166] Fernandes (2005), p. 296.

[167] For relevant criteria for distinguishing crimes from misdemeanours, see D'Avila (2009), pp. 81–103.

[168] Dias (2011), pp. 103–104.

[169] The relationship between the expansion of Criminal Law and negotiation mechanisms will be critically analysed in Sect. 4.1.1 of this book.

2.2 Bargaining as a Consensual Expression of Opportunity: Definition, Foundations, and Assumptions (an Introductory Analysis of the US Scenario for the Delimitation of the Negotiation Mechanism)

After defining the spaces and principles through which negotiation mechanisms are implemented in criminal justice, an in-depth study of the characteristics of the fundamental theme of this work: bargaining. To this end, this section will primarily use the US example of plea bargaining,[170] as the analysis of the mechanism that is internationally recognised as a benchmark in transactional terms[171] and whose contours have been developed by US legal literature and caselaw for decades, will greatly contribute to the understanding and critique of proposals to expand spaces for consensus in the field of criminal law in Brazil.

In this vein, this topic will be structured as follows: illustratively, brief outlines of the US criminal justice model will be introduced, especially describing the guilty plea, the mechanism through which the bargain is implemented; next (subtopic 1), the concept of bargain will be discussed based on problematisations in relation to plea bargaining. After that, (2) the justifications commonly used to legitimise agreements between prosecution and defence in criminal proceedings will be analysed, by critically questioning each of these foundations. Finally, (3) a scheme of the prerequisites for accepting the bargain in US justice will be structured, which will contribute to the critique of Brazilian proposals.[172]

Once aware that the intention to describe the US criminal procedural model in detail goes beyond the scope of this work,[173] this book will analyse points relevant to the study of plea bargaining and the circumstances that led to its expansion, whereas criminal convictions in this country are obtained by means of this

[170] It should be noted that the US criminal procedure presents several variations due to different legislations at the federal level and among the states. Therefore, this study will be primarily based on the federal jurisdiction model of plea bargaining, although relevant state comparisons may be added. Pedro Albergaria (2007), p. 11, for example, questions whether one can truly speak of a "real American criminal procedural system", concluding that "one cannot disregard a certain *common core* of that country's criminal justice and, thus, the existence of common traits to the various systems (state and federal), deducible from different sources".

[171] It should be noted that other common law countries also have mechanisms such as plea bargaining intrinsically linked and constantly used in their criminal justice system. On this, see: Vogler (2002), p. 281–307.

[172] As it will be described in Sect. 2.3 of this paper, the proposals for expanding spaces for consensus in the Brazilian criminal procedure, based on mechanisms similar to bargaining, disregard important aspects of the limitation of agreements based on prerequisites for their approval. Therefore, the study of the US model of plea bargaining, addressed by foreign legal scholars for decades, will contribute to demonstrating the insufficiencies of national projects.

[173] On the American criminal procedural system, see: Hendler (1996), pp. 159–223; Ramos (2006); Heringer (2013), pp. 21–50.

mechanism in up to 98% of cases, depending on the region studied.[174] It is thought that two characteristics in particular determine the possibility of agreements between prosecution and defence: the broad discretion of the prosecutor and the delimitations of the due process of law.

Initially, one can point out that this scenario is enabled by the broad discretion of the representative of the Prosecutor's Office (prosecutor), stating that "in the system of plea bargaining, everything is possible, and negotiation encounters virtually no barriers".[175] The idea contained in the principle of compulsoriness, common to continental legal systems, is incompatible with the North American procedural construction,[176] while judicial review over the accusation is rejected, in addition to being dismissed by the attitude of the members of the Judiciary themselves.[177] Thus, given a discretion described as absolute[178] or nearly unrestricted,[179] it is possible to handle the accusations so as to adapt to the various types of negotiations (and pressures on the accused),[180] since, for example, the prosecutor is authorised to withdraw certain charges or to capitulate to a fact less serious than what actually occurred.

On the other hand, the contours of the due process of law and the rules about the beginning of criminal trial, in which the accused, in their first speech, states their position regarding the criminal acts alleged against them, establish the space for waiving the trial and for imposing the penalty agreed. Unlike the typically described assimilation with due process,[181] the meaning of the due process of law is established as a right of the accused to trial, since they have pleaded not guilty. Thus, the

---

[174] It is pointed out, as already mentioned, that the percentages of convictions obtained from bargaining in the United States are reported at rates ranging from 90 to 98%. On this, see, for example: Fisher (2003), p. 223.

[175] Giacomolli (2006), p. 41.

[176] "The idea that the prosecutor could be obliged by the legislator to initiate criminal prosecution in general terms—as imposed by our Article 71 of the Penal Code (Argentinian) —, or for a certain type of crimes, is unimaginable for a US scholar, since the system does not admit that the prosecutor may be obliged by the judge to pursue a specific case" (Bovino 2005, p. 57–58).

[177] "We can state, therefore, that the discretion attributed to the Public Prosecutor's Office does not explicitly derive from legal texts—or at least from a reading of them that does not go beyond the obvious meaning of the words—, but rather from its sanctioning by a judicial power that, while being especially vigilant and active in relation to the other powers of the State, curiously guides its action in relation to the Public Prosecutor's Office by a discretion, deference and passivity that are hardly understandable" (Albergaria 2007, p. 54).

[178] Easterbrook (1983), p. 299.

[179] According to Pedro Albergaria, there are two forms of review: the prohibition of "selective prosecution" and of "vindictive prosecution".

[180] Lippke (2011), p. 1.

[181] As per Kant de Lima (1999), p. 29, the term "due process of law" is "erroneously translated into Portuguese too freely and hastily as 'devido processo legal'", as there are distinctions, given that "this legal-political institution of the USA is an option for the accused, to whom the State owes a certain judicial proceeding, stipulated by the fifth and sixth constitutional amendments". Similarly, Gonçalves Ferreira (2004), p. 102, states that "the differences are striking and forceful, as, examining the categories that guide the judicial procedures of Brazilian and US legal traditions, it is concluded that their formation and fulfilment greatly differ".

US legal scholarship supports the possibility of waiving,[182] since, upon a finding of guilt, punishment is directly imposed, without judicially investigating the facts.[183]

This manifestation generally occurs in a hearing called arraignment, in which the participation of the accused takes place after the indictment has been filed,[184] with the purpose of clarifying its terms and questioning the stance of the accused on their innocence.[185] At this point, based on the information provided by the prosecuting body, the alleged perpetrator of the criminal acts can adopt three positions: plead guilty (guilty plea), innocent (not guilty), or not contest the charges (*nolo contendere*).[186] By pleading not guilty the State must prove all elements of the crime in a trial with due guarantees, usually in a jury trial, that is, the minimum parameters of the due process of law are established.[187] As for *nolo contendere*, it is an option accepted in the criminal justice systems of half the states and in federal jurisdictions in which the accused does not contest the charges, but also does not acknowledge their guilt.[188] In other words, there is acceptance of the imposition of a penalty in more restricted cases, without effects for a subsequent civil compensation, for example.[189]

On the other hand, the guilty plea represents the recognition of guilt in relation to the imputed acts, accepting the immediate imposition of a sentence,[190] waiving fundamental rights[191] and not imposing the burden of proof on the prosecutor, that is, the proceeding is rendered useless in its essence. As **Alberto Bovino** points out, "guilty pleas are not a piece of evidence or a confession, but a conviction in itself,

---

[182] For all, see: Easterbrook (1992), p. 1.975.

[183] "Thus, Brazilian scholars bring us the idea of the accused being forcibly subjected to the jury court, while the due process of law of the US criminal justice administration system reflects the idea of a desire of the accused that represents a tool of defence, an option against the power of the State" (Ferreira 2004, p. 78).

[184] Although, in certain procedures, this act may occur earlier, and also more informally. See: Albergaria (2007), p. 64.

[185] Hendler (1996), p. 195.

[186] Rodríguez García (1996), pp. 83–84.

[187] Ferreira (2002), p. 72.

[188] Rodríguez García (1996), pp. 37–38; Bibas (2003), pp. 12–13.

[189] Diego Díez (1999), pp. 40–41.

[190] Turner (2009), p. 8.

[191] "Certainly, the *guilty plea* implies the waiver of, at least, three fundamental constitutional rights: the right not to incriminate oneself, the right to cross-examine the prosecution witnesses through *cross-examination* and the right to be tried by a jury" (Diego Díez 1999, p. 32) .

as decisive as the jury's verdict".[192] It is a unilateral act, which does not require the consent of the other parties (except when the Court refuses it, in accordance with the requirements that will be analysed later) or any kind of motivation.[193]

In this vein, three basic forms in which this act can be characterised are usually identified. They can be (1) voluntary or uninfluenced, when the accused chooses to recognise their guilt either in the face of overwhelmingly unfavourable evidence, or out of remorse, or even when they find no advantage in denying it,[194] that is, there is no direct or indirect influence from other procedural actors; (2) structurally induced or "unilateral", when the law establishes a more severe penalty for those who insist on trial or due to a custom of more lenient stance by prosecutors and judges to those who renounce it, even if not formally agreed[195]; and, (3) negotiated, when the negotiations take place explicitly, aiming at the waiving of the trial, addressing the crime or the penalty to be imposed[196]—it is the plea bargaining in essence.[197]

2.2.1 Defining the Conceptual Boundaries of the Bargaining Institution

The conceptualisation of bargaining is permeated by several complexities caused by the distinctive characteristics of the models adopted in legal systems, especially by what might be called a pattern of peculiarities in the negotiation mechanisms of common law and civil law. Issues such as the need for explicit negotiations between prosecution and defence, the legal definition of the extent of sentence reduction, and the inclusion of "turn state's evidence" as a phenomenon encompassed by the bargain are examples of essential points for the delimitation of the topic studied and, certainly, will be addressed here. We will begin with plea bargaining[198] to then structure a broad definition that encompasses both the characteristics of this mechanism and its counterparts present in continental legal systems. Although it is known that simply listing concepts related to a mechanism should be avoided, it was considered acceptable here due to the intention to outline a broader concept of bargaining in more general terms. Therefore, the passages quoted here will be accompanied by a critical analysis of their contributions and limitations.

---

[192] Bovino (2005), p. 60. Thus, also: Langbein (1979), p. 267.

[193] Rodríguez García (1997), p. 39.

[194] Diego Díez (1999), pp. 33–34.

[195] Rodríguez García (1997), p. 41.

[196] Diego Díez (1999), p. 35.

[197] However, as will be seen, the term bargain will be defined to include both negotiated and structurally induced cases, for reasons that will be explained later.

[198] According to Rodríguez García (1997), p. 29, one can also use terms such as "plea negotiation, compromise of criminal cases, negotiated plea, plea conference, plea discussion, compromising, settling cases, trading out, etc.". For critical considerations on this denomination, see: Lynch (1998), p. 307; Albergaria (2007), p. 12.

We will begin with **John Langbein's** characterisation, who defines five fundamental points of *plea bargaining*: (1) it is a mode of procedure without trial; (2) thus, it subverts the constitutional design that guarantees the right to trial (by an impartial jury); (3) to do so, it becomes burdensome for the accused to exercise their constitutional right, as, in the event of a conviction by ordinary trial, the accused is more severely punished; (4) this mode of procedure without a trial precludes the defence and does not require that the conviction be established by a criterion beyond reasonable doubt; and, (5) all of this is legitimised for reasons of efficiency.[199] This framework satisfactorily clarifies important points of criticism of the bargain, but before doing so, a more precise definition of its contours is required.

Milton Heumann points out that "plea bargaining is the process by which the defendant in a criminal case relinquishes his right to go to trial in exchange for a reduction in charge and/or sentence".[200] This definition is thought to be appropriate in that it focuses on the accused's waiver of trial, rather than on the negotiation between the parties. However, the perception that the exchange is given in return for a reduction in the charge and/or sentence unduly restricts its scope.

It is argued that the rewarding nature[201] is not exclusively characterised by sentence reduction, even in a situation in which the accused does not obtain any direct benefit from their punishment, but, for example, chooses to waive their defence in order to begin immediately the effective fulfilment of the sentence, instead of remaining as a provisional prisoner due to the imposition of a precautionary restriction for an extended period during the trial.[202] This may occur because certain rights provided for in the Penal Execution Law are guaranteed only to those detained with a final sentence. In other words, even without explicit negotiations or direct mitigations of the imposed punishment, there is a benefit to the accused, resulting from the waiver of resistance to punitive power. Thus, one concludes that the advantage does not necessarily have to be perceived in the imposed punishment or concession by any of the public actors in the criminal proceeding; it can rather come from the operation of the criminal system itself, or even from an unfulfilled hope of more lenient treatment.

---

[199] Langbein (1979), pp. 261–262.

[200] Heumann (1981), p. 1.

[201] According to Leite (2013), p. 27, when addressing the commonly established connection between the reward and the sentence of the case in question, "a characteristic always present is the *premialidade*, granting the accused a reduction of sentence, benefits for the fulfilment of the sanction, non-payment of procedural expenses, among other advantages".

[202] Here stands out an example of the irrationality and ideological inversion of the thought favourable to the agreements on penalty, which support a supposed advantage to the accused, which, as a rule, is caused by an artificial solution to the problem resulting from the State's violating stance of fundamental rights. For example, there are those who argue that the bargain favours the accused by granting certainty to their situation in a quick trial, turning an indefinite precautionary imprisonment (due to slowness of the State) into a determined penalty. On the fallacy of this argument, see: Córdoba (2005), pp. 241–242. Furthermore, reference is made to item 1.2.2 of this work, in which the supposed justifications of plea bargaining will be addressed and criticised.

Jenia Turner defines that the studied mechanism "means the process of negotiation and explicit agreement between the defendant, on one hand, and the prosecution, the court, or both, on the other, whereby the defendant confesses, pleads guilty, or provides other assistance to the government in exchange for more lenient treatment".[203] This definition highlights a commonly perceived issue: the central role of the need for negotiation between the parties.[204] Conversely, it is argued that the structurally induced recognition of guilt should also be included in the concept of bargaining, because, although there is no express negotiation between prosecution and defence, the two characteristic elements stand out: the waiver of trial through a proceeding with due guarantees and the reward for this act (or at least the hope of its fulfilment), usually a more lenient punishment. Furthermore, in a critical sense, revealing the non-existence of an effective agreement, but rather of mechanisms of coercion and pressure, **John Langbein** points out that "plea bargaining occurs when the prosecutor induces a criminal accused to confess guilt and to waive his right to trial in exchange for a more lenient criminal sanction than would be imposed if the accused were adjudicated guilty following trial".[205]

As a rule, legal scholars define this consensual mechanism based exclusively on the US model. Thus, it is outlined that the object of negotiation may vary, based on the broad discretion of the prosecuting authority[206]: for example, it is possible to agree on the withdrawal of some of the charges or the classification of the facts as a lesser offence (charge bargaining),[207] the prosecutor's agreement on a reduced sentence or the granting of benefits such as probation[208] (sentence bargaining).[209] In an attempt to conceptualise bargaining in broad terms, it becomes clear that such differentiation should not be encompassed, but rather a generic term such as "benefit", since continental systems do not admit negotiation about the charges to be formulated in the indictment, since the prosecutor's action is, as a rule, more regulated and less discretionary.[210]

Therefore, given these considerations, *bargaining* is defined as the procedural tool that results in the waiver of defence,[211] through the accused's acceptance (and

---

[203] Turner (2009), p. 1.

[204] Similarly, Albergaria (2007), pp. 20–21; Dias (2011), p. 17; Dias and Andrade (1997), p. 484; Leite (2013), p. 73.

[205] Langbein (1978), p. 8.

[206] Dias (2011), p. 17; Martínez (1999), p. 379.

[207] Some scholars even point out only charge bargaining: Dias, Andrade (1997), p. 484.

[208] It is important to distinguish plea bargaining from probation: "One should not confuse the plea bargaining system with the probation system, according to which the application of the punishment—sentence—is suspended upon the fulfilment of certain conditions, for a probationary period. However, there is a judgement of guilt conviction" (Giacomolli 2006, p. 44).

[209] Duarte and Marques (2008), p. 66; Fernandes (2006), pp. 194–195.

[210] Damaška (2010), p. 91.

[211] Turner (2009), p. 35.

possible cooperation) of the charge, usually presupposing their confession,[212] in exchange for some benefit (usually, sentence reduction), negotiated and agreed between the parties[213] or merely expected by the accused.[214] Thus, the essential elements of bargaining are the waiver of defence (distorting the accused stance of resistance and contestation), the imposition of an anticipated punishment, and the hope of the accused of receiving some benefit for such consent (or of avoiding punishment due to the exercise of their rights).[215] Regarding this last characteristic, **Albert Alschuler** aptly states that "the threat of differential punishment, whether phrased in terms of rewarding a plea of guilty or of penalising the exercise of the right to trial, is the essence of the plea bargaining process".[216]

First, the waiving of the defence occurs because, with the bargain, stages of the procedure are suppressed or, as a rule, the entire proceeding, moving immediately to applying the agreed sentence.[217] Although some argue that the right to defence is not violated,[218] in our view, its non-existence in the case of an agreement remains crystal clear, since it presupposes no questioning of the terms of the charge and, usually, even the obstruction of the possibility of appeal.[219] Thus, it is noteworthy that consensual mechanisms that, with the accused's agreement, suppress some of the procedural stages (preliminary or intermediate stage of the proceeding, for example), but safeguard the core of the oral trial, are excluded from this definition,

[212] The confession, however, is waived in mechanisms such as the Brazilian criminal settlement, the American *nolo contendere* or some abbreviated procedures, which use the concept of conformity. On the non-recognition of the accused's guilt in the criminal settlement, see: Fernandes (2012), p. 214. However, it is thought that, although the legal system artificially determines that such procedures do not entail the guilty plea, the acceptance of the imposition of a punishment at a certain point leads to the perception that there is such recognition.

[213] It is worth noting that, in some legal systems, the judge can actively participate in obtaining the bargain, which expands the conceptualisation on this issue. See: Albergaria (2007), p. 19.

[214] As pointed out, it is argued that there is no need for direct negotiations between prosecution and defence, as the bargain can occur in a scenario of leniency entrusted from the recurring stance of the actors or even from benefits unrelated to the case or its specific punishment.

[215] Regarding the inherent coercibility of the bargain proposal, see item 3.1.3 of this work. As for the distinction between reward for recognising guilt and punishment for exercising a right, see item 4.1.6 below.

[216] Alschuler (1983), p. 952.

[217] In this sense, Wálter Maierovitch (1991), p. 205), points out that plea bargaining "consists of a transaction, agreement, which abbreviates the resolution of the case by eliminating the collection of evidence and suppression of debates between the parties. The accused, in exchange for benefits, admits their guilt and declares himself responsible for the crime committed (plea of guilty)".

[218] Therefore, it is important, from now on, to position oneself against the construction that, although it expresses a commendable intention to reconcile the negotiation mechanisms with the constitutional dictates, it accepts them in cases in which they are perceived as an expression of the use of the right to defence, in search of a more favourable situation for the accused. It is thought that the bargain excludes any possibility of defence and is inexorably guided by influences and coercions for applying a punishment in advance, being thus incompatible with the exercise of the right to defence.

[219] Dias (2011), p. 93.

which does not make the exercise of the defence complex. Next, the accused's acceptance of the charge is discussed, encompassing both cases requiring a confession and those in compliance with the charges.[220]

Also, despite the opposing views,[221] the concept outlined includes the mechanism of turn state's evidence (cooperation agreement),[222] as an expression of negotiated justice, already regulated in Brazil. This mechanism presupposes the recognition of guilt (confession) and, based on this, cooperation with the State's criminal prosecution, usually with the incrimination of co-authors and the unveiling of important information for evidence production; seeking more lenient treatment (usually, a sentence reduction).[223] It is known that, according to current Brazilian rules, the accused cannot be convicted solely based on the plea, requiring the search for confirmatory evidence.[224] However, by contributing to the State's prosecution, the accused moves away from their position of resistance, thus becoming incompatible with the effective exercise of the right to defence. Therefore, some identify bargaining and turn state's evidence mechanisms in the category called "reward law", which is guided by the accused's cooperation in criminal prosecution.[225]

Furthermore, it is necessary to point out some distinctions. First, one can distinguish bargaining from non-prosecution based on spaces for opportunity. As already mentioned, the former is instrumentalised in criminal proceedings through the latter,[226] because, in a scenario where only the compulsoriness of criminal action prevails, there would be no authorisation for the prosecuting body to refrain from promoting the proceeding until the imposition of the due penalty with its natural conclusion by a court decision based on the evidence produced.[227] However, one can consider the hypothesis in which the representative of the Prosecution Office uses opportunities not to offer the indictment or prematurely end the proceeding, without any imposition of penalty on the accused. Thus, bargaining is distinguished, as it involves the imposition of a punishment on the accused, without the course of the trial with its intrinsic guarantees.

---

[220] Regarding the distinction between confession and plea agreement, see: Martínez (2002), pp. 374–375. However, it is clear that, in both situations, there is a confession, although implicitly perceived in the second case, since, given the imposition of the State punitive power, one may not speak of a simple acceptance that is not based on spontaneous confession or imposed by coercion (especially in cases in which the bargain results in criminal records, which is the rule in foreign legal systems, except, for example, the North American *nolo contendere* and the Brazilian *transação penal*—which apply only to minor offences).

[221] Excluding the turn state's evidence from the definition of bargain, see: Alschuler (1979), p. 213; Tulkens (2005), p. 675.

[222] Including the turn state's evidence in the concept of bargain, see: Albergaria (2007), p. 20; Zanatta (2001), pp. 21–22.

[223] Pereira (2013), pp. 23–27. The rewarded collaboration as an expression of the negotiation justice in Brazil will be analysed in item 3.2 of this work.

[224] Silva (2014), pp. 71–74.

[225] Ortiz Pradillo (2014), pp. 388–390.

[226] See item Sect. 2.1.3 of this work.

[227] Bovino (2005), p. 16.

Moreover, one must distinguish bargaining from consensual justice in broad terms.[228] It is known that the former is an expression of the latter, as one of its typical mechanisms; however, it is thought that bargaining presupposes waiving defence, or the possibilities of its effective action. Nevertheless, in contrast, one can cite, for example, a procedural mechanism that, by means of an agreement between the accused and the prosecution, defines which proceeding should be followed, yet maintaining a procedure that allows the exercise of the right to defence and due process[229]; this mechanism would be consensual, but not bargaining in the terms proposed here. One can also mention alternatives affecting stages of the proceeding that suppress an intermediate stage[230]—in which provisional instruction is carried out to verify the viability of the prosecution—[231]–provided that this measure was agreed by the parties and kept the stage of oral judgement with its essential characteristics.

Finally, it is essential to analyse individualisation between plea bargaining and the simplified procedure, typical of Latin American legal systems. According to **Cynthia Alkon**, there are two points worth noting: the need for negotiations, typical of the US mechanism, and the legal fixation of the penalty reduction, common to Latin mechanisms.[232] On the one hand, the dispensability of real agreements between prosecution and defence has been previously discussed and affirmed. Furthermore, it is thought that the essence of these phenomena is the same, so that, in fact, these distinctions are the contours that the negotiation model acquires in the common law system and in the continental ones. Therefore, both mechanisms are expressions, in broad terms, of the bargaining mechanism analysed in this work.

---

[228] Armenta Deu (1991), p. 220.

[229] Imagine a hypothetical (and unfeasible within the Brazilian legal system) situation in which prosecution and defence agree to submit a jury trial case for judgement by a single judge through ordinary procedure.

[230] Fernandes (2005), pp. 215–225.

[231] The intermediate stage is, as a rule, reduced in the Brazilian criminal procedure to a mere decision to accept the indictment (which, in many cases, is accepted without further depth, almost automatically). It can be said that the jury proceeding presents an intermediate stage of the *iudicium accusationis* before the single judge in its first stage, which may culminate in the commitment of the accused for trial. For a comparative analysis of the intermediate stages in foreign criminal procedure, see: Armenta Deu (2008), pp. 109–133.

[232] Alkon (2010), p. 387.

2.2.2 *Causes and Justifications: Bargaining Between Necessity and Utility to Punitive Power*

In the study of the characteristics of bargaining, after clarifying the contours of its definition and the possible modalities of implementation, an analysis of the causes of its origin, advancement, and triumph[233] in the US legal system (and in several other countries) and the justifications for its use are required. First, the reasons for the development of consensual mechanisms will be studied, based on two main arguments: necessity due to the overload of criminal justice by the number of cases and the greater complexity of the trials. Next, the foundations typically indicated to justify the transaction on the resolution of the criminal act and the reduction of the accused's penalty will be examined. Therefore, it is a matter of questioning the arguments raised by scholars (and, to a certain extent, by US caselaw) so as to defend and legitimise the introduction and routine use of bargaining in the legal-criminal field. Indeed, aligned with the critical stance adopted in this work, each thesis will be questioned, with the aim of considering the real legitimacy of negotiation mechanisms in criminal proceedings.[234] The outcome of this topic will point to the conclusion that the bargain originated and spread from the actions of the actors in criminal justice, due to their full adherence to their personal conveniences, which, certainly, deviate from the agenda of legitimate interests of criminal justice in a Democratic Rule of Law.

When studying the US legal scenario, the dissatisfaction of a large part of legal scholarship in relation to the expressive number of guilt admissions, through plea bargaining, as the basis of criminal convictions, is crystal clear.[235] It is argued that, in an "ideal" world,[236] this mechanism could not be accepted, but, in practice, its abolition would be unfeasible,[237] since it supposedly became a necessity of the system[238] and has always been an inherent trait of common law.[239] However, some scholars strenuously maintain that these statements are incorrect[240]; on the one hand they claim the possibility of extinguishing the agreements and, on the other, they unveil that historically they were not constant in the US. This argument is also recurrent in the Latin American debate, as, for example, in Argentina, where one of the advocates (and proponent) of the *juicio abreviado*, fundamentally justifies its

[233] Fisher (2003), p. 239.

[234] Questions that should be added to the theoretical and practical critical considerations woven into Sects. 4.1 and 4.2 of this work.

[235] Rodríguez García (1996), p. 92.

[236] Heumann (1981), p. 162.

[237] Bibas (2004), pp. 2527–2528.

[238] Albergaria (2007), pp. 131–132.

[239] Rodríguez García (1997), p. 31; Heumann (1981) p. 28.

[240] Schulhofer (1984), p. 1037.

construction on the idea of "obtaining sentences in a reasonable time, with strong savings of judicial resources and without harm to justice".[241]

Regarding the supposed inevitability of plea bargaining, this idea derives from a mix of myth and swiftness,[242] while examples of US states that, somehow, have abolished this mechanism and achieved positive results, or, at least, did not collapse,[243] as most scholars had predicted. This is also true in certain US jurisdictions, where concessions were not offered in exchange for guilty plea.[244]

Furthermore, this mechanism is intrinsically linked to the criminal justice system and any attempt to abolish it would be flawed, since the agreements would become informal, even if against the law.[245] At this point one may question the basis of this estimate,[246] since there is no legitimate explanation.[247] Finally, the hypothesis that the prohibition of agreements would result in an increase in punishments[248] and, therefore, would harm the accused parties is extremely weak, as there is no theoretical support for it and one may not assume that the penalties currently imposed in the case of the exercise of the right to trial would be the rule in a scenario without plea bargaining.[249] Yet, considering the Brazilian legal system, these arguments are even more emphatically rejected. There is no need to talk about the necessity or imposition of the system in relation to a mechanism that has not yet been introduced into the legal system.

Regarding the justification for the acceptance of the bargain in the United States, the Supreme Court decisions that legitimised such mechanism are paradigmatic. In cases judged in 1970 and 1971, in particular, not only did the highest body of the American Judiciary address the theme of plea bargaining but also approved its use.[250] In *Brady v. United States*, it was agreed that the guilty plea benefits all parties by avoiding trial responsibilities.[251] Finally, in *Santobello v. New York*, it was determined that plea bargaining "is not only an essential part of the proceeding, but also highly desirable".[252]

Later, in 1977, *Blackledge v. Allison* clarified that "whatever the situation in an ideal world may be, the fact is that the guilty plea and the often-accompanying plea bargaining are important components of this country's criminal justice system.

---

[241] Cafferata (1998), p. 143.

[242] Fine (1987), p. 615.

[243] Examples cited include the case of Alaska and other cities, which abolished plea bargaining for some period of time and achieved positive results. See: Fine (1987), pp. 628–630. Some question these results, see: Hessick and Saujani (2002), p. 233.

[244] Schulhofer (1984), p. 1106.

[245] Heumann (1981), p. 158; Albergaria (2007), p. 132.

[246] Schulhofer (1984), p. 1046.

[247] Alschuler 1979, p. 964.

[248] Albergaria (2007), p. 131.

[249] Alschuler (1981), pp. 724–730.

[250] Heumann (1981), p. 13.

[251] Bibas (2003), p. 7.

[252] Diego Díez (1999), p. 55.

When properly administered, they can benefit all parties involved".[253] In his critique, **Albert Alschuler** argues that these decisions are flawed, revealing that, in essence, their arguments are flawed and rhetorical, always guided by the supposed need of the mechanism and never by its constitutional compatibility or effective contributions to the criminal system, beyond the desired swiftness.[254]

On the other hand, the thesis that bargaining is a typical and original mechanism in the US common law system, supposedly used since its dawn,[255] is weakened by the scholars who criticise it based on a significant historical survey.[256] According to **Albert Alschuler**, plea bargaining was not used before the late nineteenth century[257] and, in its early days, was even rejected by the Judiciary.[258] It can therefore be said that this mechanism does not fit as a systemic characteristic and "is not, so to speak, inscribed in the genetic heritage of the American criminal procedure, but rather shows a phenotypic trait of it, acquired and consolidated in the course of the nineteenth century".[259]

After weakening the supposed inevitability of plea bargaining, we now move on to the study of the causes normally indicated as promoters of its emergence. They essentially relate to the difficulty of managing a system capable of properly judging all criminal cases, due to the increase in their number and the complexity of their trials.[260] Regarding the first reason—the growth of procedural pressure[261]—scholars usually describe the scenario of social effervescence typical of the nineteenth-century United States, which witnessed a multiplication and diversification of the forms of conflicts and the need for appeal to formal resolution mechanisms, resulting in a drastic increase in the number of cases to be judicially tried.[262] Thus, bargaining would have emerged as the only necessary instrument for the State's response to this panorama.[263]

However, some scholars challenge this idea of an overloaded judicial system as a cause of the expansion of plea bargaining: according to **Milton Heumann**, based

---

[253] Albergaria (2007), p. 47.

[254] Alschuler (1975b), p. 71.

[255] Heumann (1981), p. 157.

[256] See, among others cited: Fisher (2003); Friedman (1979).

[257] Alschuler (1979), pp. 212–213. In this sense, also: Langbein (1974), p. 261.

[258] Alschuler (1979), pp. 214–217; Dervan, Edkins (2012), p. 7.

[259] Albergaria (2007), p. 27.

[260] George Fisher (2003), pp. 6–10, describes three waves of historical studies that aimed to explain the causes of the emergence of plea bargaining: (1) increase in workload; (2) greater complexity of trials; and (3) development of preliminary investigation. Regarding the third, it is said that, with the development of the preliminary investigation stage, more solid evidence was secured at this initial stage of prosecution, thus reducing the importance of a subsequent trial. However, this hypothesis is not deeply addressed by legal literature, being considered only sporadically.

[261] This reason is also presented by German scholars to describe the scenario of introducing agreements in the German criminal procedure. See: Rauxloh (2011), p. 301.

[262] Albergaria (2007), p. 30; Fisher (2003), pp. 40–44.

[263] Leite (2013), p. 47.

on a statistical study tracking the levels of cases and bargains, a direct proportionality between these variables is dismissed, concluding by objecting to the thesis of pressure from the workload[264] and by pointing out that, even in courts not affected by the workload, the percentage of agreements was increasing.[265] Based on another theoretical framework, but sharing the intention to dismiss the explanation that procedural pressure was the cause of the emergence of plea bargaining, **Mary Vogel** builds a thesis of political and cultural nature for the origin of this mechanism, seeking to clarify that, in the scenario of social struggles of the city of Boston between 1830 and 1860 (the scope of the study), bargaining emerged as a political tool to deal with popular revolts stemming from sporadic episodes of lenience by the government.[266]

In this vein, one could cite an argument that alludes to the supposed benefit brought by plea bargaining in a scenario of judicial overload. It is argued that reaching agreements contributes to the reduction of the number of pre-trial detention,[267] while it would supposedly resolve the criminal case swiftly, imposing the definitive punishment.[268] The fallacious tone of the thesis is evident, as it aggravates the situation of the accused from their waiving of the fundamental right to trial in order to supposedly improve a situation (the prolongation of a pre-trial detention in terrible conditions, due to the delay in the proceedings) caused by the inefficiency of the State itself, that is, the government "intends to solve the situation, whose responsibility is entirely their own, by transferring the burden to the accused".[269]

Another element of the scenario that supposedly fostered the triumph of agreements between prosecution and defence, in addition to the increase in the number of cases to be resolved judicially, is the growing complexity of trials[270]—especially based on the widespread participation of legal counsel, and the increase in their powers and possibilities to act,[271] the length of proceedings has increased.[272] This slowness in the course of the evidentiary stage is particularly attributed to the system of trial by lay judges, which, theoretically, is the right of all individuals accused

---

[264] Heumann (1981), p. 32. Heumann (1981), p. 154, develops an argument based on a study about the adaptation of criminal system actors to bargaining, concluding that this mechanism is also routinely used in scenarios different from the overloaded one usually described. For a critique of Heumann's thought, see: Fisher (2003), pp. 9 and 294. For a study on procedural pressure in cases of minor offences, see: Feeley (1992), pp. 247–261.

[265] Heumann (1981), p. 154.

[266] Vogel (2007), pp. 3–9; Vogel (1999). For a critique of the author's thesis, see: Fisher (2003), pp. 45–46 and 138–152.

[267] On the issue of pre-trial detention in Brazil and its unlimited and illegitimate use, see: Vasconcellos (2013).

[268] Alkon (2010), p. 404.

[269] Córdoba (2005), pp. 241–242. In this sense, also: Bovino (2005), p. 76.

[270] Albergaria (2007), pp. 30–32.

[271] On the strengthening of the defence with advocacy and its relationship with the development of the adversarial system, see: Malan (2009), pp. 14–15; Feeley (1997), pp. 192–194; Langbein (2003), pp. 291–310.

[272] Feeley (1997), pp. 202–204.

of a crime,[273] with their rules of jury selection, exclusions of evidence, and deadlines against undue delay of the case.[274]

Therefore, the history of plea bargaining is linked to the improvement of the criminal justice system aimed at respecting fundamental rights,[275] since in the past the cases would have been solved swiftly, without major guarantees to the accused.[276] However, some challenge this description of the US scenario, stating, on the one hand, that trials would not be not as swift as it is commonly described[277] and, on the other, downplaying the relevance of this greater complexity to the increase in the number of bargains.[278]

In any case, it can be stated that the improvement of the US adversarial model based on jury trials was, in theory, implemented in a way inversely proportional to its practical implementation, that is, "the expansion of the adversarial system as a normative model led to a degradation of it as a historical/concrete model".[279] In contrast to this scenario, without succumbing to bargaining, Stephen Schulhofer proposes the adoption of the bench trial model in the United States, which is characterised by a trial conducted by a single non-lay judge.[280] Thus, the option that would enable the trial of the accused by the US justice system is already the general procedure in the Brazilian system, which, once again, eliminates the need for expansion of spaces for consensus, through the mechanism of the bargain, in the Brazilian legal system.

In addition to justifying plea bargaining due to its necessity in a context of an overloaded judicial systems, it is also necessary to present some theoretical constructs that aim to support and legitimise these agreements between prosecution and defence in criminal justice. Essentially, this is based on three propositions that characterise bargaining as: (1) a sentencing device that benefits all actors in the criminal proceeding; (2) a form of conflict resolution by consensus[281]; and (3) an administrative proceeding with its own rules.[282]

Firstly, the agreement between the parties—and the consequent sentence reduction—is justified as a sentencing device, especially on the grounds of a supposed

[273] Langbein (1992), pp. 119–123.

[274] Diego Díez (1999), pp. 37–38, describes that the jury selection system allows for extensive questioning and exclusion of lay judges, which can prolong this process for days or even months; also, the complexity of the rules on evidence increases the workload for the solidification of the accusatory thesis; and, finally, the right to a speedy trial imposes respect for legally established deadlines, which, if not met, result in the archiving of the case.

[275] Alschuler 2009, p. 240.

[276] Langbein (1979), pp. 262–265; Langbein (1978), pp. 8–10.

[277] Fisher (2003), p. 245.

[278] Fisher 2003, p. 10.

[279] Albergaria (2007), p. 32.

[280] Schulhofer (1984), p. 1064.

[281] Alschuler (1981), p. 652.

[282] McCoy (2005), p. 16.

reward for the accused's expression of remorse in agreeing to the bargain.[283] It is ensured that accused individuals who acknowledge their guilt express remorse for their crimes and are thus rewarded with a reduced punishment.[284] In this vein, some legitimise this assertion based on the theory of positive special function of penalties, which explains punishment for its rehabilitative and resocialising nature,[285] since remorse would show that the accused is already at a more advanced stage of recovery, which would reduce the need for a longer sentence.[286]

There are several criticisms of this construction, since, on the one hand, proof of alleged remorse is unfeasible and mere adherence to the agreement does not certify it.[287] Furthermore, the exercise of the right to trial can be legitimised for various reasons, which does not lead to the assumption that the accused is not remorseful.[288] Similarly, it is argued that a sentence reduction is justified by the saving of State resources brought about by the waiver of the trial,[289] but, certainly, a benefit in punishment without any link to the act committed, and instead based on economic criteria, is highly questionable in a Criminal Law guided by the principle of culpability.[290]

In the same vein, bargaining brings benefits to all involved and actors in the legal-criminal field. In other words, the parties make concessions to obtain mutual advantages, such as reducing uncertainty and trial risks.[291] The accused avoids costs, insecurities, damages and delays of the trial,[292] besides obtaining a supposed sentence reduction for leniency[293]; their legal counsel obtains a swifter financial return and lessens their responsibilities.[294] The prosecutors reduce costs and their workloads, in addition to obtaining easy convictions that help in their professional progress[295]; similarly, the judges benefit, especially with the reduction of the caseload[296];

283 Bibas (2003), p. 40.

284 Lippke (2011), p. 97.

285 Roxin (1997), pp. 85–89.

286 Lippke (2011), p. 112.

287 Alschuler (1981), pp. 661–662.

288 McCoy (2005), p. 15.

289 Lippke (2011), p. 69.

290 Batista (2007), pp. 102–105; Roxin (1997), pp. 791–794.

291 Feeley 1997, p. 185.

292 In a study about the cases of guilty plea in terrorism-related crimes, Lucian Dervan (2011), pp. 291–296, points out that, sometimes, the accused may seek benefits not directly related to their punishment, but rather to other burdens of the trial, such as financial or social damages to their family, psychological issues, and increased stigma from media exposure if the trial is conducted.

293 Diego Diez (1999), p. 57.

294 Heumann (1981), p. 156. The relationship between the accused and the legal counsel and the dysfunctionality caused by the bargaining system will be analysed in Sects. 4.1.2 and 4.1.6. See also: Alschuler (1975a), pp. 1.210–1.270.

295 Rodríguez García (1997), p. 94.

296 Lippke (2011), p. 243.

finally, the State also profits from the saving of resources.[297] This conception was endorsed by the US Supreme Court in the case *Blackledge v. Allison*, in which it was stated: "whatever the situation in an ideal world, the fact is that the *guilty plea* and the often concomitant *plea bargaining* are important components of this country's criminal justice system. Correctly administered, they can benefit all those involved".[298]

However, this understanding is criticised based on two observations. On the one hand, it is clear that the benefit to the accused is fallacious, especially in a scenario of over-charging,[299] but not limited to, as, in many cases, the reduction of the sentence is negligible, so that the punishment imposed with the agreement resembles that which would be determined after the trial.[300] Thus, it is evident that "this supposed 'exchange' is a perverse lie; the only one who gives in is the individual pursued criminally and they give up the only thing they have, each and every one of their guarantees, that is, all limitation to the exercise of criminal power".[301] On the other hand, some argue that the concessions and benefits between prosecution and accused cannot be compared, as there is no possible calculation between the time of freedom and the costs of a trial.[302] Therefore, as **Gabriel Anitua** points out, "who ends up benefiting more from this system is the punitive intention of the State, which thus achieves its objective in greater number, at a lower cost and more quickly".[303]

Also, following a similar line of reasoning, some point out that the negotiation mechanism contributes to the promotion of the dignity of the accused, thus bringing benefit by enabling their participation in the case decision,[304] besides valuing their freedom of choice.[305] On this respect, some even point out a perversity in the argument[306]: there is no real participation in the agreement, which, in most cases, is

[297] Diego Díez (1999) p. 61.

[298] Albergaria (2007), p. 47. Also in: Dias, Andrade (1997), p. 487.

[299] "However, what happens is just the opposite for the charges are inflated in a way that allows, after the bargain, the accused to receive the sentence that, through due process of law, they should receive if found guilty and convicted" (Paschoal 2001, p. 119).

[300] Alschuler (1981), pp. 654–656.

[301] Bigliani (2005), p. 189.

[302] Alschuler (1981), pp. 670–671.

[303] Anitua (2005), p. 155. The (autophagic) relationship between the bargain and the scenario of Criminal Law expansion will be analysed in Sect. 4.1.1 of this work.

[304] Diego Díez (1999), p. 58; Rodríguez García (1997), p. 93.

[305] Lippke (2011), p. 169.

[306] "[...] this perspective on things suffers from a great dose of cynicism, as it pretends to ignore that that negotiation and that agreement are most often imposed on the accused through forms of pressure and through the erosion of rights and procedural guarantees that are, themselves, pledge of a participation (effectively, materially) constitutive in the words of the law of the case" (Albergaria 2007, p. 116).

imposed on the accused due to threats of higher penalties in case of trial[307]; and, moreover, their role would be much more significant during the regular trial.[308]

After analysing the bargain as a sentencing device, which would bring advantages to all actors in the criminal trial and revealing its weaknesses, we move on to the second position justifying agreements between prosecution and defence in the criminal proceeding: regarding it as a form of conflict resolution by consensus.[309] It is argued that plea bargaining, based on the rational adjustment of trial risks,[310] promotes conflict resolution by means of the agreement between the accusatory claim and the defensive resistance.[311] Indeed, there is also the premise that both parties end up benefiting, but, unlike the previous idea, it is affirmed that this contributes to achieving a fair outcome.

Be that as it may, the legitimacy of such an agreement is weakened by the observation that the presumption of freedom of decision is often violated by the pressures and coercions that permeate the bargaining scenario.[312] A significant shift is noted in the legitimising premises of the negotiation mechanism, as, at first, it was authorised in cases of presumed certainty of conviction, that is, when the situation of the accused did not allow for further discussions. However, within a rational risk-adjustment framework, the agreements aim to reduce the dangers of an uncertain trial, in which neither party is in a position of advantage due to the evidentiary basis produced.[313] Therefore, the malleable discourse of the bargain is highlighted, which is inverted to legitimise its expansion.

One of the theoretical defences of plea bargaining is developed by **Frank Easterbrook**. Initially, the author argued that agreements between prosecution and defence were an integral part of a criminal justice system guided by economic considerations,[314] that is, an "element in a well-functioning market system".[315] Thus, this mechanism is seen under the light of the invocation of contractual law models and economic theory to characterise it as voluntary transactions that maximise the welfare of both parties.[316] Based on the premise that the function of criminal law and, specifically, punishment is deterrence/intimidation (negative general

---

307 Alschuler 1981, p. 668–669.

308 Córdoba (2005), p. 247.

309 Lippke (2011), p. 167.

310 Church (1979), pp. 516–518.

311 Alschuler (1981), p. 683.

312 Tulkens (2005), pp. 712–714. Regarding the coercibility of the proposal, see Sect. 4.1.3 of this work.

313 Alschuler (1981), pp. 693–694.

314 Regarding his considerations about economic thinking in Law, see: Easterbrook (1989). According to the author, criminal procedure is a method of allocating scarce resources (Easterbrook 1983, p. 290). For a critical analysis of economic logic in the pursuit of an efficient trial, see: Rosa and Marcelino Junior (2012), pp. 14–53.

315 Easterbrook (1983), p. 289.

316 Ross (2010), p. 116.

prevention),[317] the author defines that the "price" of committing a crime is the amount of the penalty multiplied by the probability that it will be imposed.[318] Thus, the discretion of the Public Prosecutor and plea bargaining operate based on market rules, so that both prosecutor and accused guide their attitudes similarly to buyers and sellers.[319] Not only would this mechanism be a necessary evil, but also a desirable tool to optimise criminal prosecution with the least expenditure of State resources.[320]

In a later work, **Easterbrook** reaffirms his convictions, refining certain concepts, such as the idea of bargaining as a contract, to ultimately state that "plea bargains are commitments" and thus, "autonomy and efficiency legitimise them".[321] Indeed, this construction deserves criticism in various ways[322]: first, the author assumes that the freedom of the accused and their right to due process may (and he even asserts that they must) be sold in a market like any other consumable good[323]; also, the premise that the bargain is a commitment between the parties presents an aporia when it is revealed that the accused's will is not free to make such a decision[324]; finally, he takes the current scenario of the US criminal justice system (in which criminal law has expanded to incomparable parameters) as a basis without further questioning about the legitimacy of this action—in other words, according to him, plea bargaining is a necessary tool in this scenario, but, in truth, it may be a reflection of a pathological punitive power.[325]

Finally, the last of the three theories that explain the bargain and the consequent reduction in the accused's punishment defines this institution as an administrative proceeding with its own rules[326] and, therefore, specific parameters for respecting fundamental rights. In this sense, **Gerard Lynch** proposes that the agreements between prosecution and defence be analysed as a system in itself,[327] not perverting the traditional criminal justice model,[328] but rather presenting potentially reasonable

---

[317] Regarding the theory of negative general prevention, see: Roxin (1997), pp. 89–93. For a critique of the categories of substantive criminal law: Albrecht (2010), pp. 86–90; Lorenzi (2020).

[318] Easterbrook (1983), p. 292.

[319] Lippke (2011), p. 124. According to Easterbrook, plea bargaining sets the price in the same way as a negotiation in the market of goods and services (Easterbrook, 1983, p. 308).

[320] Easterbrook (1983), p. 309.

[321] Easterbrook (1992), p. 1.978.

[322] Lippke (2011), pp. 125–145.

[323] Langbein (1992), p. 125.

[324] See the following Sect. 4.1.3 of this work, in which the coercibility of the bargain proposal and the consequent problematic in relation to the punishment of innocents is analysed.

[325] Regarding the contours of plea bargaining and its relationship with the expansion of Criminal Law, see the following Sect. 4.1.1 of this work.

[326] "[...] the negotiation of a guilty plea should be seen, above all, as a process within which the Public Prosecutor makes multiple decisions and constantly evaluates and updates all those possibilities" (Albergaria 2007, p. 65).

[327] Lynch (2012), p. 39.

[328] Lynch (1998), p. 298.

rules capable of structuring a complex process of attributing responsibility to the accused.[329]

Therefore, the power to judge the criminal case would be shifted to the Public Prosecutor,[330] but this would not be a problem in itself,[331] so an analysis would be required to verify whether this system is capable of producing fair, appropriate and free decisions (bargains).[332] Thus, the author proposes that this model be accepted and, instead of ineffective criticisms, regulations and improvements be sought, such as, for example, the establishment of criteria for the prosecutor's decision, the implementation of the adversarial principle and even the structuring of an internal appeal system for higher-ranking officials within the Public Prosecutor's Office.[333] In a similar vein, one can point to the statements of **Silva Jardim**, who, when analysing the criminal settlement introduced by Law 9.099/1995, attested that there is no violation of the principle of compulsoriness and the need for a proceeding to impose a penalty, since the offering of the settlement is the exercise of the criminal action by the representative of the Prosecutor's Office and that there is, thus, a "due legal process" for the imposition of these sanctions.[334]

Criticism of this line of thinking is consistent. Indeed, as **Geraldo Prado** points out, regarding the supposed due legal process, "one may conclude that in reality it does not exist and that the criminal settlement consists exactly in the accused 'waiving' the due legal process".[335] An administrative proceeding for criminal accountability is inadmissible in a Democratic Rule of Law, as it violates several of its premises, such as impartiality and the adversarial principle (which cannot be an option of the prosecutor as Lynch points out).[336]

In light of the above, by way of conclusion, it has been revealed that the explanations for the mechanisms of bargaining and negotiation between prosecution and defence for the imposition of an anticipated punishment are weak and questionable, failing to provide an acceptable basis to these mechanisms. In other words, there is no rational explanation, much less a justification compatible with the premises of criminal procedure. The common trait between the origin and development of plea

---

329 Lynch (1998), p. 300.

330 Dervan (2011), p. 246.

331 According to Lynch (2012), p. 320, the practical infeasibility of implementing the American accusatory theoretical model led to the creation and development of the plea bargaining system, so its characteristics should be analysed from the observation that its imposition is legitimate in reality.

332 Turner (2006), p. 516.

333 Lynch (1998), pp. 321–327.

334 Jardim (1998), pp. 100–101. Geraldo Prado (2006c), p. 225, initially adopted this position, stating that it is "merely the due legal process of a special form of conflict resolution". Later, in contrast: Prado (2006c), p. 177.

335 Prado (2006c), p. 224.

336 Lynch (1998), p. 302.

bargaining and the various other similar mechanisms in foreign legal systems is the stance of the actors in the criminal-legal field.[337]

Indeed, what determines the success of bargaining is its full adherence to the interests of those directly involved and responsible for managing criminal justice,[338] especially those with the greatest power in administering the punitive sphere of the State: members of the prosecuting body (the Public Prosecutor's Office) and judges (the judiciary). Thus, it is "a construction of the procedural actors, something created by them and meant to satisfy, above all, their interests".[339] Therefore, bargaining is a mechanism that starts with the power of those who benefit from its consequences,[340] and expands to a point that, according to **George Fisher**, it acquires its own powers and ends up influencing the entire criminal justice system, strengthening it and those who defend it while also weakening any attempt to reduce its effectiveness.[341]

2.2.3 Requirements: The Illusory Attempt to Rationalise and Limit Negotiation Metastasis

In order to structure a legal framework of requirements aimed at determining, the admissibility of agreements within the criminal procedure depending on the specific situation, three conditions for their validity have been defined by legal scholarship and caselaw: voluntariness, intelligence and adequacy.[342] This subtopic will address these assumptions based on the example of the plea bargaining in the United States by clarifying its delimitations and questioning its real possibilities of limiting the punitive power imposed through agreements between prosecution and defence. In a brief introductory summary, an agreement is legitimate if it is accepted by the accused under conditions of voluntary freedom, without pressures or coercion, with knowledge of its terms and of its consequences, especially the waiver of fundamental rights, such as the right to defence and adversarial principle,[343] besides presenting, at last, a minimum factual basis to attest its adequacy to the case.[344] As pointed out by the critical view of some legal scholars, in practice, these requirements do not fulfil their objectives, so that they only certify a fallacious procedural legitimisation

[337] On the influence of the actors' stance on the management of criminal justice and the imposition of the punitive power of the State, see: Carvalho (2010), pp. 59–111.

[338] The relationship between bargaining and the interests of the criminal justice actors will be analysed in detail in Sect. 4.1.2 of this book.

[339] Albergaria (2007), p. 33.

[340] As already mentioned, the benefit brought to the accused is fallacious and not determinant in the instrumentalisation of the bargain in its triumph in criminal justice.

[341] Fisher (2003), p. 175.

[342] Diego Díez (1999), pp. 68–73.

[343] Armenta Deu (2012), p. 32.

[344] Ross (2010), p. 109.

to the bargain due to its inefficient real review, which attests a false and illusory democratic nature to the negotiation mechanism.[345]

These assumptions are analysed in the judge's statement, usually titled "ratification of the agreement", which questions the attention to certain rights and guarantees allegedly secured for the accused.[346] In theory, the US judge can reject the plea bargaining for reasons beyond the violation of any of the requirements, such as due to "public interest in the effective administration of justice", as there would be discretion in this decision-making function.[347] However, this judicial review, in the vast majority of cases, has become a mere formality,[348] given the negligible brevity of this analysis,[349] the lack of evidential basis for making an informed decision,[350] and the judiciary's interest in minimising the number of cases in which a regular trial is necessary.[351]

In this respect, it is relevant to briefly discuss the judge's position regarding the agreement. According to most scholars and the rules of most US states, the judge shall remain passive in negotiations between prosecution and defence, reviewing the terms of the bargain after its signing.[352] However, in practice, the judge's involvement in the negotiations is routine[353] and some even advocate for its legislative authorisation in favour of greater predictability of the outcomes of the bargains and more respect for fundamental rights with the direct involvement of the judge.[354] It is thought, along with the mainstream view, that the proposal for direct action inevitably violates the necessary impartiality of the judge, as well as breaking with the system of consensual justice. Therefore, the judge shall maintain a position of post-agreement review, aiming to ensure the protection of the accused's fundamental rights and respect for procedural rules.

---

345 Rodríguez García (1997), p. 89.

346 Bovino (2005), p. 61.

347 Albergaria (2007), p. 96. For example, the case *United States v. Ammidown* is cited, in which the agreement that reduced the punishment by downgrading a first degree murder in exchange for the confession and the turn state's evidence in which the sanction to the perpetrator of the crime was considered disproportionate to the gravity of the crime (Albergaria 2007, p. 98).

348 Taruffo (2008), p. 220. Similarly, Garcez Ramos (2006), p. 188, states: "theoretically, the judge should review the bargain and verify whether it meets minimum procedural ethics requirements. In practice, it seems, the bargain request is entirely dominated by the parties" .

349 Rodriguez García (1996), p. 76, asserts that the time taken by the Court to accept the bargain is extremely short and, based on empirical studies, points out the following data: in more serious cases the average is 9.9 min and in less relevant ones, 5.2 min, resulting in an overall average of 7.8 min per approval.

350 Fernandes (2005), p. 266.

351 According to Pedro Albergaria, besides the factual difficulty in reviewing such requirements, what determines the futility of judicial review is the "judicial interest (shared with the Public Prosecutor's Office) in keeping the trials at the lowest possible rate" (Albergaria 2007, p. 100).

352 Turner (2009), p. 23.

353 Albergaria (2007), p. 80.

354 Alschuler (1976), pp. 1.107–1.113. The German example of agreements in criminal proceedings can be cited, in which the judge plays an active role in their implementation (Turner 2009, p. 520).

2.2.3.1 Voluntariness: The Alleged Freedom of Choice to Negotiate and Waive the Trial

The first condition for the validity of the bargain is the free voluntariness of the accused to accept the proposal for early implementation of punitive power. This analysis is initially related to the capacity of the accused to be in court,[355] but, fundamentally, it aims to prevent the acceptance of the agreement due to threats or pressures, which would taint the will to decide.[356] According to the decision of the US Supreme Court in the case *Brady v. United States,* the statement is voluntary as long as it is not induced by actual or threatened physical violence or by mental coercion that taints the will of the accused.

Several hypotheses of violation of the accused's voluntariness to make the bargain were raised in cases tried by the US judiciary, but, as a rule, the ratification of the agreement as legitimate was maintained. Two cases tried in the Supreme Court are emblematic and will be discussed later in this book. Still, for now, it is worth pointing them out: (1) in *North Carolina v. Alford,* plea bargaining was upheld upon the accused's acceptance, but without their admission of guilt. In other words, even though they declared themselves innocent, they did not oppose a long prison sentence, because, if they opted for trial, they could be sentenced to death (therefore, they accepted the agreement claiming to be innocent, under the coercion that, if they did not, they could be sentenced to death)[357]; and, (2) in *Bordenkircher v. Hayes,* a bargain was accepted; it imposed a five-year prison sentence for the offence of issuing a forged check for the amount of $88.30, because, due to a disproportionate law that allowed for life imprisonment for repeat offenders,[358] the accused was threatened by the prosecutor, who stated that if he exercised his right to trial, he would be indicted and tried by a jury under the said law.[359]

The limitations imposed by caselaw on the Public Prosecutor's Office stipulate that they cannot conceal evidence favourable to the defence or fabricate false clues to encourage a deal; moreover, theoretically, the prosecutor's vindictiveness due to the accused's exercise of the right to trial is prohibited.[360] However, these restrictions have little applicability given the discretion and openness of interpretation that allows various types of agreements and counteroffers.[361] For example, in *United States v. Nuckols*, a plea bargaining was approved, threatening the accused that if he did not accept the proposal, his wife would be jointly accused.[362] Therefore, the

---

[355] According to Pedro Albergaria, the assumption of the accused's ability to make a statement of guilt is understood as the "general criterion of 'competence to stand trial'"(Albergaria 2007, p. 81).

[356] Rodríguez García (1996), pp. 86–87.

[357] Diego Diez (1999), pp. 68–69.

[358] For a critical analysis of this model of legislation, see: Almeida (2021), pp. 196–198.

[359] Turner (2009), p. 38.

[360] Hessick and Saujani (2002), pp. 203–204.

[361] Diego Díez (1999), p. 69.

[362] Hessick and Saujani (2002), p. 204.

dogmatic fragility of the requirement of voluntariness in a scenario driven by bargaining is evident, given the inherent coerciveness of the proposal to reduce punishment in the event of renouncing the trial and the caselaw construction of its contours which, as it will be seen in the next subsection (since both requirements share this reason for weakening), is extremely relativised if any violation is cured by the presence of legal counsel.[363]

2.2.3.2 Information/Intelligence: The Fictions of Informed Decision and Rational Choice

In addition to voluntariness, the accused's decision to admit their guilt and accept the early imposition of a criminal sanction must be informed/intelligent. The Court must ensure that the accused is aware of their situation regarding the charges made and the facts described by the prosecutor, as well as the consequences of their acceptance of the bargain, both in relation to the rights they are waiving and the punishments that will be imposed on them, as well as their collateral effects.[364] In this regard, according to the US Supreme Court, in the decision of *Henderson v. Morgan,* the accused must receive accurate information about the nature of the charge against them.[365]

Therefore, this condition aims to prevent the accused from being deceived by the prosecutor or from making a decision without essential knowledge of their conditions and consequences.[366] To this end, one must take three aspects into account. First, it is essential to understand the charges, that is, the nature of the allegations for which they are held responsible, as well as to clarify which facts need to be proven to authorise a guilty verdict.[367] It is also essential to understand the consequences of the agreement, especially the penalty to be imposed and its possible repercussions, such as the maximum and minimum punishment's thresholds, the terms for progression of regime or probation, the possibility of conversion into a non-restrictive sentence, the need to repair the damages caused, among other consequences.[368] Finally, there must be an understanding of the rights that are objects of waiving from the consensus to the bargain, such as, for example, the right to defence, the right to legal counsel throughout the proceeding, to the adversarial proceeding, to non-self-incrimination, to trial by jury, and, in some cases, to appeal.[369]

---

[363] The demystification of the effectiveness of technical defence monitoring to prevent violations of the accused's rights will be analysed in Sects. 4.1.2 and 4.1.6, in which the distortion of the accused-legal counsel relationship caused by the possibility of bargaining will be pointed out.

[364] Albergaria (2007), p. 82.

[365] Turner (2009), p. 39.

[366] Diego Díez (1999), pp. 69–70.

[367] Rodríguez García (1997), pp. 47–48.

[368] Rodríguez García (1996), pp. 87–88.

[369] Rodríguez García (1997), p. 49.

As noted, both requirements—voluntariness and intelligence—are relativised in practice, making the review of the bargain a mere formality.[370] Furthermore, it is widely accepted that the accused's having a legal counsel implies the fulfilment of both prerequisites of the agreement,[371] which is clearly questionable in a scenario in which the relations between accused and legal counsel in many cases become dysfunctional and pathological.[372] Moreover, the possibility of nullifying the plea bargaining would only occur upon proof that the technical assistance was ineffective or incompetent, coupled with the demonstration of the resulting harm,[373] which, based on the criteria determined by the Supreme Court, proves to be unfeasible due to its unique complexity.[374] Finally, **Albert Alschuler** asserts that the contours of the defence deficiency hypotheses were developed by the US judiciary based on cases in which there was a jury trial proceeding, which, as it is well-known, is the exception in the criminal justice cases of that country.[375] Thus, it becomes unfeasible to demonstrate this in cases of plea bargaining, since such requirements cannot be proven without the entire trial taking place, which does not occur in the situation of accepting the agreement.

2.2.3.3 Adequacy/Accuracy: The Fallacy of Judicial Review Over the Factual Basis

The final cumulative condition for the judicial approval of the bargain is that the terms must be adequate and accurate,[376] represented by a supposed minimum correlation between the charges made by the accused and those that would theoretically correspond to the actual facts, in addition to the obligation of a factual basis that supports the recognition of guilt of the accused.[377] This is, without a doubt, the most

[370] Alberto Bovino (2005), pp. 61–62, cites two examples: both the need to inform about the maximum penalty that can be applied after the bargain and its related effects have become dispensable due to decisions of the US judiciary.

[371] According to Albert Alschuler (1975b), p. 1, three decisions are paradigmatic in this regard: *McMann v. Richardson*, *Parker v. North Carolina*, and *Brady v. United States*, in all of which the validity of bargains with clear traces of threats in case of exercising the right to trial was confirmed. Thus, Edmundo Hendler (1996), p. 199, also points out: "The carefully guarded point and on which, in essence, all the support of the system's legitimacy is based is the effective assistance of legal counsel in the negotiation".

[372] Alschuler (1986), p. 149. Also, refer to Sects. 4.1.2 and 4.1.6 of this book, in which the distortion of the accused-counsel relationship caused by the possibility of bargaining will be analysed.

[373] Albergaria (2007), pp. 76–79; Hessick, Saujani (2002), pp. 215–220; Alschuler (1986), p. 155.

[374] "Be that as it may, the mere existence of a conflict of interest will not necessarily imply the recognition that the accused received legal assistance inferior to the adequate. It will be indispensable to demonstrate that the client received an ineffective defence for this reason, which, as the Supreme Court has affirmed, is very difficult" (Rodríguez García 1997, p. 59).

[375] Alschuler (1986), p. 154.

[376] Langbein (1978), p. 15.

[377] Rodríguez García (1997), p. 49.

discussed requirement by scholarship and caselaw, whether due to the difficulty in defining it, the question of the judge's ability to seek evidence to confirm the agreement, or the need for a link between the admitted charge and the actual event,[378] especially in cases of charge bargaining.[379]

However, there is no formal procedural standard to be followed by the judiciary to fulfil this condition, such as the degree of conformity between the statement and the facts, the method for obtaining evidence for this analysis, and the level of certainty required regarding the facts.[380] According to **Jenia Turner**, some Courts have defined the parameter of certainty as sufficient evidence at the time of the agreement from which the judge can reasonably determine that the accused likely committed the offence, whereas others simply require some factual basis or exclusively the accused's solid confession.[381]

This requirement is criticised by some legal scholars, as "the idea of 'accuracy' of the factual grounds supporting the statement of guilt (i.e., the perfect correspondence between the facts stated and the crime confessed) is incompatible, not to say contradictory, with the essence of negotiation".[382] However, it is believed that the need for factual support in order to accept the bargain is essential to the minimum adequacy of the mechanism with the foundations of a democratic criminal procedure (if this is possible at all), since the confession cannot be taken as the sole basis for a conviction.[383] In the US practice, even though the judiciary has broad discretion to reject the bargain at its prudent discretion, the analysis of the factual basis as a requirement for an agreement has become a mere formality,[384] distorting this premise and thus downplaying the limitations to negotiated justice.[385]

---

[378] Diego Díez (1999), p. 71.

[379] Rodríguez Garcia (1997), p. 50.

[380] Albergaria (2007), p. 87.

[381] Turner (2009), p. 41.

[382] Albergaria (2007), pp. 86–87.

[383] On this, see Sect. 4.1.4 of this book, in which the procedural setback caused by the bargaining mechanism will be critically analysed, especially due to the repositioning of confession as the queen of evidence. Thus, the said compatibility between the negotiation mechanisms and the premises of a democratic criminal procedure proves difficult, or even impossible.

[384] Turner (2009), p. 41. In an empirical study carried out in Germany, 72% of judges stated that they are satisfied with the confession of the accused to substantiate the ratification of agreements (Rauxloh 2011, p. 311).

[385] Bibas (2003), p. 69.

2.2.4 *Types of Bargain: On the Object and Modalities of the Settlement Mechanism*

Considering that, as explained, bargaining is essentially defined by three key characteristics (waiver of defence, imposition of an anticipated punishment, and the accused's hope of receiving some benefit for this consent), the next step for properly understanding the mechanism is explaining its possible functions, that is, the types of agreement that can occur in the criminal legal field. Once again, the US example of plea bargaining will be used as a basis, for the reasons already stated and because it is the most comprehensive mechanism in transactional terms, allowing for several variations for study and comparison with continental systems. Thus, two classifications will be used: according to the object and according to the offeror of the agreement.

First, regarding the content of the bargain, one can point out agreements on the sentence, on the charge, and on the facts.[386] In the first case, it is the sentence bargaining, in which the prosecuting authority proposes offering the judge a reduced sentence recommendation,[387] the application of probation or of some benefit defined in the final resolution of the case (such as serving the sentence in a specific facility, for example), if the accused recognises guilt.[388] According to **Nicolás García**, the prosecutor can also promise to refrain from making any recommendation (leaving the sentencing solely to the judge) or not to oppose the accused's request for leniency in the sentence.[389] It is noteworthy highlighting that the prosecutor's recommendation is not binding on the judge,[390] in theory[391]; however, it can be said that, in practice, the power to sentence has been transferred to the prosecutor, as it is very rare for a criminal sanction different from the recommended one to be imposed.[392]

On the other hand, charge bargaining was the precursor to bargaining in the United States[393] and offers a greater range of discretion to the prosecutor, given the lack of a similar concept to continental compulsoriness.[394] This possibility is imple-

[386] Albergaria (2007), pp. 22–26.

[387] Leite (2013), p. 75.

[388] Giacomolli (2006), p. 41.

[389] Rodríguez García (1996), p. 86. Regarding the possibilities of prosecution and defence positions before the judge, see: Heumann (1981), p. 43.

[390] Diego Díez (1999), p. 42; McCoy (2005), p. 17.

[391] Alschuler 1976, p. 1062.

[392] By pointing out that the system of plea bargaining achieved its objectives by trying more than 90% of American criminal cases, Albert Alschuler (1976), p. 1063, states that this is because the accused individuals can trust the agreements, since, although it is possible to impose a different sentence than recommended by the prosecutor, this seldom happens. Regarding the dysfunctionality caused by the bargain to the separation of functions, see Sect. 4.1.5 of this book.

[393] Fisher (2003), p. 12.

[394] McCoy 2005, p. 17.

mented through the alteration/distortion of the charge,[395] either by replacing the original one with a less serious one by removing one of the charges in case of multiple crimes, or by both.[396]

Generally, scholars argue that the new charge needs to have at least a link to the actual event. However, one may argue that, in practice, clearly illogical charges are accepted.[397] Criticisms to this form of bargaining are varied,[398] and the alleged benefit brought to the accused by the agreement is often seen as illusory,[399] because it has, been found, for example, that judges consider the original charges when sentencing the newly formulated charges.[400]

Furthermore, some people add the species of bargaining to the facts narrated in the charge. This is the so-called "fact bargaining", according to which it is possible to agree on the facts to be criminally charged,[401] which expresses the wide flexibility of the US criminal prosecution. Besides these possibilities, various others are authorised in a scenario of wide discretion, like the US one, so that bargaining can involve numerous other objects and conditions.[402] Given these types of agreement, **Pedro Albergaria** concludes that they all share a common essence: they aim to end the proceeding before the trial stage, imposing a lighter sentence, in broad terms. Therefore, "it is not unreasonable to assert that all negotiation is, in direct terms, sentence bargaining ".[403]

The other classification of bargaining concerns the proponent of the agreement, or rather, the official actor in the criminal proceeding who directly influences and reviews the agreement. This involves debating the participation of the judge in the settlement, a matter discussed among US scholars and authorised only in some of the judicial systems of the US states.[404] On the one hand, the system of prosecutorial bargaining is highlighted, in which the prosecutor exclusively assumes the initiative and determination of the agreement, leaving the judge in a passive position for the review of the formal requirements of the bargain.

On the other hand, judicial bargaining authorises the judge to propose and negotiate the terms of the agreement directly with the accused or their legal counsel.[405]

---

395 Rodríguez Garcia (1997), p. 42.

396 Diego Díez (1999), p. 43.

397 Diego Díez (1999), p. 43.

398 Alshuler (1976), pp. 1136–1145.

399 Alschuler (1968), pp. 95–97; Langbein (1978), p. 16.

400 Alschuler (1976), p. 1079.

401 Lippke (2011), p. 219.

402 Examples can be cited, such as scheduling the hearing on a specific date, deducting the time of pre-trial detention from the definitive sentence, refraining from accusing a third person, sending the convicted to a rehabilitation centre, among other conditions (Diego Díez 1999, p. 46).

403 Albergaria (2007), p. 26.

404 Turner (2006), pp. 539–558.

405 Fisher (2003), p. 130. As a rule, the example of the bargaining mechanism implemented in the German legal system is pointed out, in which the judge plays a crucial role in finalising the agreement. See: Turner (2006), pp. 517–539.

The criticisms and advantages attributed to this model are numerous. While, on the one hand, it increases the predictability of the penalty and the transparency of the negotiation, on the other, it questions the judge's impartiality to manage the possibilities of agreement.[406] According to **Albert Alschuler**, even though it is prohibited in some jurisdictions, the judge's participation or influence is common in the United States.[407]

Finally, it is necessary to describe a phenomenon typical of the American context, made possible by the broad discretion of the prosecutor, and used in conjunction with charge bargaining to obtain a heavy sentence, even in a bargaining situation. This is overcharging, which, knowing that the initial accusation delimits the scope for negotiation and sentence reduction, translates into charging the accused of a crime of which they are innocent in order to induce their acceptance of the agreement.[408] In other words, a more serious charge is filed without legitimate basis, ultimately obtaining a conviction for minor offences, which, supposedly, would have been appropriate to the facts from the outset.[409]

This practice can occur vertically, when a more serious crime is charged, or horizontally, when non-existent crimes are added.[410] Criticism of this phenomenon is heavy and widely debated[411]: it is indeed an instrument of pressure on the accused, intending to intimidate them and force the recognition of guilt.[412] Furthermore, the existence of any advantage to the accused, a benefit in return for their waiving of the right to defence, is challenged.[413] In fact, this is a significant issue, closely related to and driven by the bargain, which reveals a possible ethical dysfunction on the part of the prosecuting body in formulating charges.[414]

---

406 Leite (2013), pp. 74–75.

407 Alschuler (1976), p. 1061.

408 Alschuler (1968), p. 85.

409 Therefore, when "the Public Prosecutor's Office begins by pointing to particularly harsh forms of criminal liability, with the purpose of, by means of negotiation, ending up agreeing on a charge—that is to say a much more lenient sentence" (Dias and Andrade 1997, p. 486). See also: Rodríguez García (1997), pp. 68–69; Lippke (2011), p. 31.

410 Albergaria (2007), p. 66. It can be said that this practice has also occurred in the Brazilian criminal legal field, in situations as drug trafficking (commonly reported in conjunction with association to trafficking) or homicides (in which questionable aggravations are added), for example. Its occurrence in Germany is also described: Rauxloh (2011), p. 306.

411 It is pointed out that one of the main causes of the widespread use of plea bargaining is the coercion brought about by threats of harsher penalties. On this, see: Bowers (2008), p. 35; Bibas (2004), p. 2519. Some even question the efficiency benefits of overcharging: Alschuler (1968), p. 104.

412 Dias and Andrade (1997), p. 486; Naves (1995), p. 237.

413 Alschuler (1968), p. 97.

414 This description reveals the importance of judicial review for the criminal action in the Brazilian legal system usually undervalued and even automated, when receiving the charge. On this, there is a debate about the possibility of the judge changing the factual capitulation when receiving the charge. See: Lopes Jr. (2012), pp. 1098–1100.

References

Achutti D (2009) Modelos Contemporâneos de Justiça Criminal: Justiça Terapêutica, Instantânea e Restaurativa. Livraria do Advogado, Porto Alegre

Achutti D (2013) Justiça Restaurativa no Brasil: possibilidades a partir da experiência belga. Civitas. Revista de Ciências Sociais 13(1):154–181

Albergaria PS (2007) Plea Bargaining. Aproximação à justiça negociada nos E.U.A. Almedina, Coimbra

Albrecht PA (2010) Criminologia. Uma fundamentação para o direito penal. Lumen Juris, Rio de Janeiro

Alkon C (2010) Plea bargaining as a legal transplant: a good idea for troubled criminal justice systems? Transnat Law Contemp Probl 19:355–418

Almeida VR (2014) Transação penal e penas alternativas. Uma pesquisa empírica nos Juizados Especiais Criminais do Rio de Janeiro. Lumen Juris, Rio de Janeiro

Alschuler AW (1968) The prosecutor's role in plea bargaining. Univ Chic Law Rev 36:50–112

Alschuler AW (1975a) The defense attorney's role in plea bargaining. Yale Law J 84(6):1179–1314

Alschuler AW (1975b) The supreme court, the defense attorney, and the guilty plea. Univ Colo Law Rev 47:1–71

Alschuler AW (1976) The trial judge's role in plea bargaining, part I. Columbia Law Rev 76(7):1059–1154

Alschuler AW (1979) Plea bargaining and its history. Law Soc Rev 13:211–245

Alschuler AW (1981) The changing plea bargaining debate. Calif Law Rev 69:652–730

Alschuler AW (1983) Implementing the criminal defendant's right to trial: alternatives to the plea bargaining system. Univ Chic Law Rev 50(3):931–1050

Alschuler AW (1986) Personal failure, institutional failure, and the sixth amendment. N Y Univ Rev Law Soc Change 14:149–156

Alschuler AW (2009) Plea bargaining and the death penalty. DePaul Law Rev 58:671–680

Andrés Ibañez P (1997) Por um ministério público dentro da legalidade. Rev Minist Público Lisboa 18(70):9–41

Andrés Ibañez P (2001) Justiça de oportunidade: uma alternativa não jurisdicional ao processo penal. Rev Minist Público Lisboa 22(85):25–36

Anitua GI (2005) El juicio penal abreviado como una de las reformas penales de inspiración estadunidense que posibilitan la expansión punitiva. In: Maier JBJ, Bovino A (comps) El procedimiento abreviado. Del Puerto, Buenos Aires

Anitua GI (2010) El principio de legalidad y el principio de oportunidad: interrogantes y aporías en los sistemas anglosajones y continentales. In: Anitua GI (ed) Ensayos sobre enjuiciamiento penal. Del Puerto, Buenos Aires

Anitua GI, Borinsky M (1999) Principios de legalidad y oportunidad en los sistemas procesales penales europeos. In: Hendler E (dir) Sistemas procesales penales comparados. Ad Hoc, Buenos Aires

Antonucci E (2021) The evolution of the principle of mandatory prosecution in Italy. A problematic case of gradual institutional change. Int J Law Crime Just 66

Armenta Deu T (1991) Criminalidad de bagatela y principio de oportunidad: Alemania y España. PPU, Barcelona

Armenta Deu T (2008) Juicio de acusación, imparcialidad del acusador y derecho de defensa. In: Bachmaier Winter L (coord) Proceso penal y sistemas acusatorios. Marcial Pons, Madrid

Armenta Deu T (2012) Lecciones de derecho procesal penal, 6th edn. Marcial Pons, Madrid

Armenta Deu T (coord) (2013) La convergencia entre proceso civil y penal. ¿Una dirección adecuada? Marcial Pons, Madrid

Azevedo RG (2000) Informalização da justiça e controle social. IBCCrim, São Paulo

Anziliero DL (2008) Descaminhos da informalização da justiça penal no Brasil: entusiasmo e crise nos Juizados Especiais Criminais. Dissertation, Pontifícia Universidade Católica do Rio Grande do Sul, Porto Alegre

Barros Pellegrini FM, Carvalho MFC, Guimarães NC (2005) O consenso compreendido a partir do paradigma do Estado Democrático de Direito: uma crítica ao conceito de justiça consensual. Rev Informação Legislativa 168(42):147–153
Batista N (2007) Introdução crítica ao direito penal brasileiro, 11th edn. Revan, Rio de Janeiro
Bergalli R (1998) Principio de legalidad: fundamento de la modernidad. Jueces Democ 32:58–63
Bibas S (2003) Harmonizing substantive-criminal-law values and criminal procedure: the case of Alford and nolo contendere pleas. Cornell Law Rev 88(6):1–74
Bibas S (2004) Plea bargaining outside the shadow of trial. Harv Law Rev 117(8):2463–2547
Bigliani P (2005) El juicio abreviado y su recepción en el orden jurídico argentino. In: Maier JBJ, Bovino A (comps) El procedimiento abreviado. Del Puerto, Buenos Aires
Binder AM (2005) Legalidad y oportunidad. In: Baigún D et al. Estudios sobre justicia penal: homenaje al profesor Julio B. J. Maier. Del Puerto, Buenos Aires
Borges CMR (2013) Um olhar para além dos sistemas processuais penais. Rev Bras Ciênc Crim 104(21):147–171
Bovino A (2005) Principios políticos del procedimiento penal. Del Puerto, Buenos Aires
Bowers J (2008) Punishing the innocent. Univ Penn Law Rev 156:1–55
Caeiro P (2000) Legalidade e oportunidade: a perseguição penal entre o mito da justiça absoluta e o fetiche da gestão eficiente do sistema. Rev Ministério Público Lisboa 21(84):31–47
Cafferata NJI (1998) Cuestiones actuales sobre el proceso penal. Del Puerto, Buenos Aires
Carvalho S (2010) Antimanual de criminologia, 3rd edn. Lumen Juris, Rio de Janeiro
Casara RRR (2011) O acordo para aplicação da pena: novas considerações acerca da verdade e do consenso no processo penal brasileiro. In: Coutinho JMM, Carvalho LGG (eds) O novo processo penal à luz da Constituição. Análise crítica do Projeto de Lei n. 156/2009, do Senado Federal, vol 2. Lumen Juris, Rio de Janeiro
Church TW Jr (1979) In defense of "bargain justice". Law Soc Rev 13(2):509–525
Córdoba GE (2005) El juicio abreviado en el Código Procesal Penal de la Nación. In: Maier JBJ, Bovino A (comps) El procedimiento abreviado. Del Puerto, Buenos Aires
Costa Andrade M da (1977) Consenso e oportunidade. In: CEJ (org) O Novo Código de Processo Penal. Jornadas de Direito Processual Penal. Almedina, Coimbra
Costa EM (2001) Princípio da oportunidade: muitos vícios, poucas virtudes. Rev Ministério Público Lisboa 22(85):37–49
Coutinho JM (2001) Introdução aos princípios gerais do direito processual penal brasileiro. Rev Estudos Criminais 1:26–51
D'Avila FB (2009). Ofensividade em Direito Penal. Escritos sobre a teoria do crime como ofensa a bens jurídicos. Livraria do Advogado, Porto Alegre
Damaška M (2010) Negotiated justice in international criminal courts. In: Thaman S (ed) World plea bargaining. Consensual procedures and the avoidance of the full criminal trial. Carolina Academic Press, Durham
Delgado Barrio J (1990) El principio de oportunidad en el proceso penal: aplicación de la doctrina de los conceptos jurídicos indeterminados. Actualidad Penal 1(1/26):147–153
Dervan LE (2011) The surprising lessons from plea bargaining in the shadow of terror. Ga State Univ Law Rev 27(2):239–298
Dervan LE, Edkins V (2012) The innocent defendant's dilemma: an innovative empirical study of plea bargaining's innocence problem. J Crim Law Criminol 103(1):1–48
Dias JF (2004) Direito processual penal, 1st edn. Ed Coimbra, Coimbra
Dias JF (2011) Acordos sobre a sentença em processo penal. O "fim" do Estado de Direito ou um novo "princípio"? Conselho Distrital do Porto, Porto
Dias JF, Andrade MC (1997) Criminologia: o homem delinquente e a sociedade criminógena. Ed Coimbra, Coimbra
Diego Díez LA de (1999) Justicia criminal consensuada. Algunos modelos del derecho comparado en los EE. UU., Italia y Portugal. Tirant lo Blanch, Valencia
Divan GA (2014) Processo penal e política criminal: uma reconfiguração da justa causa para a ação penal. Tese (Doutorado em Ciências Criminais)—Faculdade de Direito, Pontifícia Universidade Católica do Rio Grande do Sul, Porto Alegre
Duarte HG, Marques LAM (2008) Justiça consensual e tutela dos direitos individuais. PHRONESIS: Revista do Curso de Direito da FEAD 4:65–74

Easterbrook FH (1983) Criminal procedure as a market system. J Leg Stud 12:289–332
Easterbrook FH (1989) The inevitability of law and economics. Legal Educ Rev 1:3–28
Easterbrook FH (1992) Plea bargaining as compromise. Yale Law J 101:1969–1978
Feeley MM (1992) The process is the punishment. Handling cases in a lower criminal court. Russell Sage, New York
Feeley MM (1997) Legal complexity and the transformation of the criminal process: the origins of plea bargaining. Isr Law Rev 31:183–222
Fernandes AS (2005) Teoria geral do procedimento e o procedimento no processo penal. RT, São Paulo
Fernandes AS (2006) Reflexões sobre a justiça consensual no Brasil. Bol IBCCrim 166:2–3
Fernandes AS (2012) Processo penal constitucional, 7th edn. RT, São Paulo
Ferreira MAG (2004) O devido processo legal: um estudo comparado. Lumen Juris, Rio de Janeiro
Formmann M (2009) Regulating plea-bargaining in Germany: can the Italian approach serve as a model to guarantee the impartiality of German judges? Hanse Law Rev 5(1):197–220
Fine RA (1987) Plea bargaining: an unnecessary evil. Marquette Law Rev 70(4):615–632
Fisher G (2003) Plea bargaining's triumph. A history of plea bargaining in America. Stanford University Press, Stanford
Friedman LM (1979) Plea bargaining in historical perspective. Law Soc Rev 13(2):247–259
Gazoto LW (2003) O princípio da não obrigatoriedade da ação penal pública. Uma crítica ao formalismo no Ministério Público. Manole, Barueri
Gerber D, Dornelles ML (2006) Juizados Especiais Criminais. Lei n. 9.099/95. Comentários e críticas ao modelo consensual penal. Livraria do Advogado, Porto Alegre
Giacomolli NJ (2006) Legalidade, oportunidade e consenso no processo penal na perspectiva das garantias constitucionais. Livraria do Advogado, Porto Alegre
Gimeno Sendra V (1987) Los procedimentos penales simplificados (Principios de oportunidad y proceso penal monitorio). Bol Inf Minist Just 1457:3–22
Goldschmidt J (2010) Problemas jurídicos y políticos del proceso penal. In: Goldschmidt J, Quiroga J (eds) Derecho, derecho penal y proceso. Marcial Pons, Madrid
Guariglia FO (1993) Facultades discrecionales del ministerio público e investigación penal preparatoria: el principio de oportunidad. In: Roxin C et al (eds) El Ministerio Público en el proceso penal. Ad Hoc, Buenos Aires
Guinchard S, Buisson J (2013) Manuel procédure pénale, 9th edn. LexisNexis, Paris
Hassemer W (1988) La persecución penal: legalidade y oportunidad. Jueces para la Democracia 4:8–11
Hendler ES (1996) Derecho penal y procesal penal de los Estados Unidos. Ad Hoc, Buenos Aires
Heringer B Jr (2013) O sistema de justiça criminal dos Estados Unidos: um modelo em crise? Nuria Fabris, Porto Alegre
Hessick A, Saujani R (2002) Plea bargaining and convicting the innocent: the role of the prosecutor, the defense counsel, and the judge. Brigham Young Univ J Public Law 16:189–242
Heumann M (1981) Plea bargaining. The experiences of prosecutors, judges, and defense attorneys. The University of Chicago Press, Chicago
Jakobs G (1997) Derecho penal. Parte general. Fundamentos y teoría de la imputación. 2nd edn. Marcial Pons, Madrid
Jardim AS (1998) Ação penal pública: princípio da obrigatoriedade, 3rd edn. Forense, Rio de Janeiro
Kant de Lima R (1999) Polícia, justiça e sociedade no Brasil: uma abordagem comparativa dos modelos de administração de conflitos no espaço público. Revista de Sociologia e Política 13:23–38, Curitiba
Karam ML (2004) Juizados Especiais Criminais. A concretização antecipada do poder de punir. RT, São Paulo
Langbein JH (1974) Controlling prosecutorial discretion in Germany. Univ Chic Law Rev 41(3):439–467
Langbein JH (1978) Torture and plea bargaining. Univ Chic Law Rev 46(1):3–22
Langbein JH (1979) Understanding the short history of plea bargaining. Law Soc Rev 13:261–272

Langbein JH (1992) On the myth of written constitutions: the disappearance of criminal jury trial. Harv J Law Public Policy 15(1):119–127
Langbein JH (2003) The origins of adversary criminal law. Oxford University Press, Oxford
Le LC, Mai ST, Hoang YH, Nguyen DQ, Pham TN, Luong HT (2025) Mandatory prosecution in the changing time: a systematic literature review. Crim Just Ethics 44(1):78–106
Leite RV (2013) Justiça consensual e efetividade do processo penal. Del Rey, Belo Horizonte
Lippke RL (2011) The ethics of plea bargaining. Oxford University Press, Oxford
Lopes A Jr (2012) Direito processual penal, 9th edn. Saraiva, São Paulo
Lopes A Jr, Badaró GH (2006) O direito ao processo penal no prazo razoável. Lumen Juris, Rio de Janeiro
Lorenzi FC (2020) Justiça negociada e fundamentos do direito penal. Marcial Pons, São Paulo
Lynch G (1998) Plea bargaining: el sistema no contradictorio de justicia penal en Estados Unidos. Nueva Doctrina Penal A:293–330, Buenos Aires
Lynch G (2012) Frye and Lafler: no big deal. Yale Law J Online 122:39–43
Maierovitch WF (1991) Apontamentos sobre política criminal e o plea bargaining. Rev Inf Legis 28(112):203–210, Brasília, out.-dez
Malan DR (2009) Direito ao confronto no processo penal. Lumen Juris, Rio de Janeiro
Martínez S (2002) Algunas cuestiones en torno a los principios de la legalidad y oportunidad. Cuad Doctr Jurispr Penal 8(14):513–533, Buenos Aires, dez
McCoy C (2005) Plea bargaining as coercion: the trial penalty and plea bargaining reform. Crim Law Q 50:1–41
Meirelles HL (2006) Direito administrativo brasileiro, 32nd edn. Malheiros, São Paulo
Montero Aroca J (2008) Proceso penal y libertad. Ensayo polémico sobre el nuevo proceso penal. Thompson Civitas, Madrid
Moraes MZ (2022) Processo Criminal Transformativo. D'Placido, Belo Horizonte
Moreira RA (2013) Uma crítica à teoria geral do processo. Magister, Porto Alegre
Moura MTA (2001) Justa causa para a ação penal: doutrina e jurisprudência. RT, São Paulo
Naves LF (1995) Plea bargaining: a transação penal nos Estados Unidos da América. Revista da Fundação Escola Superior do Ministério Público do Distrito Federal e Territórios, n. 5, ano 3, p. 219–260, Brasília
Ortiz Pradillo JC (2014) El principio de oportunidad procesal y la igualdad en la aplicación judicial de la Ley. In: Martín López T, Velasco Retamosa JM (coord.) La igualdad de género desde la perspectiva social, jurídica y económica. Civitas, Madrid
Pallamollla R (2009) Justiça Restaurativa: da teoria à prática. IBCCrim, São Paulo
Paschoal JC (2001) Breves apontamentos relativos ao instituto do plea bargaining no direito norte-americano. FMU Direito 15(23):115–126, São Paulo
Paulo AR (2013) Justiça restaurativa e transação penal. Boletim IBCCrim 252, ano 21:15–16, São Paulo, nov.
Pereira CJ (2002) Princípio da oportunidade e justiça penal negociada. Juarez de Oliveira, São Paulo
Pereira FV (2013) Delação premiada. Legitimidade e procedimento, Juruá, Curitiba
Prado G (2002) Justiça penal consensual. In: Carvalho S, Wunderlich A (eds) Diálogos sobre a Justiça Dialogal. Teses e antíteses sobre os processos de informalização e privatização da Justiça Penal. Lumen Juris, Rio de Janeiro
Prado G (2006a) Da delação premiada: aspectos de direito processual. Boletim IBCCrim 159:10–12, São Paulo, fev
Prado G (2006b) Sistema acusatório. A conformidade constitucional das leis processuais penais. 4th edn. Lumen Juris, São Paulo
Prado G (2006c) Transação penal, 2nd edn. Lumen Juris, Rio de Janeiro
Prado G (2014) Prova penal e sistema de controles epistêmicos. A quebra da cadeia de custódia das provas obtidas por métodos ocultos. Marcial Pons, São Paulo
Ramos JGG (2006) Curso de processo penal norte-americano. RT, São Paulo
Rauxloh RE (2011) Formalization of plea bargaining in Germany: will the new legislation be able to square the circle? Fordham Int Law J 34(2):296–331

Rivera JC, Araque CA (2010) Principio de oportunidad: reflexiones jurídico políticas. Universidad de Medellin, Medellin

Rodrigues AM (1998) A celeridade no processo penal: uma visão de direito comparado. Revista Portuguesa de Ciência Criminal 8(2):233–250

Rodríguez García N (1996) A justiça penal e as formas de transação no direito norte-americano: repercussões. Revista Brasileira de Ciências Criminais n. 13, ano 4:79–92

Rodríguez García N (1997) La justicia penal negociada. Experiencias de derecho comparado. Ediciones Universidad de Salamanca, Salamanca

Rosa AM, Marcellino Junio JC (2012) O processo eficiente na lógica econômica. Desenvolvimento, aceleração e direitos fundamentais. Univali, Itajaí

Ross JE (2010) The entrenched position of plea bargaining in United States legal practice. In: Thaman SC (ed) World plea bargaining. Consensual procedures and the avoidance of the full criminal trial. Carolina Academic Press, Durham

Roxin C (1997) Derecho penal: parte general, vol I. Civitas, Madrid

Salas D (2010) Du procès pénal. Quadrige/PUF, Paris

Schünemann B (2013) Audiência de instrução e julgamento: modelo inquisitorial ou adversarial? Sobre a estrutura fundamental do processo penal no 3.° milênio. In: Schünemann B, Greco L (eds) Estudos de direito penal, direito processual penal e filosofia do direito. Marcial Pons, São Paulo

Schulhofer SJ (1984) Is plea bargaining inevitable? Harvard Law Review 97(5):1037–1107

Sica L (2009) Mediação, Processo Penal e Democracia. In: Prado G, Malan D (eds) Processo Penal e Democracia. Estudos em homenagem aos 20 anos da Constituição da República de 1988. Lumen Juris, Rio de Janeiro, pp 289–319

Silva EA (2000) Ação penal pública: princípio da oportunidade regrada, 2nd edn. Atlas, São Paulo

Silva EA (2014) Organizações criminosas. Aspectos penais e processuais da Lei n.º 12.850/13. Atlas, São Paulo

Taruffo M (2008) El proceso civil adversarial en la experiencia americana. El modelo del proceso de conotación dispositiva. Temis, Bogotá

Teixeira CA (2000) Princípio da oportunidade. Manifestações em sede processual

Tovo PC, Tovo JBM (2008) Princípios de processo penal. Lumen Juris, Rio de Janeiro

Tulkens F (2005) Justiça negociada. In: Delmas-Marty M (org) Processos penais da Europa. Lumen Juris, Rio de Janeiro

Turner JI (2006) Judicial participation in plea negotiations: a comparative view. Am J Comp Law 54:501–569

Turner JI (2009) Plea barganing across borders. Aspen, New York

Vasconcellos VG (2013) A inserção de medidas cautelares diversas no sistema processual penal brasileiro: entre a expansão do controle punitivo e sua limitação. Rev Estud Crim 51:125–142

Vasconcellos VG, Capparelli B (2015) Barganha no processo penal italiano: análise crítica do patteggiamento e das alternativas procedimentais na justiça criminal. Rev Eletrôn Dir Process 15:435–453

Vogel ME (1999) The social origins of plea bargaining: conflict and the law in the process of state formation, 1830–1860. Law Soc Rev 33(1):161–246

Vogel ME (2007) Coercion to compromise. Plea bargaining, the courts, and the making of political authority. Oxford University Press, Oxford

Vogler R (2002) Justiça consensual e processo penal. In: Choukr FH, Ambos K (eds) Processo penal e Estado de Direito. Edicamp, Campinas

Zaffaroni E, Pierangeli JH (2008) Manual de direito penal brasileiro, vol 1, 7th edn. RT, São Paulo

Zanatta A (2001) A transação penal e o poder discricionário do Ministério Público. SAGE, Porto Alegre

Chapter 3
Spaces for Consensus in Brazilian Criminal Justice and their Expansion Trends: Current Mechanisms and Critique of Proposals for Broadening

After analysing the principled premises and conceptual contours of bargaining, the discussion now turns to the examination of spaces for consensus in the criminal justice system, both in their current manifestations and in proposed expansions. The focus will be on the Brazilian scenario, with an analysis of the spaces for consensus currently authorised by law, namely the mechanisms of the Small Claims Courts, the turn state's evidence and the non-prosecution agreement, outlining their essential features within Brazilian negotiation justice. Next (Sect. 3.4), the study will examine legislative proposals aimed at broadening the spaces for consensus in the Brazilian criminal justice system, particularly through a critical assessment of the provisions on the fast-tracked proceedings and bargaining, as regulated in Senate Bill No. 156/2009 (comprehensive reform of the Code of Criminal Procedure)[1] and Senate Bill No. 236/2012 (comprehensive reform of the Penal Code). Finally (Sect. 3.5), a comparative analysis will be presented between the Brazilian model and the international trend towards expanding conviction mechanisms without trial, similar to plea bargaining.

[1] Senate Bill (PLS) 156/2009 was approved in its house of origin and forwarded to the Chamber of Deputies, where it was renumbered as Bill 8.045/2010.

V. G. de. Vasconcellos, *Criminal Agreements and Negotiated Justice*,
https://doi.org/10.1007/978-3-032-16962-4_3

3.1 Small Claims Courts and the Informalisation of Criminal Procedure. The Fast-Tracking of Fundamental Guarantees. Boundaries of the Precursor Mechanisms to Bargaining in the Brazilian Legal System

Undeniably, the main milestone of consensual justice in Brazil occurred with Law 9.099/1995, which regulated the Small Claims Courts. Preceded by unsuccessful proposals that sought to introduce mechanisms[2] inspired by settlements and by the example of Small Claims Courts in the civil sphere,[3] their structuring was imposed by item I of art. 98 of the 1988 Federal Constitution,[4] which mandated the creation of special courts[5] and legitimised criminal settlements within the Brazilian legal system, thereby weakening part of the scholars' criticisms raised against them.[6] However, this constitutional mandate the enactment of a federal regulatory law, which was delayed, thus allowing State attempts to implement small claims courts in their jurisdictions.[7] These, however, were struck down by the Federal Supreme Court as unconstitutional.[8]

It is noted that Law 9.099/1995 structured a "microsystem" within the Brazilian legal system,[9] aiming, according to part of the legal scholars, to favour swiftness and efficiency in the adjudication of criminal cases,[10] which, supposedly, would

[2] According to Gerber and Dornelles (2006), pp. 41–42, the 1981 Frederico Marques's draft Code of Criminal Procedure already provided for a kind of agreement to resolve the criminal case, a mechanism similar to today's criminal settlement. In 1983, Bill n.° 1.655/1 proposed the termination of the proceedings without a trial on the merits, provided that the accused, in their formal reply, agreed to pay a fine to be determined by the judge.

[3] Leite (2013), pp. 144–148.

[4] "Art. 98. The Union, in the Federal District and the Territories, and the states shall establish: I—small claims courts, staffed by non-lay or lay judges competent for agreement, judgment and execution of less complex civil cases and minor criminal offenses, through oral and very summary procedures, with the possibility, in cases provided by law, of settlements and of appeals being judged by panels of first-instance judges".

[5] Prado (2006a), pp. 9–10; Tourinho Filho (2003), p. 6; Giacomolli (2006), p. 308.

[6] It should be noted that this constitutional provision, entitled "constitutional foundation of consensus" (Leite 2013, pp. 148–149), is, in many cases, used by scholars favourable to negotiation mechanisms to dismiss any questioning about the constitutionality of the consensual mechanisms; in other words, it becomes an escape subterfuge, which hinders the necessary dogmatic criticism of this point, and, therefore, shall be debated.

[7] Commonly, the examples of the states of Mato Grosso do Sul, Paraíba and Mato Grosso are cited. On this point, see: Leite (2013), pp. 149–150.

[8] Grinover et al. (2005), p. 38.

[9] Giacomolli (2006), p. 312.

[10] Leite (2013), p. 153.

bring Brazilian procedural law closer to international trends[11] and would break with a pattern of repressive criminal policy typical of the time.[12] In this sense, there are those who dismiss any influence of the US model,[13] while others point to the alignment of the Brazilian scenario with the characteristics of European consensual mechanisms.[14]

Therefore, although one cannot forget the significant mechanism of turn state's evidence,[15] it is essentially within the Small Claims Courts that *consensual justice in Brazil* is established,[16] through the civil composition of damages, the criminal settlement, and the conditional suspension of the criminal prosecution.[17] These are limited spaces for consensus, restricted to minor transgressions, referred to as *minor offences*, which initially were limited to misdemeanours and offences punishable with a maximum sentence of up to 1 year, later being expanded to the abstract limit of 2 years.[18] Furthermore, over time, subsequent laws have used the consensus mechanisms implemented, aiming to expand their scope of action.[19]

In order to understand the applicability of the mechanisms of Law 9.099/1995, in summary, the trial procedure begins with the preliminary stage, in which the police authority drafts a police investigation[20] (since the police inquiry is waived) and refers to the perpetrator and the victim to the court (or establishes a commitment to be in court). A preliminary hearing is then scheduled, at which time, depending on the case, an attempt is made to reach a civil redressing of damages and a criminal settlement. If unsuccessful, the indictment is filed and a date is scheduled for the evidentiary hearing and trial hearing, during which evidence will be pro-

---

[11] Ada Grinover points out the similarities of the Brazilian criminal procedure to the Model Code of Criminal Procedure for Ibero-America: Grinover (2000), p. 73.

[12] Grinover et al. (2005), p. 47.

[13] Regarding the differences pointed out between Brazilian and US mechanisms, see: Grinover et al. (2005), p. 45; Gerber and Dornelles (2006), p. 48. However, the influence of the United States model is undeniable, even if its impact is debatable. On this, see: Miranda (2004), p. 212.

[14] "The analysis of foreign consensual alternatives does not advise following the breadth of the North American settlement model, distant from the traditions of the Brazilian criminal procedure, which is closer to the foundations of the European criminal procedure: a) regulation of these mechanisms by law, with the establishment of their prerequisites and requirements; b) limitation of the Public Prosecutor's Office's power of action, which operates under the principle of compulsoriness of the criminal action and the strict application of the principle of legality; and c) granting a more relevant role to the criminal judge" (Fernandes 2005, p. 269).

[15] About turn state's evidence and its expression in terms of consensus, see Sect. 3.2 of this work.

[16] Grinover et al. (2005), p. 42.

[17] "[...] in the field of consensual criminal justice, the 1995 law not only regulated the criminal settlement provided for in the Constitution, but also created the reparatory agreement and the conditional suspension of the criminal prosecution (probation)" (Grinover 2000, p. 74). In this sense, also: Leite (2013), p. 152.

[18] Leite (2013), pp. 153–154. In criticism of the criteria for defining the competence of the Small Claims Courts, see: Prado (2006b), pp. 122–139.

[19] Giacomolli (2006), pp. 309–311; Leite (2013), pp. 217–243.

[20] In a critical analysis of the "police report", see: Prado (2006b), pp. 139–147.

duced and the case adjudicated. However, at the beginning of this second hearing, after the judge has received the accusatory petition, if its prerequisites are met, a proposal for the conditional suspension of the criminal prosecution is authorised.[21]

3.1.1 The Consensual Mechanisms Precursors: Civil Redressing, Criminal Settlement and Conditional Suspension of the Criminal Prosecution

The regulation of the fast-tracked procedure, provided for in the Small Claims Courts Law for the trial of minor offences, establishes three mechanisms that relate in different ways to the subject of this book: negotiated justice. Although each mechanism has distinct characteristics—some more akin to bargaining, others less so—they share a fundamental trait: the accused's agreement to comply with the obligations established by mutual consent. It is important to note that this section does not aim to provide an exhaustive analysis of each mechanism, but rather to highlight their essential features as examples of spaces for consensus in the contemporary Brazilian criminal procedure.

Initially, it should be noted that, regarding the *civil redressing of damages*, as previously mentioned, in a narrow conception of the principle of opportunity (which presupposes the qualification of the accusatory duty of a public authority),[22] it is believed that such a mechanism does not represent the weakening of the rule of compulsoriness, while it expresses, in truth, the broad discretion of the private accuser/victim in suits that depend on their action (private criminal action and conditional public criminal action). On the other hand, starting from a broad concept of consensus (which goes beyond the negotiation mechanisms between prosecutor and defence, encompassing the idea of conflict resolution between victim and aggressor),[23] the redressing provided for in Law 9.099/1995 is among the typical mechanisms of consensual justice.[24]

The civil redressing is provided for in articles 72 to 74 of the Small Claims Courts Law, and shall[25] occur at the first moment of the preliminary hearing of the proceeding (or, in a second attempt, at the beginning of the evidentiary hearing and trial hearing), aiming at a negotiated solution between the victim and the alleged

[21] Lopes Jr (2012), pp. 976–982; Grinover et al. (2005), pp. 104–182.

[22] On this, see Sects. 2.1.2 and 2.1.3 of this work.

[23] Here, in consideration of most scholars' constructions, a conception broader than that previously developed in the conceptual delimitation of consensual justice, undertaken in Sect. 2.1.3, is used.

[24] "It is important to note that the composition, despite having a civil interest as its object, undoubtedly presents consensual elements that significantly impact criminal prosecution, thus falling within the sphere of consensual criminal justice" (Leite 2013, p. 157).

[25] "The criminal settlement and the practice of procedural acts without a prior attempt at redressing civil damages, whenever present, are tainted" (Giacomolli 2009, p. 103).

aggressor, through dialogue mediated by the judge or conciliator,[26] with the mandatory presence of their respective legal counsel.[27] It is, therefore, an "agreement or a self- redressing procedural mechanism of conflict resolution".[28]

Once the agreement is concluded, its term must be ratified[29] by the non-lay judge through an unappealable judgement, which results in the waiving of the right to file a complaint or representation, respectively, in private or public conditional criminal actions, leading to the extinction of the accused's criminal liability.[30] However, if concluded in an unconditional action, it does not constitute an impediment to the Public Prosecutor's Office, which may subsequent submit a proposal for a criminal settlement or file an indictment.[31] Since there is no legal limitation, the redressing may be concluded repeatedly, without any temporal restriction.[32] Provided that the alleged perpetrator fails to comply with the agreement, the criminal proceeding cannot be resumed, while the ratifying judgement must be enforced in the civil sphere, as it constitutes a judicial enforcement instrument.[33]

The other consensual mechanism of the fast-tracked procedure, which clearly expresses the negotiated nature of the agreement between prosecution and defence, is the *criminal settlement*. Indeed, it is a mechanism with similarities and distinctions to the US plea bargaining[34] and, more broadly, to the various abbreviated procedures in Latin America or Europe. If the attempt at civil redressing is unsuccessful, this is the moment when the Public Prosecutor's Office, provided that the legal requirements are met, must submit a proposal for the "immediate imposition of a restrictive penalty or fine", pursuant to Article 76 of Law 9.099/1995, in accordance with the implementation of the constitutional mandate of Art. 98, I.

It is an agreement made between the accused (necessarily represented by legal counsel) and the prosecutor,[35] in which the former accepts the immediate application of a criminal sanction,[36] without following the regular course of the proceeding,

[26] Leite (2013), p. 156.

[27] Grinover et al. (2005), p. 133.

[28] Giacomolli (2009), p. 101.

[29] "The judge, dealing with available rights, shall not modify the civil redressing, either in terms of facts or the extent of compensation. The decision serves to ratify the parties' agreed will" (Giacomolli 2009, p. 104).

[30] Grinover et al. (2005), pp. 143–145.

[31] Leite (2013), p. 157. According to Nereu Giacomolli, in this situation, the redressing may potentially be used as a special mitigating factor for reducing the penalty (Giacomolli 2009, p. 100).

[32] Giacomolli (2009), p. 100.

[33] Grinover et al. (2005), pp. 142–143.

[34] Although the legal literature highlights various distinctions, it is understood that their common essence allows the identification of certain characteristics and pertinent criticisms. For these distinctions, see: Leite (2013), pp. 162–165.

[35] The victim cannot interfere in the execution of the criminal settlement, even if the previous attempt at civil redressing was unsuccessful (Grinover et al. 2005, p. 165).

[36] "In the criminal sphere, the settlement is an agreement between the holder of the criminal action and the alleged author of a minor offense, whereby the latter agrees to immediately submit to a

that is, with the "anticipated exercise of the power to punish".[37] In return, the prosecutorial interest is favoured by the swift imposition of a sanction, reducing resource expenditures. In other words, it is characterised as a pact in which, theoretically,[38] both parties benefit. Although it reflects consent to the proposed sanction,[39] according to mainstream legal literature, the accused does not acknowledge their guilt, which is thought to safeguard the presumption of innocence.[40]

According to the provided procedure, after the attempt at civil redressing, the Public Prosecutor's Office must assess whether the case presents good cause to preclude dismissal.[41] This is a fundamental obligation, which must be primarily fulfilled by the public prosecutor, since the criminal settlement can only be accepted if there is sufficient evidentiary support indicating the occurrence of a minor offense; in other words, the accused will be subject to a restrictive penalty or fine at this initial stage only if a potential conviction at the end of the proceeding is feasible.[42] If the case is of a criminal prosecution conditioned on a complaint, the proposal will depend on the prior representation of the injured victim. Regarding the applicability of this mechanism in a private—initiative action, the legal literature presents divergent views.[43] Furthermore, the judge will act in ratifying the proposal, issuing a sentence of debated legal nature,[44] which, however, under the law, does not generate prior convictions or recidivism.[45] This decision is appealable, that is, subject to judicial review, although there is debate regarding the possible scope of appeal—whether it is limited to potential defects in the accused's consent or extends to cases of abuse in modifying the terms agreed upon by the judge.[46]

---

restrictive penalty or fine, with the aim of avoiding the judicial proceeding and satisfying the *jus puniendi*" (Leite 2013, p. 158).

[37] Karam (2004), pp. 34–49.

[38] Regarding criticisms of the supposed benefit to the accused, see Sects. 4.1.2 and 4.1.6 of this work.

[39] "The prosecution's proposal must be clear and precise, so as to give the accused and their legal counsel full knowledge of the proposed penalty, along with its practical consequences. It will refer to the fact narrated in the occurrence report, but without any legal qualification. This is because the imposition of the sanction does not indicate guilt recognition of" (Grinover et al. 2005, p. 158).

[40] "Under the law's technical framework, the legal nature of accepting the proposal is the voluntary submission to the criminal sanction, but it does not constitute criminal guilty plea nor civil liability" (Grinover et al. 2005, p. 164).

[41] Leite (2013), p. 161.

[42] Similarly: Giacomolli (2009), p. 130; Karam (2004), pp. 90–91

[43] On this, see: Carvalho, Nunes Júnior, 2005. Affirming its possibility: Grinover et al. (2005), pp. 150–151; Leite (2013), pp. 172–176.

In the opposite sense: Prado (2006b), pp. 167–171.

[44] Affirming its merely homologatory nature: Grinover et al. (2005), pp. 167–170. Conversely, attesting to its condemnatory efficacy: Karam (2004), pp. 98–99.

[45] Gerber and Dornelles (2006), pp. 80–81.

[46] Leite (2013), p. 160.

Moreover, certain requirements are provided in the legal text for a criminal settlement to be authorised. Besides not having been definitively sentenced to a custodial penalty for an offence, the perpetrator must also not have entered into a similar agreement within the previous 5 years. In other words, this negotiation mechanism can only be concluded once every 5 years. Finally, the personality of the accused and the factual circumstances of the illicit conduct are analysed.[47]

Based on the verification of the suitability of the specific case to these prerequisites, a fundamental debate arises among scholars: may the public prosecutor refuse to offer the criminal settlement proposal if these requirements are met? Although the legal text uses the term "may", it seems dogmatically unquestionable that the prosecutor does not have discretion to refrain from proposing the agreement in a case compatible with the conditions provided for in the law.[48] The arbitrariness of an attitude that, for any other extralegal reason, denies the accused the possibility of resorting to the said mechanism is clear. Then another question arises: what should be done in the face of an unjustified refusal in this regard? One school of thought (1) asserts that this mechanism becomes a public subjective right of the accused when applicable to the case and, thus, it would be up to the defence to request the criminal settlement from the judge, who would either ratify or reject the request, "ensuring the compliance of the accused's rights ".[49] On the other hand (2), some argue that the proposal should be formulated by the judges themselves,[50] a thesis that, in the face of criticism of violation of the accusatory system through usurpation of the activities of the Public Prosecutor's Office, is defended by Tourinho Filho on the basis of a questionable authorisation of the Brazilian criminal procedural law for the judge's active stance.[51] Moreover (3), it is also argued that the judge might reject the complaint[52] due to the lack of a condition of action, namely, procedural interest,

---

[47] Giacomolli (2009), pp. 126–128.

[48] In this regard, most scholars affirm the compulsory nature of the prosecutorial proposal whenever the requirements established by the law are met: Grinover et al. (2005), p. 153; Karam (2004), p. 91; Giacomolli (2009), p. 121.

[49] Leite (2013), p. 166.

[50] Giacomolli (2009), pp. 129–130.

[51] "Moreover, in our legal system, the Criminal Procedure is not predominantly accusatory. The cornerstone of the accusatory proceeding is separating the functions of the prosecutor and the judge. Otherwise, the judge could not, *ex officio,* order the production of evidence (see, for example, CPP arts. 156, 176, 209, 234, 241, 276, 407, 425, among others). Tasks that should be the parties' responsibility were also allowed to the judge" (Tourinho Filho 2003, p. 101).

[52] According to Fernando Fernandes (2001), p. 602, two situations should be distinguished: first, when a public prosecutor does not offer the criminal settlement because they believe the case should have been dismissed earlier; second, when the prosecutor recognizes good cause for prosecution but states that the criminal settlement is not applicable. In the former, art. 28 of the CPP should be used, but not in the latter. In the second situation, the judge shall reject the subsequently filed complaint if they find that the prerequisites for the criminal settlement are met. In summary, "In essence, under the procedure provided for in art. 28.° of the CPP, what is at stake is the *jus pursequendi in judicium*, and since the Public Prosecutor's Office holds this right, only its hierarchical superior has the ultimate authority on this matter; concerning the criminal settlement, what is at stake is the accused's subjective right to the proposal, and it is up to the judge only to deter-

since the proposal offering in this case would be a prerequisite for the initiation of the proceedings.[53] Finally (4), the fourth position, adopted mainly by higher courts of the country, imposes the application, by analogy, of Art. 28 of the Code of Criminal Procedure, which determines the referral of the case to the Attorney General of Justice if the judge disagrees with the prosecutor's stance, thus preserving the separation of functions typical of the accusatory system.[54]

In view of such theories, contrary to the majority view, it is thought that the entry into the agreement is a right of the accused if the specific case meets the legal requirements, and thus, the refusal of the public prosecutor shall not occur, as it is patently arbitrary.[55] Therefore, whether upon a request by the defence or even *ex officio*, the judge must ensure its implementation, provided that there is consent from the alleged perpetrator. In the last instance, it also seems legitimate to reject the indictment, which is even a preferable option, as it shifts the burden caused by the unjustified refusal back onto its source, the member of the Prosecutor's Office. What is certainly unacceptable is any obstruction to the exercise of such a right, whether by prosecutors's decision or their superior's (Chief Prosecutor).

Such a conclusion, however, does not undermine the characterization of the Brazilian criminal settlement as an expression of consensual justice[56] for two reasons: (1) the notion of consensus in criminal proceedings fundamentally concern the accused's agreement to the early implementation of the State's punitive power; it is the accused who waives their position of resistance, their right to defence, and accepts the penal sanction, thus establishing a consensual/negotiated essence; and,

---

mine whether the legal requirements are present. Indeed, it is the judge who will later verify whether the legal requirements for ratifying the settlement are met (art. 76.°, §§ 3.° and 4.°)".

[53] In this regard, Maria Lúcia Karam (2004), pp. 93–94, states: "If the criminal action is improperly filed, it is not the judge who should 'offer the settlement'. Nor should the judge refer the case to the Chief Prosecutor by analogy to art. 28 of the CPP. These solutions, proposed since the enactment of Law 9.099/95, do not seem to recognise that an unfounded refusal by the Public Prosecutor, author of the criminal action, to comply to the rules of art. 76 of Law 9.099/95 is nothing more than an illegitimate exercise of the right of action, which requires the legally and traditionally established solution". Similarly: "The mechanisms of agreement (art. 74) and of the criminal settlement (art. 76) constitute a mandatory preliminary stage through which legal operators must pass before filing a criminal action. Thus, for the offences covered by this law, all extrajudicial forms of conflict resolution must be exhausted; only afterwards, if the se means remain fruitless or inapplicable, may the interested party validly file a criminal complaint against the accused. […] The action will lack procedural interest (interest-necessity) when the parties are not given the opportunity to seek pre-procedural consensus through agreement or criminal settlement" (Moraes 2000, pp. 82–83). In contrast: Leite (2013), pp. 171–172.

[54] Grinover et al. (2005), p. 155; Zanatta (2001), pp. 81–111; Gerber and Dornelles (2006), p. 77.

[55] Giacomolli (2013), pp. 123–125.

[56] From a different perspective, Rosimeire Leite (2013), pp. 170–171, points out that, due to its consensual nature (and so as not to undermine this nature), the agreement is bilateral and, therefore, the Public Prosecutor's representative has discretion, making the appropriate course of action to refer the matter to the Chief Prosecutor.

(2) this characteristic is not negated by making the offer of the proposal a duty of the prosecutor when if the legal requirements are met, because the accused's will (reflecting the traditional idea of agreement) can—and indeed must be bound by law, in line with the principle of legality that shall govern the conduct of public agents, particularly in the criminal sphere.[57]

Furthermore, another important issue concerns the consequences of the accused's non-compliance with the penal sanction. Initially, the possibility of converting it into a custodial sentence, in accordance with the rules of criminal law for cases of non-compliance with a sentence restricting rights, was considered. However, this option blatantly violates the right to due process, as it imposes the imprisonment of an accused without the proper course of proceedings, in addition to infringing the rights to a full defence and adversarial proceedings.[58] Thus, a theory emerged authorising the resumption of criminal prosecution through the filing of an indictment. Nevertheless, this approach has been criticised for unduly disregarding the court decision approving the agreement, which produced *res judicata* and, therefore, became immutable.[59]

According to Nereu Giacomolli, the only acceptable alternative under the current legal framework is execution within the scope of the Small Claims Courts, with the possible summoning of the parties to a hearing, aimed at reaching a consensual resolution to the issue.[60] However, a binding precedent from the Federal Supreme Court (number 35) established that: "The ratification of the criminal settlement provided for in art. 76 of Law No. 9.099/1995 does not produce *res judicata*, and if its terms are not complied with, the *status quo ante* is restored, allowing the Public Prosecutor's Office to continue criminal prosecution through the filing of an indictment or the request for a police investigation".

Finally, the third mechanism that exemplifies a space for consensus and negotiated justice in the Brazilian criminal procedure is the *conditional suspension of the criminal prosecution*.[61] Certainly inspired by foreign models,[62] this mechanism entails the suspension of the procedure, after the indictment has been filed, for a specified period, during which the accused agrees to comply with certain conditions. If these conditions are met, the accused's criminal liability (and, consequently,

[57] "Thus, the action of the Public Prosecutor's Office is not a pure expression of the principle of opportunity, that is, the discretion to bring an alternative claim, but rather an action determined by law" (Giacomolli 2009, p. 121).

[58] Leite (2013), p. 180; Giacomolli (2009), pp. 144–145.

[59] Grinover et al. (2005), p. 170.

[60] Giacomolli (2009), pp. 145–146. Alternatively, it has also been suggested to convert the non-complied restrictive penalty into compensation for loss and damage, with the determination of a monetary value and execution (Gerber, Dornelles 2006, p. 78). Some authors assert the impossibility of any consequence in the event of non-compliance with a restrictive penalty, due to the legal gap: Karam (2004), pp. 105–106.

[61] Leite (2013), p. 184.

[62] Giacomolli (2009), pp. 188–197; Ishida 2003, p. 17–26.

the proceeding) is extinguished at the end of that period.[63] According to its legal provision (Art. 89 of Law 9.099/1995), this option is admissible for offences carrying a minimum statutory penalty of one year or less, making it broader in scope than other mechanisms limited to minor offences.[64] Furthermore, it requires that the accused is not facing prosecution for other alleged offences, nor has been convicted of a crime, and that the measure is appropriate considering the circumstances of the act and the personal conditions of the accused.[65]

The suspension proposal must be submitted by the public prosecutor along with the filing of the indictment, whether in ordinary,[66] summary, or simplified proceedings, provided that a criminal settlement has not been previously carried out. This raises the same issue previously discussed regarding the compulsoriness to make the proposal and the consequences of an illegitimate refusal by the representative of the Public Prosecutor's Office.[67] Similarly, it is argued that the fulfilment of the legal requirements establishes a right of the accused, whereas any refusal is arbitrary, and should be rectified by the judiciary either *ex officio* or upon request of the defence.[68] However, the mainstream view, following Supreme Court Precedent No. 696, holds that the matter shall be referred to the Chief Prosecutor, analogously to art. 28 of the Code of Criminal Procedure.[69]

Once the agreement is reached, the proceeding and the statutory period of limitation are suspended by an interlocutory decision of the judge, and the probation period begins, which may last from 2 to 4 years, as determined in the ratified proposal. During this time, the accused must fulfil the agreed-upon obligations, under penalty of revocation and resumption of prosecution.[70] According to most scholars, the implementation of this mechanism does not imply an acknowledgement of guilt by the alleged offender, nor does it result in a criminal record or recidivism.[71]

Given the description of the three mechanisms introduced by Law 9.099/1995 of the Small Claims Courts—prominent examples of spaces for consensus and, to some extent, of negotiated criminal justice—, their shared essence stands out: the accused's acceptance of obligations,[72] coupled with the waiver of their right to defence and their typical position of resistance in the proceeding, in exchange for a purported benefit.[73] Together with the provision for turn state's evidence mecha-

[63] Grinover et al. (2005), p. 369.

[64] Leite (2013), p. 185.

[65] Grinover et al. (2005), p. 310.

[66] Regarding the timing of the submission of the suspension proposal in the ordinary proceeding in light of the 2008 reform, see: Leite (2013), p. 186.

[67] Ishida (2003), pp. 59–103.

[68] About this discussion: Giacomolli (2009), pp. 207–209.

[69] Grinover et al. (2005), pp. 317–320.

[70] Leite (2013), pp. 187–188.

[71] Grinover et al. (2005), p. 369.

[72] Giacomolli (2009), p. 199.

[73] Similarly, although affirming the recognition of the claim "regardless of the acknowledgement of the infraction", Maria Lúcia Karam highlights the defence's concession to resistance (Karam 2004,

nisms, this scenario unmistakably reflects the expansion of spaces for consensus in the Brazilian criminal justice system, particularly in response to the contemporary need for cooperation in punitive enforcement, highlighting the increasing inadequacy of the State's response to the complex phenomenon of crime. Finally, it is important to note the alignment of these mechanisms with the criticisms of bargaining outlined in this work.[74]

3.2 Cooperation and Leniency Agreements: The Debate on Ethical Minimums in State Criminal Prosecution and the Distortion of the Allocation of Evidentiary Burdens in Criminal Proceedings

Together with the insertion of spaces for opportunity in the Brazilian criminal procedure through the negotiation mechanisms of the Small Claims Courts, the expansion of the scope of applicability of cooperation mechanisms with the justice system represents a significant trend in the Brazilian legal-criminal field.[75] This phenomenon is closely linked to the expansion of consensus possibilities within the consolidation of the so-called "reward-based criminal law".[76] The present section therefore seeks to outline the fundamental features of "turn state's evidence"[77] in the Brazilian legal system, without claiming exhaustiveness given the complexity of their con-

p. 167). Asserting that the acceptance of the settlement entails an admission of guilt, Cezar Bitencourt observes: "The moment the perpetrator accepts the immediate application of an alternative penalty, they are assuming guilt, which is natural under the principle of *nulla poena sine culpa*" (Bitencourt 1997, p. 103).

[74] See, especially, Sect. 2.2.2 (criticism of the justifications for negotiation mechanisms) and this chapter (description of the aporias of bargaining in criminal justice).

[75] Coutinho and Carvalho (2006), p. 77; Cordeiro (2010), pp. 274–275.

[76] "Turn state's evidence is a form of the so-called reward-based criminal law. It represents the exercise of authority in offering benefits to the perpetrators themselves, in order to facilitate the dismantling of criminal organisations" (Lamy 2014, p. 23). On this, see Sect. 2.2.1 of this work and also: Pereira (2013), pp. 23–27.

[77] Although part of the legal scholars chooses, euphemistically, to use only the term "colaboração premiada", pointing to the supposed negative charge of the term "delação", in this work both terms will be used to refer to the mechanism under analysis. Defending the adequacy of the term" colaboração premiada" alone, but later employing several others ("delação premiada", "colaboração premiada", "arrependimento processual" and "arrependidos"), Frederico Pereira (2013), pp. 27–28 states: "The designation by certain equivocal terms, such as 'delação premiada' or 'arrependidos', does not help in the task of defining the precise contours of the procedural cooperation instrument. The word "delação" suggests that, having been caught committing the offence, it would suffice for the agent to deliver another's offence, thereby carrying a negative ideological and ethical burden, marking a harmful position, besides failing to correctly identify the content of the instrument. Nor does it fit its nature and *raison d'être*, which encompasses cooperative behaviours aimed at clarifying crimes, individualising their perpetrators or the *modus operandi* of a criminal organisation, and even recovering, totally or partially, the proceeds of crime, without imputing facts to third parties

tours, but aiming to relate them to bargaining as expressions of negotiated justice.[78] To this end, the section first sets out its concept; next, it compares it to agreements between prosecution and defence for the recognition of guilt;, finally, based on the study of its legal regulation (as detailed in Law 12.850/2013), it considers possible contributions to the criticism of bargaining.

Regarding its conceptualisation, it can be affirmed that the turn state's evidence is "a mechanism of criminal law that guarantees to the investigated, indicted, accused or convicted, a reward—a reduction that may even reach exemption from the sentence—in exchange for their confession and assistance in the persecutory proceedings, provided voluntarily (that is, without any form of coercion)".[79] On the other hand, some authors emphasise the prosecutorial purpose of such mechanism, as an "investigative technique sustained by the cooperation of a suspect ",[80] which, as will be pointed out later, constitutes one of the main criticisms of this mechanism: the unveiling of the State's dependence on the cooperation of the accused themselves due to its inefficiency in gathering sufficient evidence to overcome the presumption of innocence; in other words, an undue inversion of the procedural burdens.[81]

Furthermore, it is important to mention a mechanism of growing importance in the Brazilian criminal-legal field, closely connected to reward mechanisms[82]: the leniency agreement. It is a "form of turn state's evidence", materialised through a specific legal regime regulated in antitrust legislation. Its main distinction, according to Anna Lamy, lies in the authority empowered to propose the agreement: in leniency, it is the Ministry of Justice and not the Prosecutor's Office.[83] Gradually introduced into the national framework by provisional measures later converted into

---

in two of these situations." For an attempt to distinguish "delação" and "colaboração", see: Silva (2014), pp. 52–53.

[78] For further study, refer to: Vasconcellos (2023), Rosa (2024), Mendes (2020).

[79] Bittar (2011a), p. 5. According to Eduardo Silva (2014), p. 52, "cooperation agreements, also called procedural cooperation (cooperative procedure), occurs when the accused, still in the criminal investigation stage, in addition to confessing their crimes to the authorities, prevents other infractions from being consummated (preventive cooperation), as well as concretely assists the police in their activity of gathering evidence against the other co- perpetrators, enabling their arrests (repressive cooperation)". However, the author limits cooperation only to the criminal investigation stage, which seems to restrict its applicability to the pre-trial stage. Such a statement proves inadequate, since turn state's evidence, as provided for in Law 12.850/2013 (and even later acknowledged by the author himself), may be implemented in the investigation, during the trial, or even in the execution phase of the sentence.

[80] Pereira (2013), p. 35.

[81] Together with Aury Lopes Jr (2012), pp. 100–106 and James Goldschmidt, the terminology" procedural burden" was adopted, following the theory of the procedural legal situation. On this, see: Gloeckner (2009), pp. 255–262; Goldschmidt (2010), pp. 829–830. Regarding the term "burden of proof", see: Badaró (2003), pp. 156–193.

[82] "In the case of cartel crimes, the legislator gave the mechanism the name 'leniency'. Both are, so to speak, two sides of the same coin. It is the same mechanism that, more generally, can be referred to as 'cooperation agreement'" (Mendroni 2014, p. 60).

[83] Lamy (2014), p. 47.

law,[84] these mechanisms were consolidated in the legislation structuring the Competition Defence System (Law 12.529/2011). Certainly, this mechanism presents significant features for the ongoing expansion of spaces for consensus in criminal procedure, so that its peculiarities require specific analysis, which goes beyond the scope of this work.[85]

The legal nature of the cooperator 's statements is controversial amongst scholars and, at this point, reveals an important distinction in the critical approach to the mechanism. On the one hand, some scholars point to its dual nature: a confession with respect to the cooperator and testimonial evidence in relation to those implicated.[86] However, such a view is subject to criticism,[87] since the cooperator cannot technically be considered a witness,[88] as they are a party with a vested interest in the outcome of the trial.[89] Thus, this mechanism would assume a *sui generis*[90] character, or the form of an "improper testimony", given its evidentiary limitations.[91]

As an expression of negotiated justice, together with agreements for recognition of guilt, cooperation agreements have been incorporated into the Brazilian legal system, permeated by recurrent discourses that call for swiftness and efficiency in criminal prosecution, or, in other words, "the improvement of the operability of the

[84] "The Leniency Programme was introduced into Law no. 8.884/94 by Provisional Measure no. 2.055, of 11 August 2000. After three editions, the Provisional Measure was converted into Law no. 10.149/2000, which consolidated, among others, articles 35-B and 35-C of the Competition Defence Law. [...] The programme is also regulated by Ordinance no. 456 of the Ministry of Justice, of 15 March 2010, which addresses various types of administrative proceedings, specialising in the investigation, prevention, and repression of infractions against the economic order within the Secretariat of Economic Law" (Salomi 2012, pp. 128–129).

[85] On this, see, for example: Salomi (2012), pp. 127–267; Lamy (2014), pp. 47–115.

[86] Grinover et al. (2001), p. 161.

[87] "From a technical point of view, it is incorrect to extend the legal treatment of testimony, confession, or any other means of proof to this type of statement without prior caution. This is because the individual in question is not a witness, understood as a third party unrelated to the object of the case, but rather someone directly linked to the alleged acts, and therefore with an interest both as a party to the proceedings and as a beneficiary of a potential reward. Nor is it a pure and simple confession; statements unfavourable to third parties cannot fall within the scope of the confession genre; their legal nature is different, as they entail the direct imputation of acts to others; thus, the evaluation of such evidence cannot disregard these circumstances" (Pereira, 2013, p. 160).

[88] Badaró (2014), p. 314.

[89] In this sense, Frederico Pereira (2013), p. 157, asserts that the accusatory statements of the repentant co-defendant cannot "rationally confer the attributes of certainty and security, as the information provided by the cooperator comes from a party with a vested interest in the case", thereby preventing a conviction from being based solely on such contributions.

[90] Bittar (2011b), p. 189.

[91] Silva (2014), p. 68. The author, however, points out that, after Law 12.850/2013, the cooperator's statements came to have the force of testimony, which would require observance of the adversarial principle (with the possibility of questions by the defence of the incriminated co-defendants). Such a view is debatable, as the author himself warns, since that legislation expressly confirms the insufficiency of cooperation statements as the sole basis for a conviction.

punitive judicial system'" .[92] Admittedly, these are debatable[93] influences, driven by criminal policy objectives,[94] that enter the criminal procedure under the justification of an alleged necessity to confront new forms of criminality and evidentiary difficulties in complex cases.[95] Undeniably, however, this mechanism stands out a significant trend in the international legal sphere, having been implemented in numerous jurisdictions[96] and even recommended by international organisations.[97]

As previously stated, the broad notion of bargaining also includes the mechanism of turn state's evidence.[98] Although undeniably influenced by the *common law* legal culture—particularly the American tradition—[99] and by their close association with the principles of opportunity and consensus,[100] some scholars highlight distinctions in their fundamental features.

According to Valdez Pereira, distinctions arise regarding the foundations of its emergence, since in *common law* legal systems, cooperation agreements essentially arise legitimised by the system's governing principle (opportunity), while in those of Roman-Germanic tradition, its introduction was motivated by "a need for effectiveness in controlling serious offences, with a pronounced criminal policy orientation".[101] Admittedly, the distinction regarding the premises of the systems (opportunity or obligation) is unquestionable; however, one can state that: (1) continental systems, guided by the principle of compulsoriness, are gradually adopting broader spaces for exception, in which, generally within legally defined parameters, cases of non-compulsoriness of public criminal prosecution are permitted; and (2) similar demands for swiftness and efficiency cannot be dismissed in either

---

[92] Pereira (2013), p. 20.

[93] For criticism of violations of fundamental rights under the pretext of pursuing swiftness and efficiency, see Sect. 4.1.1 of this work. In this regard, and specifically on turn state's evidence, see: Valle (2012), p. 113.

[94] Fernandes (2001), pp. 73–77; Dias (2011), pp. 37–39.

[95] Pereira (2013), p. 68.

[96] On the regulation of cooperation agreements in the United States, Spain, and Italy, see: Bittar (2011a), pp. 7–30.

[97] According to Eduardo Silva (2014), p. 54, the United Nations Convention against Transnational Organised Crime, adopted in New York on 15 November 2000, and ratified in Brazil (Decree 5.015/2004), recommends that State Parties adopt measures to encourage members of organised criminal groups to cooperate with criminal justice.

[98] On this, see Sect. 2.2.1 of this work, where bargaining was defined as a "procedural instrument that results in the waiver of defence, through the acceptance (and possible cooperation) of the accused with the prosecution, generally presupposing their confession, in exchange for some benefit (usually sentence reduction), negotiated and agreed between the parties or only expected by the accused".

[99] Lamy (2014), p. 34.

[100] "The agreement is an application of the principle of opportunity or of consensus, depending on the procedural stage in which it occurs" (Mendroni 2014, p. 44). For the contours of the principle of opportunity (non- compulsoriness) and consensual justice, see Sect. 2.1 of this work.

[101] Pereira (2013), p. 39.

scenarios, so the supposed necessity is argumentatively shared in most, if not all, legal systems internationally.[102]

Furthermore, the author also highlights a distinction between turn state's evidence and *plea bargaining* regarding the nature of their reward-based consequence.[103] However, it can be observed that, compared to bargaining, both mechanisms are essentially guided by the incentive for the accused to confess, with the expectation of a benefit or reward in their procedural position[104]—generally achieved through a reduction of their future punishment—with the purpose of facilitating the State's prosecutorial activity for a swift and less costly exercise of punitive power.[105] The distinction lies in the consequences of the agreement for third parties: in bargaining, the accused 's admission of guilt is aimed at their own criminal sanction, whereas in turn state's evidence its primary function is the incrimination of third parties (although it usually results in the conviction of the informant due to their confession).[106]

Cooperation agreements have been provided for in Brazilian law through various statutes since the 1990s. However, the most detailed regulation was only enacted in 2013, with Law 12.850/13. The implementation of cooperation agreements involves certain basic procedural characteristics and requirements that must be met, primarily aimed at safeguarding the fundamental rights of the accused in the criminal proceedings.[107] In this regard, studying these particularities may contribute to a critical analysis of the (potential future) legal regulation of bargaining,[108] since many aspects, as noted, are shared by both mechanisms. Thus, in addition to examining specific points of turn state's evidence, the following aspects should be particularly observed, as they reflect issues that will also be discussed in relation to

---

[102] Regarding the calls for swiftness and efficiency in the US legal system, see, Heumann (1981), pp. 1–6. Some authors even argue that the Brazilian legal system has not faced criminal phenomena that internationally legitimised the introduction of cooperation mechanisms, such as mafias or terrorist groups (Bittar 2011a, p. 2).

[103] Pereira (2013), p. 42.

[104] According to Gabriel Anitua (2010), p. 154, these mechanisms "share the common feature of granting the State (represented by the Judiciary or the Public Prosecutor's Office) the ability to reduce the sentence or even pardon the accused based on pacts or agreements".

[105] According to Frederico Pereira (2013), p. 43, these mechanisms are similar to mechanisms designed "to encourage engagement between the investigated party and the prosecution authority in order to meet the legal requirements authorising the 'positive sanction' for the evidentiary contribution provided by the accused—an assessment that is not immune to judicial review".

[106] In this regard, as will be discussed in Sect. 3.3, a potential confession made for a "bargain" agreement, if it does not include a turn state's evidence cause (with an added reduction of penalty), shall not be used against possible co-defendants.

[107] Badaró (2014), p. 319.

[108] It is believed that studying the legal framework (especially of Law 12.850/2013) and the scholarly theoretical background on turn state's evidence can contribute to critical assessment of any legislation that expands consensual mechanisms within the Brazilian legal system, since the study of the mechanism of cooperation agreement although still recent, is more consolidated in criminal-law scholarship

bargaining[109]: (1) the accused's consent must be free, informed and voluntary; (2) there must be an evidentiary basis to confirm the confession; (3) legal counsel must be present during all acts; (4) the judge must maintain a passive stance (prohibited from participating in negotiations); (5) the possibility of retraction must be ensured; and, (6) the use of the confessions is prohibited if the negotiation fails.

Firstly, as already noted, both negotiated mechanisms are grounded on a common denominator: the confession (1).[110] In the case of turn state's evidence, in which an accused implicates co-offenders, self-incrimination is required[111]; in other words, "the whistleblower's revelations must be related to the specific offence for which they are being prosecuted, or to the organisation or group of which they were a member or with which they collaborated".[112] Such a statement must be made or confirmed before the judge of competent jurisdiction during the procedural stage of criminal prosecution.[113] Moreover, it must be the expression of free,[114] informed and conscious will,[115] and therefore voluntary.[116]

---

[109] Later, in Sect. 3.4 of this work, proposals for expanding spaces for consensus in the Brazilian criminal process will be analysed, particularly through the critique of the comprehensive reform projects of the Code of Criminal Procedure (PLS 156/2009) and the Penal Code (PLS 236/2012), which clearly does not establish a system that protects fundamental rights—essential to a democratic criminal process. Thus, although subject to criticism, the regulation of turn state's evidence in Law 12.850/2013, provides elements that suitably limit the mechanism and can serve as a point of comparison.

[110] "It is understood as a prerequisite of procedural cooperation agreement that the accused confesses the facts in which they have participated, expressly waiving their constitutional right to silence, and appearing in the proceedings as a witness/informant, what the British call a crown witness […]" (Pereira 2013, p. 30). The author cites the example of Spain, which attempted to remove the requirement of a confession of the facts for turn state's evidence in drug trafficking, aiming at greater effectiveness of the mechanism. However, such an approach resulted in a distortion of the cooperation mechanisms, as it encouraged illegitimate statements merely to avoid the accused's responsibility (Pereira 2013, p. 31). On the scholars' divergences regarding the need for confession in the turn state's evidence, see: Carvalho, Lima (2009), p. 242.

[111] Eduardo Silva (2014), p. 73, further stresses the importance of the "non-existence of the purpose of acting to reduce or eliminate one's own criminal responsibility" in the cooperator's statement, since they must attest to the "full admission […] of their participation in the investigated facts."

[112] Pereira (2013), p. 36. However, the author later notes: "It is understood that it is not necessary that, if a criminal organization is established, the agent be part of it in order to claim the reward […]. This allows the use of the mechanism by minor external cooperators, not belonging to the organised structure of the association or criminal organisation" (Pereira 2013, p. 120).

[113] Bittar (2011b), p. 96.

[114] "The voluntariness of the cooperator's initiative is one of the most sensitive aspects of the mechanism in practice, given the real possibility of coercion for effective cooperation. If excesses in extracting a confession during investigations are foreseeable, nothing prevents them from also occurring in the search for efficient cooperation, which will inevitably lead to the illegality of the evidence obtained [...]" (Silva 2014, p. 57).

[115] Regarding the delimitation of such requirements from the American legal literature on plea bargaining, see Sect. 2.2.3 of this work. Regarding turn state's evidence, see: Pereira (2013), p. 115.

[116] With respect to the voluntariness in cooperation, debates amongst scholars are particularly relevant in light of the wording of the Heinous Crimes Act, which also required "spontaneity" in the cooperator's action—meaning that such conduct could not be initiated or encouraged by any State authority. However, it is stated that "a consensus was reached that voluntariness is sufficient for the

Furthermore, and here lies the main difference from bargaining, it is essential to provide an effective cooperation with the criminal prosecution, through an active stance of the whistleblower.[117] Thus, a procedural obligation is established for the them,[118] "a duty to cooperate permanently with the authorities", so that their presence is mandatory in all cases in which it is requested by the police or the judicial authority.[119] This derives essentially from the waiver of the right to silence resulting from the acceptance of the turn state's evidence agreement, a matter widely debated in legal literature,[120] but determined by the provisions of Law 12.850/2013.[121]

Indeed, one of the most important points in the regulation and implementation of turn state's evidence agreements is the insufficiency of the cooperator's statement to solely ground a conviction (2).[122] This is the mainstream, if not unanimous, position of Brazilian legal scholars and caselaw,[123] since, similarly to the confession regulated in the Code of Penal Procedure, its probative value cannot be the exclusive determinant for resolving the case, under penalty of a return to a system in which the accused's word becomes the "queen of evidence".[124]

In this regard, the express provision of Law 12.850/2013, in paragraph 16 of art. 4, amended by Law 13.964/19, is commendable: "§ 16. None of the following measures shall be decreed or issued solely based on the cooperator's statements: I—real or personal precautionary measures; II—receipt of a criminal complaint or indictment; III—conviction."[125] This requirement will be revisited later, in the critical analysis of a possible regulation of bargaining, since, as a mechanism structured on the basis of the confession, it shall also be corroborated by the examination of the evidentiary basis of the criminal procedure.

---

implementation of turn state's evidence, spontaneity not being indispensable [...]" (Lamy 2014, p. 34).

[117] "An active stance on the part of the agent is also required. Conducts that demonstrate the unequivocal will to cooperate with the authorities in clarifying the facts" (Bittar 2011b, p. 169).

[118] Pereira (2013), pp. 133–134.

[119] Silva (2014), pp. 57–58.

[120] On this, see: Pereira (2013), pp. 54–55; Silva (2014), pp. 67–68. Regarding the waiving of the accused's fundamental rights, resulting from the acceptance of bargaining, see criticism in Sect. 4.1.6 of this work.

[121] According to § 14 of art. 4 of Law 12.850/2013: "In the testimonies provided, the cooperator shall, in the presence their counsel, waive the right to silence and shall be subject to the legal duty to tell the truth".

[122] Bittar (2011b), p. 194.

[123] "One must emphasise that the prevailing view denies the possibility of a conviction being founded solely on the statements of a co-defendant who benefits from the reward-based mechanism; indeed, it is often said that virtually all scholar works and positions consulted do not admit that this evidentiary element has the strength to, by itself, sustain a conviction" (Pereira 2013, p. 64).

[124] Lopes Jr. (2012), p. 646.

[125] Silva (2014), p. 71; Mendroni (2014), p. 49.

Similarly, the aforementioned legislation should be praised for requiring the indispensable presence of the accused's counsel in all acts (3), whether negotiation, confirmation or execution (art. 4, § 15, of Law 12.850/2013).[126] Undoubtedly,[127] such technical assistance is characterised as a prerequisite for the validity of the cooperation agreement, as it is essential to ensure the whistleblower's full understanding and awareness of the act of confession.[128]

Regarding the procedure to be adopted for the execution of a cooperation agreement, prior to Law 12.850/2013, the insufficiency and confusion of the legal framework on the matter were widely noted.[129] Various legal statutes addressed the mechanism (especially, but not only,[130] the Heinous Crimes Act, the Victim and Witness Protection Act and the Narcotics Act), yet always in a deficient manner, focusing on its penal consequences rather than on procedural aspects. However, with the enactment of Law 12.850/2013, this scenario changed due to the introduction of new legal provisions into the Brazilian legal system, which, although primarily aimed at the criminal prosecution of offences related to criminal organisations, may be applied to turn state's evidence in general, by analogy.[131]

According to this law the agreement may be concluded at any stage of the criminal proceedings, whether during the preliminary investigation, the trial or, even later, during the execution stage, while the sentence is being served.[132] Thus, the authority to initiate negotiations regarding the cooperation is granted to the police officer,[133] in which case the public prosecutor must provide an express statement, or negotiations may be conducted directly with the representative of the Public Prosecutor's Office. Once the turn state's evidence agreement is reached, it must be formalised in writing, observing the formalities set for in article[6] of Law 12.850/2013,

[126] "In addition to concerns about the preservation of the cooperator's rights and the fulfillment of the benefits agreed upon, the legislator's attention to observing the legal prerequisites is once again evident [...]" (Silva 2014, p. 69).

[127] Although Frederico Pereira (2013), pp. 115–116, notes the possibility of the cooperator waiving the assistance of a legal counsel due to concerns about potential leaks of the content of the turn state's evidence, it is understood that, besides being expressly provided for in Law 12.850/2013, such a scenario would require the appointment of a public defender, who would be obliged to uphold the confidentiality of the agreement.

[128] Bittar (2011b), pp. 175–177.

[129] Pereira (2013), pp. 107–108; Bittar and Pereira (2011), p. 7.

[130] For a thorough analysis of each legal statute that regulates turn state's evidence, see: Bittar (2011a), pp. 89–158.

[131] Badaró (2014), p. 318.

[132] Silva (2014), pp. 61–65.

[133] Regarding the possibility of initiative by the police authority, some argue its unconstitutionality, given that the Public Prosecutor's Office holds the exclusive prerogative over criminal prosecution: "[...] the law is unconstitutional in granting such power to the police officer, through an agreement with the cooperator, even though it requires the opinion of the Public Prosecutor's Office and judicial approval, since it assigns a function that does not belong to police authority, namely, the pursuit of criminal prosecution in court, thereby constraining the understanding of the authority responsible for the prosecution" (Silva 2014, p. 59–60).

including, for instance, the account of the cooperation, the conditions of the offer, and the acceptance by both cooperator and their legal counsel.[134]

Two points that deserve attention are the requirement of the judge's passive stance and the possibility of retracting the agreement. In order to safeguard judicial impartiality, it is essential to exclude the judge from any negotiations regarding a possible turn state's evidence (4).[135] Accordingly, the aforementioned statute is commendable when inferring the judge's non-participation,[136] restricting their role to that of guarantor of legality and of the accused's fundamental rights through the review exercised in approving the cooperation. However, the provision authorising the judge to readjust the agreement to the specific case (art. 4.°, §8.° of Law 12.850/2013) is questionable, since altering the terms negotiated between the prosecutor and the accused undermines the very nature of the mechanism, violates the consensual will of the parties, and infringes the defence's legitimate expectations regarding the terms of the pact—expectations which determined its acceptance. Thus, as Eduardo Silva argues, the judge's intervention shall be limited to verifying compliance with the agreement's formal requirements, lest their impartiality be compromised through the usurpation of prosecutorial functions.[137]

With regard to the possibility of retracting the cooperation (5), Law 12.850/2013 provides for such a hypothesis in § 10 of art. 4.°, establishing that the self-incriminating evidence produced by the cooperator shall not be used solely against them, particularly the confession made within the scope of the agreement (6).[138]

In addition to such relevant procedural issues, the consequences of the cooperation agreement for the accused/ cooperator are essential to the study of the mechanism and its role as an expression of negotiated justice. This is the reward granted by the State in exchange for cooperation in criminal prosecution, legally regulated in the statutes that provide for the cooperation mechanism.[139] According to Walter

---

[134] Mendroni (2014), pp. 52–54.

[135] Pereira (2013), pp. 129–130.

[136] According to Art. 4, § 6, of Law 12.850/2013: "The judge shall not participate in the negotiations conducted between the parties for the formalisation of the cooperation agreement, which shall take place between the police officer, the investigated party and their counsel, with the participation of the Public Prosecutor's Office, or, as the case may be, between the Public Prosecutor's Office and the investigated or accused party and their counsel".

[137] "[...] the adequacy of the agreement shall be restricted to compliance with the legal prerequisites and requirements, as determined by § 8 of Art. 4 of the law, given the risk of an undesirable intrusion into the private sphere of the prosecution, with the inevitable compromise of impartiality, if it entails a change in the merit" (Silva 2014, p. 66). In this sense, Marcelo Mendroni states that any alteration of the n content—for example, the type of benefit granted—is only possible if expressly ratified by the parties (prosecution and defence) (Mendroni 2014, p. 45–46).

[138] In the same vein, it is affirmed, in a similar hypothesis, that, "in cases in which the agent's revelations are deemed unsubstantiated, due to the absence of any external elements of credibility, the confession, made to obtain the benefit, cannot be considered evidence against the alleged cooperator" (Pereira 2013, p. 138).

[139] According to Frederico Pereira (2013), p. 104, in order to avoid arbitrariness stemming from discretion, the benefits and their respective parameters of definition shall necessarily be strictly and objectively provided for in criminal legislation.

Bittar, in the Brazilian legal system there are four possible benefits: (1) exemption from penalty through judicial pardon; (2) reduction of the sentence by one to two thirds; (3) initial serving of the sentence in an open regime; and, (4) substitution for a right-restricting penalty.[140] The determination of the extent of the reward is based primarily on the effectiveness and scope of the cooperation provided,[141] and the judge must give reasonable grounds for the percentage of the reduction.[142]

Regarding the specific regulation of Law 12.850/2013, the following consequences are provided: (1) reduction of one to two thirds of the sentence; (2) judicial pardon; (3) substitution by a right-restricting penalty; (4) reduction of up to half or progression of regime, if the copperation occurs during the execution stage (art. 4.°, § 5.°); (5) non-filing of the indictment, if it occurs before the initiation of the criminal action (art. 4.°, § 4.°).[143] This last situation—the authorisation to the Public Prosecutor's Office to refrain from filing the indictment, if the whistleblower is the first to cooperate and is not the leader of the criminal organisation—represents an innovative possibility in the Brazilian legal system, as it advances in the introduction of exceptions to the principle of compulsory public criminal prosecution.[144] In addition, the law establishes criteria to guide the granting of the benefit: the personality of the cooperator, as well as the nature, circumstances, severity and social repercussion of the criminal act, and the effectiveness of the cooperation (art. 4.°, § 1.°).[145]

In contrast to the system established in the Brazilian legal framework, the agreements formalised within the scope of the *Lava Jato* operation introduced several innovations, such as the provision of "differentiated regimes of sentence execution", the release of assets derived from illicit activities, the granting of immunity to family members and third parties to the agreement, the waiver of access to justice and appeals, and the imposition of a vague and generic duty of cooperation. In opposition to this practice, in December 2019, Law 13.964/19 was enacted, inserting and amending relevant provisions on cooperation agreements from Law 12.850/13. For the purposes herein discussed, the new legislation amended § 7 of art. 4, expressly determining that, at the time of the agreement's approval, the judge shall analyse "II - the adequacy of the agreed benefits to those provided for in the head provision and in §§ 4 and 5 of this article, with nullity of clauses that violate the criterion of defining the initial regime of sentence execution under art. 33 of Decree-Law no. 2.848, of 7 December 1940 (Penal Code), the rules of each regime provided for in the Penal Code and in Law no. 7.210, of 11 July 1984 (Sentence Execution Act) and the requirements for regime progression not covered by § 5 of this article". However,

---

[140] Bittar (2011b), p. 181.

[141] Carvalho and Lima (2009), pp. 248–249.

[142] Pereira (2013), p. 139.

[143] Silva (2014), pp. 62–65.

[144] Regarding this innovation, see: Vasconcellos (2015a, b). In this regard: Silva (2014), p. 62; Mendroni (2014), p. 41. On the principles of compulsoriness and opportunity, and their contours in the Brazilian legal system, see Sect. 2.1 of this work.

[145] Mendroni (2014), pp. 36–37.

despite this express prohibition, Brazilian courts still tend to admit the granting of benefits not authorised by law, thereby considerably expanding the power of the parties—particularty the Public Prosecutor's Office—to dispose of criminal prosecution.

Finally, two points highlighted by scholars are pertinent. Firstly, it is noted that, after the ratification of the agreement and the implementation of the cooperation, the benefit to the accused becomes mandatory, characterising it as a subjective right.[146] Furthermore, it is worth mentioning the possibility of increasing the reduction of the sentence due to the joint consideration of the cause for reduction arising from cooperation and the mitigating factor of the confession,[147] a situation that may occur in the future through the combination of bargaining and a cooperation agreement, in which the accused should be entitled to a greater benefit.

Therefore, in summary, based on the outlined contours, particularly the provisions set out in Law 12.850/2013, the following premises shall be established as possible contributions to defining a minimum core for the potential future regulation of bargaining[148]: (1) the accused's will to enter into the agreement must be free, informed and conscious, under penalty of the agreement's illegality and the unlawfulness of any evidence produced; (2) the confession alone is not sufficient to substantiate a conviction, and must necessarily be corroborated by other evidence; (3) the accused must be assisted by legal counsel at all stages of negotiation and execution of the agreement; (4) the judge must maintain a passive stance, being prohibited from taking part in the negotiations, in order to safeguard their impartiality, and shall act as a guarantor of legality and of respect for fundamental rights through the ratification or rejection of the agreement; and, (5) it must be possible for the accused to retract, in which case the confession cannot be deemed lawful evidence.

Having analysed the main characteristics of turn state's evidence in the Brazilian criminal—legal framework and its possible contributions to the study of a potential regulation of bargaining, it is necessary to consider the criticisms raised by legal scholars regarding the mechanism of repentant. In addition to the objections that are common to consensual mechanisms—since they are fundamentally grounded in the incentive to confess in exchange for sentencing benefits,[149] which will be further

[146] "[...] once it is concretely established that the requirements for cooperation are met, and the agent's statements serve to support the actions of the police authority or the prosecution before the criminal court, with the cooperator having complied with the commitments previously undertaken, the agent acquires a subjective right to the granting of the benefit, with no room for discretion on the part of the Public Prosecutor or the judge" (Pereira 2013, p. 137).

[147] Pereira (2013), p. 137.

[148] On the criticisms and proposals for the possible regulation of bargaining within the Brazilian legal system, see Sect. 3.4 of this work.

[149] "The architecture of turn state's evidence, due to its similarity to criminal settlement, also contains another element which, in connection with a criminal policy of ever-increasing penalties, has the potential to undermine the investigation of acts, in public adversarial proceedings" (Prado 2006a, p. 12).

examined later[150]—two points deserve attention at this stage: the tacit acknowledgement of State's deficiency in the prosecution of crimes and the consequent encouragement of conduct that violates the minimum ethical standard of public action.

In the face of arguments that legitimise the reward-based mechanism through the acceptance of a "soft inquisition" in a scenario of "investigative emergency",[151] the deficit of State mechanisms—especially in a context marked by the striking expansion of punitive power in social relations—reveals the persistent insufficiency in addressing criminal matters. Such deficiency, in turn, supports discourses that seek to distort the premises of criminal procedure, for instance by reversing the burden of proof and by restricting the rights to full defence and to the adversarial proceedings, based on unduly secretive statements.[152]

On the other hand, also revealing the aporias of the reward model, some authors assert that the mechanism of turn state's evidence operates by incentivising unethical behaviour by those criminally prosecuted,[153] which completely undermines the State authorities' promise to act ethically and legitimately action of the manifestations of state power.[154] In other words, according to some legal scholars, the fundamental minimum ethical standard for the State's public action is being violated.[155] In this regard, the "prisoner's dilemma" is illustrative, highlighting the coercion exerted by the possibility of cooperation agreement, which encourages illegitimate incriminations: when two accused individuals are arrested and are offered the option of turn state's evidence, without knowing the partner's decision, they may end up cooperating with the criminal prosecution out of fear that the other will act (since joint cooperation is prohibited in the concrete case).[156] Even without a clear intent

150 On this, see Chap. 4 of this work and, for instance, regarding violations of constitutional dictates: Bittar (2011b), pp. 194–217.

151 Pereira (2013), pp. 66–69.

152 "The central point of the criticism is that turn state's evidence merely justifies deficient investigations, acting as a palliative for the State's poor performance. It would operate as a means by which the Public Prosecutor, holder of unconditional public criminal action, could seek elements of conviction capable of substantiating a summary of guilt, thus exempting themselves from collecting the necessary evidence. In other words, the burden of proof imposed on the Prosecution by the presumption of innocence would be shifted onto the very individual responsible for the conduct." (Lamy 2014, pp. 26–27). Also in this sense: Coutinho and Carvalho (2006), p. 179.

153 "The ethical disapproval of the turn state's evidence has become a common stance in the legal literature committed to the implementation of the Constitution. This is because the informer, unlike the confessor, invariably seeks to absolve or mitigate their responsibility, attributing it to others; that is, it expands incrimination, affecting third parties" (Carvalho and Lima 2009, p. 250). Describing this aporia: Rosa (2011), p. 11.

154 "Redemption becomes an integral part of the content, which is the reward for the act of informing granted in Brazilian penal laws—a more than evident example of social disintegration through the encouragement of betrayal, which indelibly affronts the principle of human dignity" (Valle 2012, p. 114).

155 Coutinho and Carvalho (2006), pp. 78–81.

156 Valle (2012), p. 123.

to whistleblow (or even without reliable information to do so),[157] the accused is pressured to act this way, fearing that failing to do so will put the accused at disadvantage.[158]

Therefore, in light of the described scenario regarding international trends in the implementation and expansion of reward mechanisms, such as turn state's evidence, and the criticisms presented, a careful analysis of the mechanism is essential, as it reveals and intensifies various tensions with constitutionally and conventionally established fundamental rights.[159]

3.3 The Non-prosecution Agreement and the Expansion of Bargaining in the 2019 Reform of the Brazilian Code of Penal Procedure

Still regarding the expansion of spaces for consensus in Brazilian criminal justice, in September 2017 the National Council of the Public Prosecutor's Office (CNMP) regulated, through Resolution 181/2017, the possibility of a "non-prosecution agreement". After strong criticism within the legal community, this mechanism was quickly amended by Resolution 183 of January 2018. In this context, the original text should first be analysed, followed by the modifications introduced.

According to the head provision of the originally approved article 18, "in crimes committed without violence or serious threat to the person, if the case is not subject to dismissal, the Public Prosecutor's Office may propose a non-prosecution agreement to the investigated party, provided that they formally and in detail confess to the crime and indicate any evidence of its commission". Thus, the investigated party would agree to the imposition (cumulative or not) of "sanctions" such as compensation to the victim, waiving of assets and rights, community service and payment of monetary damages, for example.

Therefore, such an agreement would be possible for any crime committed without violence or serious threat to the person, unless (art. 18, §2 °) a criminal settlement is applicable, the damage caused exceeds 20 times minimum wages or "waiting for the agreement to be fulfilled may result in statute of limitations". Furthermore, the agreement would not be possible in cases regulated in art. 76, §2 of Law 9.099/95, such as when the investigated party has been definitively sentenced to a custodial

157 It is also important to highlight what scholars call "professional informers", who fabricate information to unduly obtain benefits: "Moreover, in analysing this requirement, one must consider, what the Italians call *professionisti del pentitismo,* that is, people who trade half-truths in exchange for individual advantages" (Silva 2014, p. 58).

158 Lamy (2014), p. 33.

159 In this regard, even highlighting the unconstitutionality of turn state's evidence mechanism, Jacinto Coutinho states: "There is very little doubt—although some remains due to the concession that effective means of progress might be sought—that the mechanism is unconstitutional, as it currently stands; and harmful to the democratic structure of society" (Coutinho and Carvalho 2006, p. 8).

sentence for a crime, or when the measure is deemed unnecessary or insufficient considering the individual's prior record, social conduct, and personality.

The introduction of the ANPP through a CNMP resolution sparked debate regarding the violation of the principle of strict legality, which should guide (and limit) the exercise of the State's punitive power.[160] Even in criminal proceedings, legality is a fundamental premise, meaning that only the law can modify its norms. Accordingly, there was a clear unconstitutionality due to a violation of art. 22, I, of the Federal Constitution, although the Federal Supreme Court did not issue a ruling to that effect.

Besides this formal defect of origin, coupled with the imprecision of the applicability criteria, art. 18 of Resolution 181/2017 did not provide any judicial review over the proposed negotiation mechanism. Clearly, the judiciary must be the controlling and limiting body of agreements between the parties in criminal proceedings, consolidating its role as a guarantor of fundamental rights and a check on State punitive power. Thus, any consensus regarding the immediate application of a criminal sanction must invariably be submitted to judicial review, primarily aimed at preventing abuses and violations of the fundamental rights of the accused.[161]

Given these problematic issues, this mechanism faced strong resistance both in legal literature and within the Public Prosecutor's Office itself, to the point that it was even challenged in some Brazilian states.[162] As a result, in December 2017, an amendment was approved and published as Resolution 183 in January 2018, which limited the agreement to crimes carrying a minimum sentence of less than 4 years and required prior judicial review, in addition to other stipulated restrictions.[163]

Only at the end of 2019 was the ANPP inserted into art. 28-A of the CPP through Law 13.964/19, adopting terms largely similar to those established in the CNMP's amended regulation. The non-prosecution agreement (ANPP) is a negotiated criminal justice mechanism regulated in the Code of Criminal Procedure following the amendment introduced by Law 13.654/19 in art. 28-A. It constitutes a procedural legal arrangement between the prosecution and the investigated party, in which the defence and the trial are waived in exchange for a benefit, such as avoiding a prison sentence and the classification of criminal records as aggravating. Although this entails an expansion of the parties' power, the role of the Judiciary cannot be disregarded, and the agreement is therefore subject to judicial review.

The Brazilian law (art. 28-A, CPP) states that the ANPP must undergo judicial approval, during which "the judge shall verify its voluntariness by hearing the investigated party in the presence of their legal counsel, and its legality" (§ 4),

[160] Andrade and Brandalise (2017), p. 252.

[161] On the need for submission to judicial review, in accordance with the precedent of the European Court of Human Rights: Aras (2018), pp. 287–290.

[162] In Minas Gerais, the Joint Recommendation PGJ CGMP N. 2, dated 13 Sept. 2017, was issued, instructing that prosecutors and public attorneys of MG refrain from entering into the agreements provided for in art. 18 of Res. 181/2017 of CNMP. Available at: http://s.conjur.com.br/dl/mp-mg-proibe-acordo-ignorar-acao-penal.pdf.

[163] The amendment available at: http://www.cnmp.mp.br/portal/images/PROP_927_2017_69_-_Resolução_181_-_Parecer.pdf.

holding, for this purpose, a public and oral hearing. Furthermore, "if the judge considers the conditions set forth in the non-prosecution agreement to be inadequate, insufficient, or abusive, they shall return the case to the Public Prosecutor's Office so that the agreement proposal may be reformulated, with the consent of the investigated party and their legal counsel" (§ 5).

One of the fundamental requirements for the admissibility of a non-prosecution agreement (ANPP) is that the minimum sentence for the offense must not be equal to or exceed 4 (four) years, provided that the crime was not committed with violence or serious threat and the accused has not been previously convicted in another case. Unlike criminal settlements and the conditional suspension of criminal prosecution (agreements provided for in Law 9.099/1995), a confession is a prerequisite for the implementation of the ANPP. As established in the head provision of art. 28-A, the perpetrator must formally and circumstantially confess to the commission of the criminal offence. Thus, the confession can serve as a factual check on the elements set forth by the prosecution.

As a legal transaction, the accused must fulfil certain obligations provided for in article 28-A, and upon completion, will benefit from the extinction of criminal liability. In the event of non-compliance, the prosecution may subsequently file charges. The provision establishes that the conditions may be cumulative and alternative, in accordance with the principle of proportionality. The agreement cannot result in the imprisonment of the accused, but only in alternative sanctions, such as compensation to the victim, waiving of assets and rights, payment of monetary damages, community service, or other conditions agreed upon by the parties according to the specific circumstances of the case.

Negotiations must be recorded audiovisually, so that subsequent review is possible, for instance, in case of alleged undue coercion or defects biasing the voluntariness of the accused. If negotiations are unsuccessful and the ANPP is not formalised or ratified by the court, any information provided by the accused—including any confession made as a prerequisite to the agreement—cannot be used by the prosecution.

Any refusal by the Public Prosecutor's Office to propose a non-prosecution agreement must be duly justified. According to art. 28-A, § 14, "in the event of refusal by the Public Prosecutor's Office to propose the non-prosecution agreement, the investigated party may request that the case be referred to a higher body, in accordance with art. 28 of this Code". In other words, there is an internal appeal mechanism within the Public Prosecutor's Office, allowing a higher instance in the prosecution to review the refusal to enter into the agreement.

3.4 Current Proposals for the Introduction and Expansion of Bargaining in Brazilian Criminal Justice: A Critical Analysis of Trends towards Expanding Spaces for Consensus

After examining the existing spaces for consensus in the current Brazilian criminal procedure, it is now essential to undertake a descriptive and critical analysis of proposals, in broad terms, for the expansion of bargaining authorisations with in the national legal system (primarily Senate Bill 156 of 2009 and 8, 045 of 2010 in the Chamber of Deputies, which seek a comprehensive reform of the Code of Criminal Procedure, and Bill 236 of 2012, which proposes a new Penal Code). This section will present some critical considerations aimed at improving the provisions in the most significant current proposals, or, more precisely, will attempt to mitigate potential harms in the event of a problematic legislative approval.[164]

As previously noted, the characteristics of the bargaining model established in each legal system can vary in several aspects. According to Richard Lippke, eight determinants are essential in structuring this mechanism: (1) the possibility and factors for sentence reduction; (2) the possibility and factors for reduction or modification of charges; (3) the possibility and factors for procedural sanctions (due to the non-acceptance of the plea); (4) the possibility of negotiating acts and its limits; (5) the possibility of a pre-trial agreement; (6) the role of legal actors in the negotiation; (7) the list of offences for which bargaining may occur; and, (8) the scope of judicial power review over the agreement.[165] Thus, there is no single model of agreements in criminal justice, as multiple determinants exist, offering a broad range of grounds for criticism. This section will therefore focus on some of these characteristics, given the countless possible versions and potential objections, emphasising points considered particularly sensitive for the protection of fundamental rights in criminal proceedings.

It is important to point out that, besides the proposals to expand the scope of action of the Small Claims Courts, and consequently their consensual mechanisms,[166] the addition of a function to the list of attributions of the Public Prosecutor's Office (art. 129) was also discussed in the context of a Constitutional Amendment Project (PEC 230/00),[167] in the following terms: "X – negotiate the penalty of individuals

[164] Also expressing similar concern, in stating his opposition to the institution of the US plea bargaining, one of its most fervent critics, Albert Alschuler (1976), p. 1122, proposes measures to try to reduce the tensions generated by the mechanism, although maintaining his opposing, delegitimising view.

[165] Lippke (2011), pp. 6–7.

[166] In this regard, Fernandes (2005), p. 282, proposes that the settlement may be offered in cases in which, in abstract terms, the Public Prosecutor's Office concludes and substantiates the future possibility, in the event of conviction, of converting the penal sanction into a restriction of rights, that is, for custodial sentences of up to 4 years.

[167] According to the justification of the project: "The rising wave of violence affecting our country, as well as the increase in cases related to organised crime and corruption within the State structure,

under police investigation and/or accused individuals in ongoing criminal proceedings, being able to reach an agreement, compromise, waive criminal prosecution, or grant immunities so that they confess details of crimes and identify accomplices, provided that the requirements to be established in Complementary Law are met".[168] If approved, this modification would bring the system closer to the US *plea bargaining* model, at least in a general sense, although it lacked ordinary regulation regarding its prerequisites. However, in its last movement, the PEC was dismissed in 2008.

Today, the two most relevant proposals, both aiming at comprehensive reforms of the Codes, are PLS 236/12 and PLS 156/09 (PL 8.045/10). It has long been recognized in legal literature that revisions to the main criminal legislations—the Penal Code and the Code of Criminal Procedure—are necessary, given the authoritarian framework characteristic at the time of their drafting[169] and the numerous partial amendments that have generated systematisation issues.[170] Both projects introduce significant innovations in the context of negotiated justice through the expansion of spaces for consensus, particularly with the introduction of a bargaining mechanism, or the similar "fast track",[171] which breaks with the national tradition that has historically limited possibilities of settlement in criminal matters, even allowing negotiation for the imposition of custodial sentences with full recognition of guilt.[172]

Initially, the proposal for a comprehensive reform of the Penal Code (Senate Bill 236/12) has been met with objections from legal scholars due to its lack of technical precision and its development within a very short timeframe.[173]

Along the turn state's evidence, the negotiation mechanism is regulated in Title VII of the aforementioned project,[174] without further specifications regarding its pro-

has required the State itself to create mechanisms capable of making punitive measures more efficient and effective in curbing such practices, reaching their main perpetrators who, as a rule, employ third parties to achieve their criminal objectives. This mechanism already exists in developed countries under the name of 'plea bargaining'".

[168] Prado (2006c), p. 23.

[169] Malan (2010), p. 2.

[170] Regarding the stance of partial reforms adopted by the Brazilian legislator in criminal matters, see Coutinho (2009), p. 9.

[171] The Senate Bill 156/2009 also provides for modifications to the fast track applied to minor offences, repealing the provisions of Law 9.099/1995 and introducing innovations to its framework. However, in this work, the focus will be on the "fast track" mechanism, due to its notorious tendency as an expression of bargaining in criminal proceedings. For innovations to the fast track, see Leite (2013), pp. 193–201.

[172] Casara (2011), p. 148.

[173] On this, see Greco (2012), pp. 55–58; Wunderlich et al. (2013).

[174] "Art. 105. Once the complaint or charge has been definitively received, the lawyer or public defender, on one side, and the Public Prosecutor's Office or complainant responsible for the case, on the other, in the exercise of their autonomous will, may enter into an agreement for the immediate application of penalties, prior to the evidentiary and trial hearing. § 1. The requirements for the agreement referred to in the head provision of this article are: I—a full or partial confession regarding the acts imputed in the accusatory document; II—a request that the prison sentence be applied at the minimum provided by law, regardless of any aggravating circumstances or factors increasing the penalty, without prejudice to the provisions of §§ 2.° to 4.° of this article; III—the express

cedural aspects (for instance, there is no mention of the need for judicial approval of the agreement) and containing provisions very similar to those in Senate Bill 156/09, which will be examined next[175] (e.g., the requirements, the setting of the penalty at the legal minimum, and the timing of the agreement). However, there is a fundamental difference: Senate Bill 236/12 imposes no limitation on the severity of the offence, meaning that bargaining would be possible in cases involving any type of crime.[176]

According to the statement of reasons for this proposal, it draws direct inspiration from the "American plea bargain model, in the sense of granting broad autonomy to the parties to negotiate terms that may be mutually agreeable ", representing a "new and bold step" in the pursuit of swiftness through the "avoidance of criminal proceedings ", thereby breaking with the "rigid paradigm of the non-availability of criminal prosecution". In its most recent relevant legislative development, the wording of the original report presented by the commission was modified following the opinion of the Senate Bill rapporteur, Senator Pedro Taques, who, faced with numerous criticisms of the text, sought to revise its content. Accordingly, Opinion 1.576/2013 proposed the exclusion of the bargaining mechanism, due to its inappropriate placement within a Penal Code of substantive content, the distortion of existing consensus mechanisms in the Small Claims Courts, and its "difficult compatibility with Brazil's institutional culture".

Regarding the project for a comprehensive reform of the Code of Criminal Procedure, Senate Bill 156 of 2009, also drafted by a commission appointed by the Federal Senate, it was approved in a vote and sent for review by the Chamber of Deputies, but has not progressed since then.[177] According to the wording at the conclusion of its consideration in the first legislative chamber, the negotiation mechanism was regulated under the designation of "fast track" and established in the following terms:

> **Arts. 283-284**
> Art. 283. Until the start of the evidentiary stage and the hearing referred to in art. 276, once the provisions of the ordinary proceeding have been observed, the Public Prosecutor's Office and the accused, through their legal counsel, may request the immediate application of a penalty in cases of crimes whose maximum statutory sanction does not exceed 8 (eight) years.
>
> § 1.° The requirements of the agreement referred to in the head provision of this article are: I – a total or partial confession, regarding the facts alleged in the complaint; II – a request that the custodial sentence be applied at the minimum

waiver by the parties of producing evidence indicated by them. § 2. Where applicable, the substitution of the prison sentence shall be applied pursuant to art. 61 of this Code. § 3. The initial closed regime is prohibited. § 4. Upon request by the parties, the penalty referred to in § 1.° may be reduced by up to one third of the legal minimum".

[175] Due to the similarity between the two regulations, an in-depth examination will be conducted focusing on Senate Bill 156/2009, given its greater specificity (though still clearly insufficient).

[176] Rodrigues, Costa (2013); Freitas (2012), p. 22.

[177] The aforementioned bill is currently under consideration as no. 8.045/2010.

established by law, regardless of the possible incidence of aggravating circumstances or causes for increasing the penalty, and without prejudice to the provisions of §§ 2o and 3o of this article; III – the express declaration of the parties waiving the production of the evidence they have indicated.

§ 2.° Where applicable, the custodial sentence shall be substituted in accordance with the provisions of art. 44 of the Penal Code, as well as the conditional suspension under art. 77 of the same Code.

§ 3. At the request of the parties, the penalty applied under the fast track may be reduced by up to 1/3 (one third) of the statutory minimum, if the offender's personal circumstances and the lesser severity of the consequences of the crime so indicate.

§ 4. The provisions of § 3 of this article shall not apply when another cause for the reduction of the penalty is present in the case, except in the event of an attempted crime, which shall be expressly indicated in the agreement.

§ 5. If there is a cumulatively prescribed imposition of a fine, it shall also be applied at the legal minimum, and the amount shall be set out in the agreement.

§ 6. The accused shall be exempt from expenses and court costs.

§ 7. When ratifying the agreement and for the purposes of applying the penalty under the fast track, the judge shall verify compliance with the formal requirements laid down in this article.

§ 8. For all legal purposes, the ratification of the agreement shall be deemed a conviction.

§ 9. If, for any reason, the agreement is not ratified, it shall be removed from the records, and the parties shall be prohibited from making any reference to its terms and conditions, as shall the judge in any decision.

Art. 284. If no agreement is reached between the prosecution and the defence, the proceedings shall continue under the ordinary proceeding.

Similarly to what Ventura Leite advocates, an "alternative procedure" is created for allowing the early termination of the proceedings by consensus.[178]In short, this mechanism authorises negotiation between the Public Prosecutor's Office and the accused in cases in which the maximum statutory penalty does not exceed 8 years, determining the criminal sanction at its legal minimum, which may be converted into a restrictive penalty or suspended under the Penal Code.[179] So as to conclude the agreement, the accused must necessarily confess the acts alleged in the charge, and both parties must waive the production of any evidence. The judge is then required to examine the formalities of the agreement, which, if ratified, produces the effects of a conviction; in

[178] Leite (2013), p. 203.

[179] Freitas (2012), pp. 22–23.

other words, it generates criminal records and may establish recidivism. Conversely, if judicial ratification is denied, the agreement must be withdrawn from the case file, and any subsequent use in the proceedings is strictly prohibited.[180]

Given this, amongst critical positions—which include claims of the mechanism's unconstitutionality[181]—and enthusiastic supporters,[182] several points demand closer scrutiny, particularly in light of the insufficient procedural regulation contained in the proposed text. Thus, without aiming at exhaustiveness, the following issues will be addressed: (1) the agreement as a right of the accused; (2) the procedure and publicity of negotiations; (3) the timing and possible withdrawal of the agreement; (4) the judge's role and the safeguarding of impartiality; (5) judicial ratification and possibility of acquittal; and, (6) the right to appeal.

Initially (1), a widely discussed aporia arises with respect to the implementation of the consensual mechanisms currently provided for in the Brazilian legal system (criminal settlement and conditional suspension of the criminal prosecution): does the accused have a right to enter into the agreement if, in the specific case, the legally prescribed requirements are met?[183] As previously noted,[184] the arbitrariness of an unjustified refusal by the public prosecutor is evident,[185] given that the will of the Public Prosecutor's Office must be guided exclusively by statutory provisions, in observance of the principle of legality.[186] Accordingly, under the framework outlined in PLS 156/09, in which the accused confesses and waives the production of evidence in cases involving crimes with a maximum abstract penalty of less than 8 years, they should be entitled to the agreement and to the consequent reduction of punishment—an entitlement that must be safeguarded by the judge as the guarantor of individual rights in criminal proceedings.

Another problematic issue concerns the procedural formalisation of negotiations for the bargain (2). Here, particular attention must be paid to publicity in order to enable the fundamental "democratic review" of procedural acts[187]: informal agreements should be prohibited,[188] and the full content of the negotiations, as well as the

---

[180] Malan (2010), p. 2.

[181] Prado (2012), pp. 54–56; Freitas (2012), pp. 22–24; Casara (2011), pp. 155–157.

[182] Campos (2012), p. 25; Leite (2013), p. 203.

[183] In summary, for illustrative examples of such debates, see: Giacomolli (2009), pp. 129–130; Leite (2013), pp. 165–172.

[184] On this point, see Sect. 3.1.1 of this chapter.

[185] In this regard, there is a well-established body of scholarship criticising the broad prosecutorial discretion in the American model, suggesting that: "the prosecutor should offer equal opportunities to all accused individuals who plead guilty, making public the criteria that guide negotiations and listing the determining factors at the time of offering the deal" (Rodríguez García 1997, p. 92).

[186] According to Pedro Caeiro (2000), pp. 41–42, when analysing the Portuguese framework, it can be said that, if the legal requirements are met, there is a "duty to dismiss/suspend the proceeding", meaning that the prosecutor's discretionary will is not indispensable for establishing the agreement.

[187] Tulkens (2005), p. 715.

[188] It is worth recalling the German regulation of agreements, in which the conclusion of informal settlements was expressly prohibited, as negotiations must necessarily comply with statutory regulation. On this, see, among others: Weigend and Turner (2014), pp. 97–101.

terms of the agreement, should be presented in a hearing,[189] audiotaped and transcribed into the case files.[190] Transparency, therefore, constitutes a fundamental premise for ensuring at least minimal review of the bargain and for preventing undue coercion.[191]

In this regard, it is also worth noting the obligation to hold a hearing to finalise the agreement[192] and the accused's right to be present at all stages of any negotiation and its discussion.[193] Thus, although the text of PLS 156/09 does not explicitly mention this, a hearing should be conducted to formalise the bargain, ensuring that its terms and circumstances are made public and formally recorded in the case files, with the necessary presence of the accused and their legal counsel.

Regarding the timing of the bargain's implementation (3), under the project under review, the final deadline is set at the evidentiary hearing, that is, essentially at the beginning of the evidence production. Although some legal scholars consider this provision appropriate,[194] it is argued that the agreement should be allowed up until the moment immediately prior to the pronouncement of the first -instance judgement, so that the accused has full knowledge of the evidence presented and of their position in the proceeding.[195]

Finally, it is essential that the accused be allowed to retract their consent, which may occur up until the judicial ratification of the agreement, or even at the moment of the public hearing for its formalisation, after the accused has been duly informed of the circumstances and consequences of their actions.[196]

Next, the judge's role in the negotiations and the realisation of the bargain is also a fundamental issue not expressly addressed by the comprehensive reform project of the CPP (4). This debate is recurring amongst US scholars, who compare the benefits of a passive judge—respecting impartiality—to those of an active judge—who would ostensibly provide greater predictability and confidence to the

[189] "Procedural agreements must, in short, be made public at the hearing, so that their content can be reviewed by those who participated in them and, possibly, also by the appelate court" (Dias 2011, p. 72).

[190] Albergaria (2007), p. 75.

[191] Turner (2009), p. 508.

[192] Emphasising the importance of holding a hearing, Santiago Martínez (1999), p. 392, comments on the draft reform of the Criminal Procedure Code of the Argentine province of Santa Fé: "The greatest success of the draft, in our view, is the obligation of the court to summon the parties to a public hearing. At that time, the accused will be heard and, if they approve the agreement, the presiding judge will explain, clearly and simply, how the proceeding works and what its consequences are. Moreover, and this is the most important point, the accused must again be asked to confirm their express consent to the agreement".

[193] Alschuler (1976), p. 1135. One of the key reforms of the US plea bargaining system is the recognition of the need for the accused's participation in the negotiations, see: Heumann (1981), p. 167.

[194] Dias (2011), pp. 72–73. Similarly, the Italian procedure allows the agreement to be reached up until the opening of the *dibattimento* (Diego Díez 1999, p. 137).

[195] Even more broadly, in the United States, plea bargaining may take place before, during, or even after the trial. For further discussion, see: Turner (2009), p. 28.

[196] Diego Díez (1999), p. 154.

bargain.[197] The German model, in which the judge negotiates and determines the agreement, is contrasted with the Italian model, in which the judge maintains an equidistant stance.[198] In the Brazilian context, one may refer to the legislation on turn state's evidence (cooperation), Law 12.850/2013, which, as noted, prohibits judicial participation in agreement negotiations.[199] Direct judicial involvement in the negotiations is thought to undermine judicial impartiality and the presumption of innocence, given discussions concerning the evidentiary basis at the start of proceedings and the accused's situation in the case. Moreover, it may also amplify the State's coercive power to compel the accused into the bargain.[200]

The role of the judge in any negotiation is to verify the legality of the agreement at the time of its approval, particularly by ensuring that the accused's fundamental rights are respected. However, if the agreement is not ratified, complex questions arise. First, does the judge's exposure to the negotiated terms, including the accused's willingness to confess, compromise judicial impartiality? It is argued that this constitutes grounds for disqualification, meaning that the eventual trial must necessarily be conducted by another judge.[201] Second, the confession provided should be completely removed from the case files, as it becomes manifestly inadmissible in its very essence.[202]

Still regarding the judicial approval of the bargain, attention should be paid to the scope of the judicial review and the possibilities for reviewing the agreement (5). According to Senate Bill 156/09, the judge will examine the formal fulfilment of the stipulated requirements, meaning that the review is limited to procedural legitimacy, without room for considerations of merit. It could be argued that review over a minimum acceptable evidentiary basis occurs at an earlier stage, upon the filing of the indictment, through the analysis of good cause. However, this possibility cannot be restricted when assessing a potential conviction, as this constitutes a distinct and fundamentally important situation. Again, reference should be made to the regulation established by Law 12.850/2013 regarding turn state's evidence, which

---

[197] Alschuler (1976), pp. 1061–1099; Turner (2009), pp. 501–516.

[198] Formmann (2009), pp. 198–204.

[199] Law 12.850/2013, art. 4, § 6: "The judge shall not participate in the negotiations conducted between the parties for the formalisation of the cooperation agreement, which will take place between the police officer, the investigated party and the legal counsel, with the intervention of the Public Prosecutor, or, as the case may be, between the Public Prosecutor and the investigated or accused party and their legal counsel". For further discussion, see Sect. 3.2 of this work.

[200] Formmann (2009), pp. 206–210.

[201] "[…] there should be an incompatibility between the judge who conducts the agreement procedure and the one who, if the agreement is not accepted, will preside over the evidentiary and trial hearing. Only in this way can the accused be assured that they have the ability to refuse the proposed agreement without any negative psychological or procedural effect" (Schünemann 2013, p. 238). In this regard, see also: Alschuler (1976), p. 1111.

[202] "[…] even if the accused expresses a willingness to confess, or has actually done so, such willingness or confession must leave no procedural trace if the discussions do not result in a sentencing agreement: the confession cannot be mentioned in court, nor can it be given evidentiary weight" (Dias 2011, p. 77–78). See also: Albergaria (2007), p. 101; Alschuler (1976), p. 1070.

prohibits a conviction from being based exclusively on evidence produced by means of cooperation (art. 4, § 16).[203]

Furthermore, the current Code of Penal Procedure also provides in art. 197: "The value of the confession shall be assessed according to the criteria applied to other pieces of evidence, and in its assessment the judge must compare it with the other evidence in the case, verifying whether there is compatibility or agreement between them". It is argued that any bargain should comply with the same requirement: the confession shall not be the sole basis for a conviction and shall necessarily be corroborated by the existing and lawfully admissible evidentiary basis.[204] Therefore, even if both parties have consented to and signed the bargain, the judge, in addition to having the power to refuse its ratification due to formal defects, is also authorised to acquit the accused if the confession is not confirmed by the evidentiary basis available.[205]

Finally, in this brief analysis of particularly problematic points in the proposed regulation to the "fast track" under Senate Bill 156/09, it is important to examine the right to appeal against the agreement that has been made and judicially ratified (6).[206] Widely discussed in the German legal system, the condition of waiving the right to appeal at the time the agreement is concluded is rejected by German case-law and was legally prohibited with the 2009 reform.[207] Considering the various interpretations regarding the double instance of jurisdiction in the criminal sphere, it is clear that a prohibition on accessing appeal before the pronouncement of the sentence is inadmissible,[208] as it would render the review of agreements by higher courts impossible and, consequently, encourage the informal practice of bargaining contrary to what is prescribed by law.[209] Generally, however, any challenge will be limited to the formal aspects of the agreement, particularly the voluntariness of the accused's compliance.[210]

Moreover, with regard to crimes committed jointly, it is understood that the conclusion of the negotiation cannot depend on the consent of all the accused

---

[203] Silva (2014), p. 71. For further discussion, see Sect. 3.2 of this work.

[204] Rauxloh (2011), p. 321.

[205] Pizzi and Montagna (2004), p. 443.

[206] On the right to appeal in criminal proceedings, see: Vasconcellos (2017).

[207] Rauxloh (2011), pp. 320–323.

[208] "In conclusion, the waiver of the right to appeal in the context of procedural agreements does not appear to be based on any legitimate interest; on the contrary, its intended effectiveness could entail enduring risks for the maintenance of a criminal proceeding consistent with the Rule of Law" (Dias 2011, p. 97).

[209] Rauxloh (2011), p. 330.

[210] This approach also avoids the possibility of State coercion for the execution of "package deals", a practice prohibited in the United States, where the realisation of a bargain with one accused is contingent upon convincing the others (Turner 2009, p. 36).

individuals,[211] as the agreements shall have individual effect and binding force.[212] Accordingly, a confession made by a co-defendant for the purpose of the bargain cannot be used as evidence against the other defendants, unless a cooperation agreement is expressly provided for and authorised in accordance with its specific rules. In such a case, the requirements of both mechanisms must be fullfilled, which, if properly met, will result in a reduction of the criminal sanction based on the combined benefits of both mechanisms.

3.5 The Brazilian Criminal Justice Negotiation System Compared to International Mechanisms of Conviction Without Trial

Unlike most Latin American countries, Brazil has not yet undertaken a comprehensive reform of its criminal justice, which remains governed by the 1941 Code of Penal Procedure, albeit with significant amendments to some chapters. In recent years, legislative innovations have introduced mechanisms of criminal consensus, such as criminal settlement, conditional suspension of the criminal prosecution, non-prosecution agreement, and cooperation agreement. The first three mechanisms apply only to less serious offences, without the possibility of imposing imprisonment, but only non-custodial sanctions, besides not resulting in the accused's formal conviction. However, they completely dispense with the need for trial and the production of evidence to establish the accused's guilt.

The turn state's evidence, on the other hand, generally preserves the need for trial and has a distinctly evidentiary purpose, as it imposes on the accused the duty to cooperate with the prosecution in order to enable, for instance, the punishment of co-defendants. In addition, Law 12.850/13 established a system of limited negotiations which are subject to strict legality. However, the examination of the provisions introduced by that law—which, in an innovative manner for the Brazilian legal system, regulated procedural aspects of the cooperation agreement—is essential but clearly insufficient. The implementation of negotiated criminal justice in Brazil has profoundly diverged from the normative framework,[213] which may even be seen as an inevitable consequence of the gaps that invariably permeate negotiations over criminal sanctions.

The international expansion of criminal agreement mechanisms allowing for the imposition of penalties and convictions without trial has been the subject of intense

[211] Albergaria (2007), pp. 104–105.

[212] Leite (2013), p. 133. For instance, in the regulation of the Argentine "abbreviated procedure", variations exist depending on the specific legislation of each province, so the requirement of consent from all co-defendants is one of the points of divergence (Bigliani 2005, pp. 170–171). On this, regarding the Chilean system: Oliver, 2021.

[213] Bottino (2016), p. 376.

debate amongst scholars. Máximo Langer analyses the introduction of bargaining mechanisms in civil law systems (Germany, Italy, Argentina, and France) and argues that, although US influence cannot be entirely denied, these imports do not replicate the common law model in precise terms. Instead, he advances the hypothesis that what is occurring is, in fact, a phenomenon of fragmentation and divergence within civil law traditions.[214]

Furthermore, the author's criticism of the legal transplant metaphor, predominantly employed in comparative legal texts, is particularly emblematic. He underscores its limitations, especially as it suggests a mere "cut and paste" operation, which oversimplifies the complexity of transformative phenomena.[215] Instead, he advances the notions of "legal translations", emphasising that adversarial and inquisitorial systems represent distinct procedural cultures, each with unique modes of producing meaning. In this sense, the transfer of legal mechanisms must be understood in relation to the language and traditions of the receiving legal system field.[216]

In a more recent study, Máximo Langer describes the phenomenon of the administrativisation of criminal convictions, drawing on statistical data that show the spread of bargaining models and avoidance of trial worldwide. The author starts from the concept of a conviction mechanism without trial, which includes any procedural mechanism that makes it possible to reach a criminal conviction without a trial. Thus, he excludes from his analysis the mechanisms similar to cooperation agreement, as they would not eliminate the need for a trial.[217]

Furthermore, Langer develops the conceptual contours of the phenomenon of the administrativisation of criminal convictions, which he defines on the basis of two characteristics: "(a) trial-avoiding mechanisms have given a larger role to non-judicature, administrative officials in the determination of who gets convicted and for which crimes, and (b) these decisions are made in proceedings that do not include a trial with its attached defendants' rights.".[218] Although it is acknowledged that current Brazilian consensual mechanisms cannot strictly be defined as conviction mechanisms without trial, it is argued that they nevertheless exhibit these characteristics, thereby producing a phenomenon of the administrativisation of criminal justice in similar terms.

As stated, the Brazilian criminal procedure currently provides for certain mechanisms that may be characterised as agreements between the prosecution and the defence based on the accused's consent: criminal settlement, conditional suspension of the criminal prosecution, non-prosecution agreement, and cooperation agreement. In this context, the State offers incentives to the accused in order to facilitate

---

[214] Langer (2010), p. 79. Supporting the thesis of fragmentation, as proposed by Máximo Langer: Armenta Deu (2012), p. 288.

[215] Langer (2010), p. 39–42.

[216] Langer (2010), p. 8.

[217] Langer (2019), p. 16.

[218] Langer (2019), p. 2.

the work of investigative and prosecutorial authorities in criminal cases. In exchange for benefits, such as a reduced sentence, the accused accepts the accusation or cooperates with the prosecution, for instance by producing evidence against third parties, confessing, or returning unlawfully obtained assets.

In any case, by means of the incentives and benefits offered by the State, the accused refrains from opposing criminal prosecution, which takes place through agreements between the prosecution and the defence within criminal proceedings. Therefore, it can be affirmed that Brazil already has negotiation mechanisms in criminal justice system, insofar as they "function as facilitators of criminal prosecution by encouraging the accused's non-resistance, through their acceptance of the accusation in exchange for a benefit or reward (such as a reduced sentence), with the purpose of realising the State's punitive power in a swifter and less onerous manner".[219]

Undoubtedly, there are significant distinctions, which support the thesis that such international influences result in translations of legal mechanisms that align with the premises and culture of the receiving legal system.[220] Today, there are no mechanisms in Brazil that allow for a formal conviction to occur without due process.

The mechanisms of criminal settlement, conditional suspension of the criminal prosecution, and non-prosecution agreement have limited applicability to minor and moderately severe offences, without the possibility of imposing a prison sentence, only non-custodial sanctions, and without resulting in a formal conviction against the accused. Moreover, in the event of non-compliance with the agreement, imprisonment shall not be imposed nor a sentence executed; instead, criminal prosecution is resumed, allowing for the possibility of obtaining a formal conviction at the conclusion of the proceeding.

However, such mechanisms allow for the imposition of a criminal sanction based on the accused's consent, acceptance, and conformity with the accusation. In other words, even in the absence of a formal conviction, they authorise the imposition of a sanction without trial, without the exercise of defence right, and without the production of evidence, thereby excluding the need for adjudication with the corresponding rights and guarantees ordinarily afforded to the accused. As a result, there is an expansion of the powers of non-judicial actors, particularly the Public Prosecutor's Office, which establishes the terms of the agreement and, consequently, the sanction applied. In practice, judicial review in the ratification of such agreements is predominantly formal and, as a rule, superficial, since it does not involve substantive scrutiny of the accused's guilt.

The cooperation agreement, as a rule, preserves the need for a trial and also serves an evidentiary purpose, since it imposes on the defendant the duty to cooperate with the prosecution in order to enable, for example, the conviction of co-defendants. However, as previously noted, cooperation agreements have significantly expanded the parties' powers to negotiate and dispose of criminal sanctions,

[219] Vasconcellos (2018). p. 26.

[220] Langer (2010), p. 8.

including the granting of benefits not expressly provided for by law and even the authorisation to commence the execution of penalties prior to conviction, based solely on the accused's consent.

Therefore, the aim here is not to diminish the relevant distinctions between Brazilian consensual mechanisms and similar foreign examples to plea bargaining, but rather to conclude that the Brazilian scenario makes it possible to observe a phenomenon analogous to what Langer has defined as the "administrativisation of criminal convictions", which could perhaps more broadly be referred to as the administrativisation of criminal justice or of criminal sanctions.

Given the existence of criminal settlement, conditional suspension of the criminal prosecution, non-prosecution agreement, and cooperation agreement, and based on how these mechanisms are applied in Brazil, a greater role for administrative, non-judicial actors in determining the guilt of individuals and the offences and penalties applicable to them arises. Besides that, such decisions are made in proceedings that do not include a trial with the consequent rights and guarantees of the accused.

References

Albergaria PS (2007) Plea Bargaining. Aproximação à justiça negociada nos E.U.A. Almedina, Coimbra

Alschuler AW (1976) The trial judge's role in plea bargaining, part I. Columbia Law Rev 76(7):1059–1154

Andrade MF, Brandalise RS (2017) Observações preliminares sobre o acordo de não persecução penal: da inconstitucionalidade à inconsistência argumentativa. Rev Fac Dir UFRGS 37:239–262

Anitua GI (2010) El principio de legalidad y el principio de oportunidad: interrogantes y aporías en los sistemas anglosajones y continentales. In: Anitua GI (ed) Ensayos sobre enjuiciamiento penal. Del Puerto, Buenos Aires

Aras V (2018) Acordos penais no Brasil: uma análise à luz do direito comparado. In: Cunha R, Barros F, Souza R, Cabral R (coords) Acordo de não persecução penal. JusPodivm, Salvador

Armenta Deu T (2012) Sistemas procesales penales. La justicia penal en Europa y América. Marcial Pons, Madrid

Badaró GH (2003) Ônus da prova no processo penal. RT, São Paulo

Badaró GH (2014) Processo penal, 2nd edn. Elsevier, Rio de Janeiro

Bigliani P (2005) El juicio abreviado y su recepción en el orden jurídico argentino. In: Maier JBJ, Bovino A (comps) El procedimiento abreviado. Del Puerto, Buenos Aires

Bitencourt CR (1997) Juizados Especiais Criminais e alternativas à pena de prisão. Lei n. 9.099, de 26.9.95. 3 ed. Livraria do Advogado, Porto Alegre

Bittar WB (2011a) A delação premiada no Brasil. In: Bittar WB (coord) Delação premiada. Direito estrangeiro, doutrina e jurisprudência. Lumen Juris, Rio de Janeiro

Bittar WB (2011b) Observações necessárias. In: Bittar WB (coord) Delação premiada. Direito estrangeiro, doutrina e jurisprudência. Lumen Juris, Rio de Janeiro

Bittar WB, Pereira AH (2011) Breve análise do direito estrangeiro. In: Bittar WB (coord) Delação premiada. Direito estrangeiro, doutrina e jurisprudência. Lumen Juris, Rio de Janeiro

Bottino T (2016) Colaboração premiada e incentivos à cooperação no processo penal: uma análise crítica dos acordos firmados na "Operação Lava Jato". Rev Bras Cien Criminais 24:122

Caeiro P (2000) Legalidade e oportunidade: a perseguição penal entre o mito da justiça absoluta e o fetiche da gestão eficiente do sistema. Rev Ministério Público Lisboa 21(84):31–47
Campos GSQ (2012) Plea bargaining e justiça criminal consensual: entre os ideais de funcionalidade e garantismo. Custos Legis 4:1–26
Carvalho LGGC, Nunes Júnior FMA (2005) A transação penal nos crimes de ação penal de iniciativa privada. Rev EMERJ 8(31):71–85
Carvalho S, Lima CE (2009) Delação premiada e confissão: filtros constitucionais e adequação sistemática. In: Pinho ACB, Gomes MAM (coords) Ciências criminais: articulações críticas em torno dos 20 anos da Constituição da República. Lumen Juris, Rio de Janeiro
Casara RRR (2011) O acordo para aplicação da pena: novas considerações acerca da verdade e do consenso no processo penal brasileiro. In: Coutinho JMM, Carvalho LGG (eds) O novo processo penal à luz da Constituição. Análise crítica do Projeto de Lei n. 156/2009, do Senado Federal, vol 2. Lumen Juris, Rio de Janeiro
Cordeiro N (2010) Delação premiada na legislação brasileira. Rev Ajuris 37(117):274–296
Coutinho JM, Carvalho ER (2006) Acordos de delação premiada e o conteúdo ético mínimo do Estado. Rev Estud Criminais 22(VI):75–84
Coutinho JM (2009) Novo Código de Processo Penal, nova mentalidade. Rev Estudos Criminais 33:7–9
Dias JF (2011) Acordos sobre a sentença em processo penal. O "fim" do Estado de Direito ou um novo "princípio"? Conselho Distrital do Porto, Porto
Diego Díez LA d (1999) Justicia criminal consensuada. Algunos modelos del derecho comparado en los EE. UU., Italia y Portugal. Tirant lo Blanch, Valencia
Fernandes AS (2005) Teoria geral do procedimento e o procedimento no processo penal. RT, São Paulo
Formmann M (2009) Regulating plea-bargaining in Germany: can the Italian approach serve as a model to guarantee the impartiality of German judges? Hanse Law Rev 5(1):197–220
Freitas JOF (2012) PLS 156/09 e o acordo para aplicação da pena: avanço ou retrocesso? In: Pinto FM, Gonçalves GFM (eds) Processo & efetividade. Initia Via, Belo Horizonte
Gerber D, Dornelles ML (2006) Juizados Especiais Criminais. Lei n. 9.099/95. Comentários e críticas ao modelo consensual penal. Livraria do Advogado, Porto Alegre
Giacomolli NJ (2006) Legalidade, oportunidade e consenso no processo penal na perspectiva dasgarantias constitucionais. Livraria do Advogado, Porto Alegre
Giacomolli NJ (2009) Juizados Especiais Criminais. Lei 9.099/95. 3 ed. Livraria do Advogado, Porto Alegre
Giacomolli NJ (2013) O devido processo penal. Abordagem conforme a Constituição Federal e o Pacto de São José da Costa Rica. Atlas, São Paulo
Gloeckner RJ (2009) Risco e processo penal. Uma análise a partir dos direitos fundamentais do acusado. JusPodivm, Salvador
Goldschmidt J (2010) Problemas jurídicos y políticos del proceso penal. In: Goldschmidt J, Quiroga J (eds) Derecho, derecho penal y proceso. Marcial Pons, Madrid
Greco L (2012) Princípios fundamentais e tipo no novo projeto de Código Penal (Projeto de Lei 236/2012 do Senado Federal). Rev Liberdades Ed Esp Reformas no Código Penal:35–58
Grinover AP (2000) A marcha do processo. Forense, Rio de Janeiro
Grinover AP, Fernandes AS, Gomes Filho AM (2001) As nulidades no processo penal, 7th edn. RT, São Paulo
Grinover AP, Fernandes AS, Gomes Filho AM, Gomes LF (2005) Juizados Especiais Criminais. Comentários à Lei 9.099, de 26.09.1995, 5th edn. RT, São Paulo
Heumann M (1981) Plea bargaining. The experiences of prosecutors, judges, and defense attorneys. The University of Chicago Press, Chicago
Ishida VK (2003) A suspensão condicional do processo. Saraiva, São Paulo
Karam ML (2004) Juizados Especiais Criminais. A concretização antecipada do poder de punir. RT, São Paulo

Lamy ACPCF (2014) Reflexos do acordo de leniência no processo penal. A implementação do instituto ao direito penal econômico brasileiro e a necessária adaptação ao regramento constitucional. Lumen Juris, Rio de Janeiro
Langer M (2010) From legal transplants to legal translations. In: Thaman SC (ed) World plea bargaining. Consensual procedures and the avoidance of the full criminal trial. Carolina Academic Press, Durham
Langer M (2019) Plea bargaining, trial-avoiding conviction mechanisms, and the global administratization of criminal convictions. Annu Rev Criminol
Leite RV (2013) Justiça consensual e efetividade do processo penal. Del Rey, Belo Horizonte
Lippke RL (2011) The ethics of plea bargaining. Oxford University Press, Oxford
Lopes JA (2012) Direito processual penal, 9th edn. Saraiva, São Paulo
Malan DR (2010) Sobre a condenação sem julgamento prevista no projeto de reforma do CPP (PLS n° 156/09). Bol IBCCrim 17(207):2–3, São Paulo, fev
Martínez S (1999) Confesión en el juicio abreviado. Cuad Doctr Jurispr Penal 5(9B):373–398. Buenos Aires, out
Mendes FC (2020) Leniency policies in the prosecution of economic crimes and corruption. Nomos, Baden-Daden
Mendroni MB (2014) Comentários à Lei de Combate ao Crime Organizado. Lei n.° 12.850/13. Atlas, São Paulo
Miranda ALV (2004) Transação penal, controle social e globalização. Sage, Porto Alegre
Moraes MZ (2000) Interesse e legitimação para recorrer no processo penal brasileiro. RT, São Paulo
Oliver G (2021) Convenience or inconvenience of requiring the unanimous consent of the co-defendants for the negotiated criminal justice mechanisms (in a restricted sense) in the Chilean criminal procedural system. Revista Brasileira De Direito Processual Penal 7(2):1261
Pereira FV (2013) Delação premiada. Legitimidade e procedimento. Juruá, Curitiba
Pizzi WT, Montagna M (2004) The battle to establish an adversarial trial system in Italy. Mich J Int Law 25:429–466
Prado G (2006a) Da delação premiada: aspectos de direito processual. Boletim IBCCrim, n. 159, p. 10-12, São Paulo, fev
Prado G (2006b) Sistema acusatório. A conformidade constitucional das leis processuais penais, 4th edn. Lumen Juris, São Paulo
Prado G (2006c) Transação penal. 2nd ed. Lumen Juris, Rio de Janeiro
Prado G (2012) Campo jurídico e capital científico: o acordo sobre a pena e o modelo acusatório no Brasil—a transformação de um conceito. In: Prado G, Martins RC, Carvalho LGG (eds) Decisão judicial. A cultura jurídica brasileira na transição para a democracia. Marcial Pons, São Paulo
Rauxloh RE (2011) Formalization of plea bargaining in Germany: will the new legislation be able to square the circle? Fordham Int Law J 34(2):296–331
Rodrigues AB, Costa DB (2013) A barganha e o art. 105 do PLS 236/2012: dos perigos e retrocesso de uma disponibilização da liberdade mediante confissão. Rev Bonijuris, n 600, p. 23–29
Rodríguez García N (1997) La justicia penal negociada. Experiencias de derecho comparado. Ediciones Universidad de Salamanca, Salamanca
Rosa AM (2011) Delação premiada: terror e surpresa. Boletim IBRASPP, no. 1, ano 1, p 10–11, fev
Rosa LW (2024) Colaboração Premiada. Emais, Florianópolis
Salomi MB (2012) O acordo de leniência e seus reflexos penais. Faculdade de Direito, Universidade de São Paulo, São Paulo, Dissertação
Schünemann B (2013) Audiência de instrução e julgamento: modelo inquisitorial ou adversarial? Sobre a estrutura fundamental do processo penal no 3.° milênio. In: Schünemann B, Greco L (eds) Estudos de direito penal, direito processual penal e filosofia do direito. Marcial Pons, São Paulo
Silva EA (2014) Organizações criminosas. Aspectos penais e processuais da Lei n.° 12.850/13. Atlas, São Paulo

Tulkens F (2005) Justiça negociada. In: Delmas-Marty M (org) Processos penais da Europa. Lumen Juris, Rio de Janeiro

Tourinho Filho FC (2003) Comentários à Lei dos Juizados Especiais Criminais. 3 ed. Saraiva, São Paulo

Turner JI (2009) Plea barganing across borders. Aspen, New York

Valle JK (2012) Crítica à delação premiada: uma análise através da teoria do garantismo penal. Conceito Editorial, São Paulo

Vasconcellos VG (2015a) Colaboração premiada e não oferecimento da denúncia: o espaço de oportunidade do art. 4.°, §4.°, da Lei 12.850/2013. Bol IBCCRIM 268:13–14

Vasconcellos VG (2015b) Barganha no processo penal e o autoritarismo consensual nos sistemas processuais: a justiça negocial entre a patologização do acusatório e o contragolpe inquisitivo. Rev Trib 953:261–279

Vasconcellos VG (2017) Direito ao recurso no processo penal: conteúdo e dinâmica procedimental de um modelo de limitação do poder punitivo estatal pelo controle efetivo da sentença condenatória. Tese (Doutorado em Direito), Faculdade de Direito, Universidade de São Paulo, São Paulo

Vasconcellos VG (2018) Colaboração premiada no processo penal. 2ª ed. RT, São Paulo

Vasconcellos VG (2023) Colaboração premiada no processo penal. 5ª ed. RT, São Paulo

Vasconcellos VG (2024) Acordo de não persecução penal. 2ª ed. RT, São Paulo

Weigend T, Turner JI (2014) The constitutionality of negotiated criminal judgments in Germany. German Law J 15(1):81–105

Wunderlich A, Garcia RM, D'Avila FR, Oliveira RM (2013) A ideologia do projeto de reforma do Código Penal. Rev Estud Crim 50:169–171

Zanatta A (2001) A transação penal e o poder discricionário do Ministério Público. SAGE, Porto Alegre

Chapter 4
Unveiling the Tension between Bargaining and the Foundations of a Democratic Criminal Procedure. Theoretical and Empirical Criticism on the Negotiated Model

Having established the basic premises of the negotiated model and bargaining in contemporary criminal procedure and described them with in the Brazilian scenario, it is necessary to delve into the problems that inevitably permeate the establishing of agreements between prosecution and defence for the imposition of a punitive sanction based on the recognition of guilt. Based on six general critical commentaries systematically described (Sect. 4.1) and, subsequently, verified in the practical implementation of the criminal settlement in the Brazilian Small Claims Courts and the non-prosecution agreement (Sect. 4.2), the risks of expanding spaces for consensus in criminal justice and the importance of adopting a limiting stance to reduce damage will be outlined.

4.1 Criticism to the Consensual Model and the Institution of Bargaining in Criminal Procedure

This section will analyse the main criticisms directed at the negotiated model of criminal justice and, specifically, at bargaining mechanisms.[1] To this end, these considerations have been divided into six essential issues: (1) *Expansion of Criminal Law and the obstruction of due process*, which will address the procedural commodification caused by the authorisation of agreements between the parties and the resulting relativisation of fundamental guarantees, both phenomena intrinsically related to the instrumentalisation of criminal procedure as a swift means of early implementation of punitive power in response to the demands of an uncontrolled expansion of State criminal intervention[2]; (2) *Bargains, relations and concessions,*

[1] In summary, see: Alschuler (1983), pp. 932–937.

[2] Dervan (2011a), pp. 649–655.

V. G. de. Vasconcellos, *Criminal Agreements and Negotiated Justice*,
https://doi.org/10.1007/978-3-032-16962-4_4

which will unveil the distortion of the roles of criminal justice actors within the criminal system due to the primacy of their personal interests based on the power of bargaining, ultimately completely corrupting the foundations of the democratic procedure[3]; (3) *The problem of the innocent and the coercibility of the proposal,* whose function will be to clarify the pressure inherent in the possibility of bargaining, which, potentially, results in innocent individuals confessing out of fear of more severe penalties in case of exercising their right to trial[4]; (4) *The authoritarian procedural setback,* which will expose the violation of fundamental precepts of the proceeding, such as the return of the tariffed evidence system with primacy of confession and the consequent complete obstruction of the exercise of defence and adversary proceeding[5]; (5) *The imbalance of the scales between the procedural actors,* which weakens one of the fundamental premises of bargaining, the equality between the negotiating parties, in addition to exposing the undue usurpation of decision-making functions by accusers due to their pivotal role in determining the accused's guilt and penalty[6]; and, (6) *The disappearance of the trial and of the defence*, which problematises the possibility of waiving the right to defence and the supposed autonomy of will for the establishment of the pact.[7]

Regarding the applicability of the criticisms to the Brazilian scenario herein described, even though the differences in relation to the negotiation mechanisms typical of the US model are undeniable,[8] it is believed that the essential features of these mechanisms (such as criminal settlement, cooperation agreement and non-prosecution agreement, for example), namely, the conformity of the accused (usually with a confession) and the waiving of defence, as a rule, make the objections described in this chapter generalisable.[9] Indeed, a significant amount of legal

[3] On this, see, for example: Fisher (2003), p. 230; Alschuler (1981), pp. 690–691.

[4] Dervan and Edkins (2012), pp. 43–48.

[5] Giacomolli (2006a), pp. 116–118; Schünemann (2013a), p. 253.

[6] Lopes Jr. (2002), p. 120; Rodrigues (1998), p. 240.

[7] Armenta Deu (2012a), p. 284; Bovino (2005), pp. 80–84.

[8] Affirming the inapplicability to the Brazilian context of certain criticisms directed at bargaining, Ventura Leite (2013), p. 215, points out: "It should also be said that, often, there is a tendency to transfer to the criminal settlement, in a generalised way, criticisms that apply more properly to the plea bargaining, such as the excess of discretion of the accuser, the commodification and the pressures to make the agreement. There is something improper about this, since the two mechanisms are quite disparate, as are the regime of the American public ministry and the Brazilian one. One must, therefore, to keep in mind the peculiarities of each order and always seek the reference of the Federal Constitution of 1988, which authorised the consensus" (free translation). However, these restriction sustained by the author should be questioned: on one hand, any expansion of the spaces for consensus in the Brazilian criminal procedural system will, in a certain way, approach the contours of the negotiation mechanisms to the US model; on the other, it is believed that issues related to the commodification of justice due to the agreements and the pressure imposed on the accused to consent is fundamental in the critical analysis of the legal landscape, both foreign and national; and, finally, the constitutional provision that mandates the creation of settlement mechanisms (in addition to referring exclusively to minor offensive infractions) does not exempt from criticism the practical implementation of these precepts.

[9] Also in this sense: Rodríguez (2005), pp. 438–439.

literature cited has Anglo-American origins and, thus, its considerations are somewhat biased towards its reference model. However, in addition to the constant reference to European and Latin American mechanisms, the international trend towards expanding spaces for consensus (and, to some extent, convergence between the adopted models) requires a comprehensive critical examination, exposing the fundamental aporias described in both legal systems.[10]

In general terms, two critical perspectives can primarily be adopted for questioning negotiation mechanisms: (1) issues involving the weakening of the ideal of justice sought by the criminal system or the relativisation of the search for truth in the trial; and, (2) the violation of fundamental rights and guarantees of the accused and the distortion of the essence of procedure as a limiter of punitive power.[11]

The first of these is essentially based on rejecting the reduction of the punitive sanction to be imposed on the accused, which would be excessively lenient without any suitable justification.[12] In other words, there would be an injustice that would even lead to the subversion of the general preventive function of Criminal Law.[13] Furthermore, according to this stance, there would be an unacceptable violation of the principle of the search for truth, which legal scholars consider fundamental to criminal procedure.[14]

This book, however, will base its considerations primarily on the second stance described, that is, on the need to protect the fundamental rights of the accused and to uphold the limiting function of the procedure against State punitive power.[15] For

[10] It is worth mentioning the distinction drawn by Armenta Deu (2012b), pp. 135–138, between the criticisms commonly opposed to negotiation mechanisms amongst scholars of countries with a continental tradition (tensions with basic procedural principles, such as the obligation of criminal action and guarantees for the accused in criminal prosecution) and in others of US origin (in which the scope of agreements and pressures imposed on the accused are questioned). Indeed, different points present greater relevance in each legal system, according to their respective characteristics and fundamental aporias, but such finding in no way reduces the complexity of the problem of the bargain phenomenon in broad terms, so that its critical study is imposed in a profound way.

[11] Similarly, describing two currents of criticism among US scholars (which value the procedural aspects of justice and the protection of the accused's rights), see: Bibas (2003), pp. 9–10.

[12] In this sense, it is argued that the bargain violates the retributivity of the criminal sanction, as the punishment should be determined by the agent's guilt (Costa 2001a, p. 47). It is stated that: "[...] when determining the penalty to be imposed, elements such as the severity of the crime, the personality and circumstances of the accused or requirements of general and special prevention are not taken into account, but simply those subjects who accept responsibility for the committed conduct are rewarded [...]" (Rodríguez García 1996, p. 91, free translation).

[13] "For the accused to be moved to make a guilty plea, the promised mitigation of their penalty must be considerable compared to the penalty that would be expected in case of a conviction after the pre-trial hearing and the trial. This means, however, in practical terms, that the imposed penalty will not be the one that, for reasons of general prevention, would be necessary for the protection of legal goods, but rather a much lesser penalty. With this, the protective function of criminal law is subverted in the long term" (Schünemann 2013a, p. 253, free translation). On this, see also: Lippke (2011), pp. 180–183.

[14] Schünemann (2013a), pp. 244–245.

[15] Giacomolli (2006b), p. 79.

example, without delving into the complex debate about the search for truth,[16] it is believed that bargaining undermines the premises of criminal procedure by removing the imposition of the burden of proof from the prosecutor, a necessary assumption for breaking the presumption of innocence.[17] Therefore, a critical description of the agreements between prosecution and defence will be presented, in broad terms, as a cause of violations of procedural guarantees.[18] In addition to the weakening of the benefits supposedly sought by the introduction of negotiation mechanisms in the proceeding, the "annihilation of the guarantee model" is exposed.[19]

By way of example, since these objections will be explored in greater depth in the following sections, it is worth mentioning three key tensions to fundamental principles of criminal justice. First, the presumption of innocence, one of the cornerstones of criminal procedure,[20] is dissipated and inverted in a legal-criminal scenario guided by bargaining.[21] Coupled with the debatable waivability,[22] this guarantee ends up distorted with the consecration of a presumption of guilt[23] or even a "duty to confess".[24] Although some attempt to avoid this violation with theoretical arguments, by lacking express or formal guilty plea (in the Brazilian settlement) or obscuring any pressures imposed on the accused,[25] as explained earlier, there is, inevitably, a tension in the presumption of innocence in the implementation of negotiation mechanisms within the legal field.[26]

Secondly, there are issues surrounding the right against self-incrimination.[27] This is particularly complex due to the coercion inherent in the bargain proposal.[28] This aporia reveals that this mechanism "was not designed to be used by confessing accused individuals, but to generate confessing accused individuals to whom it is

[16] On the truth in criminal procedure, see: Barros (2013); Martins Pinto (2012); Khaled Jr. (2013); Badaró (2019).

[17] Rodríguez (2005), pp. 442–444.

[18] "It has been rightly said that this paradigm of consensus is more naive, less convincing and riskier in terms of procedural guarantees, as the realm of common sense, as fleeting as it is easily manipulable with the means of creating opinions available nowadays, will lead to natural law and volatile results" (Giacomolli 2006a, p. 101, free translation).

[19] Díaz Cantón (2005), p. 256.

[20] On this, see: Moraes (2010), pp. 173–261; Ferreira (2013), pp. 45–100; Sánchez-Vera Gómez-Trelles (2012), pp. 31–45.

[21] Duarte and Marques (2008), p. 71; Tulkens (2005), p. 710.

[22] "On the other hand, the presumption of innocence, as a consequence of the principle of human dignity, cannot be waived by the accused" (Rodríguez 2005, p. 444, free translation).

[23] Heumann (1981), p. 138.

[24] Lippke (2011), pp. 183–186.

[25] Leite (2013), pp. 209–212; Fernandes (2005), p. 271.

[26] Lopes Jr. (2002), p. 118.

[27] On the contours of *nemo tenetur se detegere* within Brazilian criminal procedure, see: Queijo (2012), pp. 69–105; Guedes (2014); Lopes Jr. (2012), pp. 250–251.

[28] Martínez (1999), p. 380. On this, see item Sect. 4.1.3 of this work.

applied".[29] Finally, it is crucial to perceive the emptying of the duty of judicial motivation, as the act of ratification imposes a merely formal analysis of the prerequisites for conviction, which, in reality, is often undervalued in practice by the "bureaucratic performance of the judge".[30]

Furthermore, emphasising the roots of the problems related to negotiation agreements, two considerations should be immediately noted in order to highlight the tension created. As **Albert Alschuler** points out, bargaining leads to an overemphasis of tactical choices during the procedural game, that is, it distances the establishment of the criminal sanction from the criminal act committed and aligns its criteria with the accused's attitude during trial and their decisions related to the exercise of their defence.[31] Thus, given the several possible criticisms, the characteristics of such a mechanism could be compared to the torture routinely used in medieval trials with, of course, a different degree of intensity.

According to **John Langbein**, the recognition of confession as full proof and the coercion imposed on the accused for its accomplishment are similar in both scenarios (even though the distinction in relation to intensity is acknowledged)[32]: the threat of aggressive physical suffering was replaced by the intimidation of a more severe punitive sanction in case of exercising the right to trial.[33] In this sense, regarding the German model, Bernd Schünemann states: "the German version of the agreement uses the market paradigm only as a kind of inverted mimicry, behind which hides a situation of structural coercion and with it the quite sublimated revival, it is true, of the sentence coerced by means of physical torture".[34]

4.1.1 *Expansion of Criminal Law and the Obstacle to Due Process. Utilitarian-Economic Policies, Procedural Commodification and Relativisation of Fundamental Guarantees*

Since the first edition of the book described as a landmark concerning the expansion of Criminal Law, in 1999, **Silva Sánchez** has revealed the phenomenon that is an indisputable expression of punitive power in contemporary societies. More than 10 years later, in the book's third edition, published in 2011, the author remains categorical in his epilogue: "the fundamental observation that Criminal Law is growing

[29] Bovino (2005), p. 77.

[30] Duarte and Marques (2008), p. 72. Similarly: Lopes Jr. (2002), p. 118.

[31] Alschuler (1981), p. 657. Also in this sense: Albergaria (2007), pp. 116–117. On the strategic determinants in the procedural game, see: Rosa (2014), pp. 36–46.

[32] Langbein (1978), pp. 12–15.

[33] Díaz Cantón (2005), p. 253.

[34] Schünemann (2013a), p. 321.

everywhere is undisputed".[35] Brazil is certainly an example of this scenario, having today more than half a million arrestees, many of whom has not received a definitive conviction, and more and more repressive statutes, usually guided by the idea of "law and order"[36] and zero tolerance,[37] through which new definitions of criminal offences are introduced, penalties are aggravated and fundamental guarantees of the trial are relativised.[38]

Indeed, there is a clear connection between such punitive ostentation[39] in today's social relationships and the perception of two phenomena that directly impact the legal-criminal field: the idea of risk and the construction of the figure of the enemy.[40] On the one hand, the scenario fundamentally described by **Ulrich Beck**[41] entails consequences for criminal dogmatics—for example, according to **Marta Machado**, with the dematerialisation of legal interests,[42] the increase in endangerment crimes or cumulative offences[43]—and also criminal procedural—based on mechanisms of procedural acceleration and flexibilities of guarantees.[44] Moreover, the constant resurgence (or reconstruction) of the figure of the enemy, not a person,[45] to whom the State power can direct all its repressive force without major concerns, breaking with the limitations of the trial.[46] Therefore, it can be stated that the contemporary criminal justice model is fundamentally guided by the concept of "emergency",[47] being established by punitive attitudes of the actors within the criminal legal field and directly influenced by authoritarian social influxes, resulting,

---

[35] Silva Sánchez (2011), p. 189. In this sense, also: Karam (2009), pp. 1–44; Husak (2008), pp. 3–54.

[36] "This criminal policy was based on the right-wing Hegelian tradition whose thesis consists in considering the project of modernity as accomplished (fiction of accomplished modernity). Thus, finding the rational state implemented, power would not have criminogenic elements. Therefore, crime should be seen as the result of an individual decision that, at the very least, would imply its retribution" (Rosa and Silveira Filho 2009, p. 32).

[37] On this, see: Wacquant (2011), pp. 9–46; Wacquant (2007), pp. 25–75.

[38] Campos (2010), pp. 125–206. On the influence of social defence discourses in criminal and procedural law, see: Santos (2015).

[39] Rosa (2014), pp. 43–71.

[40] Saavedra and Vasconcellos (2011), pp. 133–138.

[41] Beck (1998), pp. 25–93.

[42] On the contours of the theory of legal asset, see, for example: Santos (2015), D'Avila (2009), pp. 57–79.

[43] Machado (2005), pp. 91–152.

[44] Gloeckner (2009), pp. 203–284.

[45] Jakobs (2010), p. 35; Saavedra (2010), pp. 133–151.

[46] Malan (2006), p. 230. On the consequences of the concept of enemy in the fight against terrorism in the United States and its reflexes on the relativization of procedural guarantees, see: Galícia (2013), pp. 17–18.

[47] Choukr (2002), pp. 1–9.

thus, in a society of control[48] fuelled by a culture of fear[49] in which the criminal system is used as an instrument of governmentality.[50]

This is undoubtedly a complex topic, requiring a specific and in- depth analysis, which goes beyond the scope of this study. However, based on these introductory remarks, this topic aims to unveil the symbiotic relationship between the expansion of Criminal Law and the spaces for consensus within criminal procedure, especially through negotiation mechanisms such as bargaining.[51] The exponential expansion of its scopes of intervention in social relationships entails the need for the instrumentalisation of a functionally speedy and effective mechanism to meet the demand for swift punishments.[52] In this sense, it is important to note the growing dominance of ideas towards the pursuit of efficiency through the relativisation of fundamental rights,[53] essentially guided by mercantilist and utilitarian stances, which will also be critically analysed in this section.[54]

It is often stated that one of the main reasons for the triumph of negotiating mechanisms in criminal procedure is the expansion of substantive Criminal Law.[55] In the United States, for example, its decisive consolidation took place with the enactment of the Prohibition Act, which expanded social control through the criminally enforced prohibition of alcoholic beverages.[56] However, on the other hand, **Lucian Dervan** reveals that the widespread use of bargaining with the generalised coercion of accused individuals to waive the right to defence leads to the obstruction of judicial review over the legality/constitutionality of new types of criminal offenses or investigative procedures, since the accused consents to submit to the punitive sanction without adequate judicial review.[57] In other words, the

---

[48] Garland (2001), pp. 167–192.

[49] Glassner (2009), pp. 21–49; Pastana (2003), pp. 91–128; Wermuth (2011), pp. 25–89.

[50] Simon (2007), pp. 3–31; Rosa and Amaral (2014), pp. 19–43.

[51] Dervan (2011a), p. 645; Anitua (2005a), pp. 137–160.

[52] "This procedural reform claims to be guided, with 'efficiency' criteria, to facilitate economy in the proceeding. It is stated that the legal proceeding (both the legally current and the one ordered by the Constitution) cannot respond, at least not in a reasonable time, to the number of cases that need to be addressed. It is to achieve such objectives that an attempt is made to regulate a simpler procedure for imposing convictions" (Anitua 2005a, p. 142). On the functionalist stance in defining the basis of criminal law, which also has consequences for criminal procedure, see: Scalcon (2013), pp. 41–72.

[53] "The result of this mutation is the progressive de-jurisdictionalisation (or, if you prefer, the administrativeisation) and informalisation of criminal procedure, now obsessively reduced to an efficient management tool for problems, in a society where the idea of criminal law as the last resort of social policy has long been a mere empty proclamation, all framed against a broader backdrop of a 'control culture', in which the value of security, to the detriment of equality, truth and justice, assumes pronounced, if not exclusive, prominence" (Albergaria, 2007, p. 110).

[54] Addressing the "utilitarian commodification of criminal procedure": Giacomolli (2006a), pp. 112–114.

[55] Alschuler (1979), p. 234; Binder (2005), p. 209; Giacomolli (2006b), p. 23.

[56] Fisher (2003), pp. 19–27.

[57] Dervan (2011a), pp. 648–651.

expansion of Criminal Law also depends on and, in a way, is caused by the generalisation of bargaining, since by means of bargaining, criminal justice manages to respond to some of the punitive social demands (without the Judiciary controlling and and limitating it), thereby avoiding a possible collapse that would reveal the unsustainability of this attitude and, thus, could lead to debates about the need to reduce punitive power.[58]

Therefore, in the contemporary scenario, several legal reforms are legitimised under the argument of the pursuit of *efficiency*,[59] which proposes maximum speed in criminal prosecution to, as a rule, respond to punitive social demands.[60] It is important to note the terminological confusion involving the use of the words efficacy, efficiency and effectiveness. In a specific study on the issue, **Scarance Fernandes** argues that "an efficacious act is one that produces an expected effect", "efficiency is, in essence, the ability of something to produce a certain effect" and effectiveness occurs "due to the positive effects produced in the social environment, depending on what is expected from the criminal proceeding".[61] On the other hand, some point to a negative connotation in the concept of "efficiency", as it would be linked to an analysis of means,[62] with the goal of determining actions aimed at achieving predictable results, which, given the uncertainties inherent in criminal procedure, would lead to problems related to the context of exclusion and inequality in the application of the punitive power of the State.[63] Indeed, what must be necessarily criticised is the relativisation of the fundamental rights of the accused by distorting the primary function of criminal procedure as a limit to punitive power.[64]

---

[58] Dervan (2011a), p. 646.

[59] On the relationship between bargaining and the pursuit of efficiency in criminal justice: Fisher (2003), p. 175. In the Brazilian context, a striking example of this efficiency-driven approach is the trend of restricting access to higher courts through substitute habeas corpus appeals, which is justified solely on the alleged overburdening of the courts; on this, see: Bottino (2014).

[60] Borges (2013), p. 163.

[61] Fernandes (2008), p. 25.

[62] "In this framework, it is not admissible, under any circumstances, to consider that effectiveness is the same as efficiency, especially due to ignorance. After all, the former requires an analysis of the ends; the latter, efficiency, from a neoliberal base, responds to the means" (Coutinho 2002, p. 692, free translation).

[63] "The notion of efficiency is widespread in the market, meaning that actions must be efficient in order to achieve predictable results. Since it is impossible to correctly predict the results in the trial—explains Coutinho—attention turns to the means. In other words, the actions developed must be efficient to achieve the 'best' outcome. The outcome should be seen in the context of exclusion (social and criminal). The individual already socially excluded (hence deviant) should be the object of an effective action to obtain the (maximum and certain) punishment, which corresponds to the declaration of legal exclusion" (Lopes Jr. 2002, p. 114, free translation). According to Jacinto Coutinho (2002), p. 694: "It could, of course, be a simple exchange of words, but it is not. Allied to time, efficiency can be synonymous with exclusion. Here, in procedural reforms, stamped by the suppression of rights and/or guarantees, especially constitutional or, at least, by the reduction of their scope, manipulable by the force of hermeneutics, always without the slightest possibility of being eliminated [...]". On this, also see: Martins (2013), pp. 45–47.

[64] Vegezzi (2005), p. 343.

Thus, we witness the advancement of economic theories in search of cost reduction: "efficiency mechanisms"[65] are introduced aiming to enable the maximum number of convictions/punishments with the minimum possible resources and time. According to **Garapon** and **Papadopoulos**, plea bargaining is fundamentally based on premises of the law and economics movement, "a multidisciplinary theoretical current that tries to understand legal institutions with the aid of economic analysis".[66] One of the major exponents of this current is **Frank Easterbrook**, who, based on these ideas, describes criminal procedure as a "market system", a "method of allocating scarce resources", in which negotiations between prosecution and defence are legitimate in determining the acceptable cost (penal sanction consented to by the accused) of committing the offence.[67] However, there are many criticisms of this construction, as the resulting utilitarian stance ultimately undermines important assumptions of criminal justice.[68]

Undoubtedly, this brings up the debate about the trends towards the commodification of criminal procedure.[69] In this sense, metaphorically, **Bernd Schünemann** describes the change in legal theory, from its original foundation in religion to the contemporary premise of the market.[70] Thus, bargaining becomes a determining mechanism in characterising criminal justice as a "Persian market",[71] or a "modern supermarket",[72] where people's fundamental rights are illegitimately traded.[73]

This scenario is an expression of new criminological trends according to which risk management assumes primacy in the administration of punitive control, because, according to **Gabriel Anitua**, this current, by appealing to efficiency, "is only concerned about symbolically maintaining order in the society that is 'inside'

[65] "One can observe the submission of the trial to efficiency control mechanisms (typical of the economy), the reduction of the accused to a mere object destined for a purpose of eradicating insecurity. The issues related to the problem of punishment and the identification, in this, of a purpose seem to lose their meaning" (Gloeckner and Amaral 2013, p. 357, free translation).

[66] Garapon and Papadopoulos (2008), pp. 56–57.

[67] Easterbrook (1983), pp. 289–311. On the theoretical foundation developed by this author and its critical analysis, see Sect. 2.2.2 of this work.

[68] Tulkens (2005), p. 717; Lopes Jr. (2002), p. 99; Rosa (2010), pp. 11–37.

[69] Anitua (2005a), pp. 151–152.

[70] "It seems that the only explanation lies in a recent trend of law as a whole, which manifests itself in the agreement and which will have to be analytically explained. I will test this hypothesis here, describing, through the metaphor of the 'temple', this evolution of a Law that, in its origins, had a religious foundation, and which becomes a Law based on mere negotiation, which I express through the metaphor of the 'market'. I suspect that the agreement represents the expansion of this new model of law to the last branch of law which, so to speak, is still almost in the temple, namely, criminal law" (Schünemann 2013b, p. 309, free translation).

[71] "It is the introduction of the logic of the plea negotiation, transforming the criminal procedure into a Persian market, in its most derogatory sense. Hence our criticism of negotiated justice and Small Claims Courts, true expressions of the law and order movement, insofar as they contribute to the trivialisation of criminal law, fostering pan-penalisation and repressive symbolism" (Lopes Jr. (2002), p. 110, free translation).

[72] Feeley (1992), pp. 187–188.

[73] Giacomolli (2006a), p. 113.

the market, and aims to keep on the periphery, incapacitating or neutralising, those who are 'outside'".[74] This is the so-called actuarial thought,[75] characterised by the adoption of statistical-mechanical approaches based on data with comparisons of numerical values and risk assessment of suspects.

Given the above, it is clear that the expansion of criminal law, fueled by efficientist and mercantilist conceptions of procedure, is in lockstep with the use of bargaining and with the imposition of swift criminal sanctions based on the flexibilisation of fundamental rights, subverting the limiting procedural function[76]: all this fits into a vicious circle of symbiotic dependence and reciprocal feeding.[77] Therefore, the argument that legitimises the introduction of negotiation mechanisms is fallacious when pointing to the reduction of the Judiciary's caseload and crime rates in society as its supposed objective, while its real purpose is the continuous legitimisation of the expansion of social control by means of punitive power.[78]

4.1.2 *Bargains, Relationships and Concessions: The Corruption of the Foundations and Roles of the Actors within the Criminal Justice System*

In this section, we will analyse the consequences of this mechanism on the premises of the criminal justice system, especially in relation to the roles played by its fundamental actors and their reciprocal relationships.[79] Here, we point out an unquestionable degradation of the functions performed by judges, prosecutors, legal counsels and even accused individuals in a procedural landscape marked by negotiations and concessions, thus leading to an expropriation of the roles of the parties, in which

---

[74] Anitua (2005a), p. 139.

[75] "In brief, Actuarial Criminal Policy is understood as the preferential use of actuarial logic in the theoretical and practical foundation of secondary criminalisation processes for the purpose of controlling social groups considered high risk or dangerous through the selective incapacitation of their members. The aim of the new model is to manage groups, not punish individuals: its purpose is not to combat crime—although it knows how to use populist labels when necessary—but rather to identify, classify and manage undesirable social segments in the social order as fluidly as possible" (Dieter 2013, p. 20, free translation).

[76] Anitua (2005a), p. 142.

[77] Dervan (2011a), p. 645.

[78] McCoy (2005), p. 12. In this sense, also: "Who benefits most from this system is the punitive intention of the State, which thus achieves its goal in greater numbers, at lower cost and more quickly" (Anitua 2005a, p. 155).

[79] On the influence of the actors' stance in the management of criminal justice and the imposition of state punitive power, see: Carvalho (2010), pp. 59–111. In this sense, Geraldo Prado (2006a), p. 5, states: "The definition of one of the central problems of the dogmatics of the Brazilian criminal procedure necessarily involves the stance that scholars and legal professionals have adopted (or are adopting) in the face of the possibility of resolving criminal cases using the technique of consensus" (free translation).

their personal interests override the procedural functions of limiting punitive power.[80] In this regard, **Albert Alschuler** builds his solid criticisms of the negotiation mechanism on the premise that there is an improper subordination of justice to the personal interests of the actors in the criminal-legal field, thus weakening the idea that the prosecutor represents public interests and legal counsels represent the interests of the accused.[81] In other words, "plea bargaining was, essentially, a construction of the procedural actors, something created by them and aimed at satisfying primarily their interests".[82]

On the one hand, the judge is obviously one of the biggest beneficiaries of bargaining and the consequent immediate trial of the case, as it reduces their caseload[83]—since their duties are amortised, their concern for a possible reversal of decision on appeal is nullified and their worries about meeting efficiency targets are alleviated[84]—and, more importantly, their responsibility in determining the accountability of the accused. Although the adherence of the representatives of the Judiciary to plea bargaining in the United States has been intriguingly gradual, and not immediate,[85] its widespread adoption became significant especially because these actors began to benefit from the mechanism.[86]

The public prosecutor also benefits, as in addition to reducing their workload, the agreement ensures that convictions will be obtained,[87] thus maintaining their public image in line with the recurring social clamours for punishment.[88] Therefore, the personal interests of the prosecutor are emphasised[89] and entail an active stance, which, together with the judge, pressures the accused and the defence to accept the acceleration of the conviction.[90] Furthermore, even the accused's legal counsel has their role distorted due to the prominence of their personal interests in carrying out the bargain.[91] In addition to economic interests, as the swift conclusion of the case allows for the representation of a larger number of accused individuals,[92] the desire to maintain good relations with the other actors in the criminal-legal field is deter-

[80] Diego Díez (1999), pp. 49–50.

[81] Alschuler 1981, p. 691.

[82] Albergaria (2007), p. 33.

[83] "The judge, by no longer decisively influencing the resolution of the case, tends to accommodate the anticipated solution, seeing in it a quick way of resolving the process, stimulating and forcing the implementation of agreements" (Fernandes 2005, p. 267, free translation).

[84] Heumann (1981), p. 144.

[85] Fisher 2003, p. 58.

[86] Fisher (2003), p. 129.

[87] Bibas (2004), p. 2.471.

[88] Diego Díez (1999), p. 60.

[89] Alschuler (1968), p. 111; Hessick and Saujani (2002), pp. 191–193.

[90] Rauxloh (2011), p. 309.

[91] Regarding this, see Sect. 4.1.6 of this work, where the disappearance of the defence due to bargaining will be critically analysed, also due to the dysfunction caused to the relations between lawyer and defendant.

[92] Alschuler (1975a), pp. 1.206–1.270.

minant to the consensus-encouraging stance, aiming, even, at benefits in other, more important cases.[93]

Therefore, this scenario corroborates **George Fisher**'s description: the unquestionable and unshakeable triumph of bargaining in the criminal justice system is due to its adherence to the interests of those who hold the power in determining the implementation of the punitive power of the State.[94] This institution is, therefore, a tool serving the interests of power,[95] protected and nurtured by the actors in the legal field, and thus, decisive in shaping its intrinsic relations as well as its functioning.[96] According to **Milton Heumann**, there is a process of adaptation, in which the actors involved in the mechanics of criminal justice end up adhering to the negotiation mechanisms, not only due to a systemic imposition, but also (and more prominently) due to a process of learning and teaching,[97] essentially guided by the relations between these active characters in the legal field, in a manner similar to the phenomenon described by **Pierre Bourdieu** as "habitus" in determining a "practical sense" to their actions.[98] Furthermore, a prominent example of this scenario in the US context is the description of the "myth of written constitutions", in which the constitutional determination that all trials should be conducted by a public jury has become a dead letter due to the stance of the actors in the criminal system.[99]

There is, therefore, a "bureaucratic symbiosis"[100] that hinders the fulfillment of the primary function of criminal procedure, which is to limit punitive power, while the actors in the legal field, in favour of their private interests unrelated to the specific case and due to their perverse mutual cooperation relationships,[101] encourage (or rather, pressure and coerce) the execution of bargains for the early imposition of criminal sanctions resulting from the defendant's consented admission of guilt.

Although some argue for greater legitimacy of the criminal sanction imposed by the bargained confession,[102] the irrationality determined by such practice is evident,[103]

---

93 Hessick and Saujani (2002), p. 210.

94 Fisher (2003), pp. 229–230. According to Luis Diego Díez (1999), p. 62: "in summary, all legal operators in the criminal process and also the state itself have *a common administrative interest in a quick resolution of cases facilitated by the practice of bargaining*".

95 "Therefore, agreements transform the criminal procedure, which was previously conceived as a conflict of values decided by a third and impartial judge, into a conflict regulation governed by power criteria and not by legal criteria, which usually leads to the triumph of judicial authorities through a normative alliance [...]" (Schünemann 2004, p. 185, free translation).

96 Fisher (2003), p. 90.

97 Heumann (1981), p. 154.

98 The concept of *habitus* by Pierre Bourdieu (1989), pp. 87–93, in brief terms, represents a range of devices/determinations that induce the actors of a specific field to act and react in certain ways, which are generalisable, although not consciously coordinated or governed by a specific rule. On this, see: Azevedo (2000), pp. 87–93.

99 Langbein (1992), p. 126.

100 Hessick and Saujani (2002), p. 211.

101 Fine (1987), p. 624.

102 Fisher (2003), pp. 178–180.

103 Alschuler (1968), p. 112.

which turns the system into a production line in which accused individuals are coerced, deprived of due process, and considered less important than efficiency.[104] In this regard, it is pointed out that the functions of accusing and judging have been perverted and trivialised from the discretionary spaces granted to prosecutors and judges.[105]

In any case, the commonplace scenario in which theoretically, and presumably, opposing parties in the procedural game (prosecution and defence) benefit from mutual collaboration, fundamentally guided by such dysfunctional bureaucratic relationship is unquestionably intriguing.[106] This creates opportunities and loopholes for illegitimate displays of power, in which arbitrariness, inevitably, ends up harming those who lack the conditions for an effective defence.[107] Thus, the stance of criminal justice system actors (and the distortion of their roles, caused by negotiation mechanisms) is crucial for exacerbating one of the main aporias of bargaining (which will be analysed in the next section): the conviction of innocent individuals through agreements and recognition of guilt with undue coercion.[108]

4.1.3 The Issue of the Innocents and the Coercibility of the Proposal: When Criminal Procedure Disregards Its Main Function

The unveiling of cases in which the accused's liability, supposedly acknowledged in a bargain, is questioned has been a historical occurrence since the earliest days of such practice. It has been pointed out that even Joan of Arc and Galileo Galilei suffered coercion to accept consent in exchange for a promise of leniency—, to mention some of the most notable episodes that expose the problem of innocence in negotiating mechanisms.[109]

The scepticism towards confessions given in exchange for lenient treatment is evident even during the times of Inquisition, when such evidence was considered superior and obtained by means of torture. In other words, at that time, it was believed that statements made under physical coercion were more reliable than those motivated by the hope of benefits in criminal prosecution.[110]

---

[104] Hessick and Saujani (2002), p. 197.

[105] Rodríguez García (1997), p. 100.

[106] Alschuler (1968), p. 79.

[107] "This happens because, by proceeding in this way, spaces are opened, subtracted from the intervention of the law, to the game of forces in terms of pure power relations, in which, naturally, the strongest prevails over the weakest, the defendant, particularly when he is poor, which is usually a guarantee of insufficient defence, if not of authentic deprivation of defence" (Andrés Ibañez, 1997, p. 29, free translation).

[108] Hessick and Saujani (2002), p. 190.

[109] Alschuler (1979), p. 241; Dervan and Edkins (2012), p. 17.

[110] "Finally, the doctors of the Church believe that a confession obtained as a result of a promise of forgiveness has no validity: it must be ratified. Indeed, many defendants, fearing the rigours of

However, despite such considerations, the current scenario of expanding spaces for consensus and the State's need for the accused's cooperation to enable their criminal prosecution has led to a repositioning of the issue, placing the accused individuals of our time in the position occupied by Joan of Arc and her unavoidable dilemma: "to passively await the confirmation of her presumption of innocence, aware of the risks this implies in a environment that was coercive by nature, or to accept one of these rules and decide to resolve the issue in the quickest and most economical way available".[111]

Nowadays, there are countless examples of pressure and intimidation directed at accused individuals within the US criminal justice system,[112] so much so that two cases are routinely cited for their striking arbitrariness. In *Bordenkircher v. Hayes* (tried in 1978), the Supreme Court upheld the admissibility of a bargain made under the following circumstances: the defendant was accused of issuing a forged check, but, as a repeat offender, he was being prosecuted under a law that authorised life imprisonment for such situations (a situation coercively emphasised by the prosecutor at the time of the negotiation); thus, the prosecutor offered an agreement with a five-year sentence in a legal provision of a minimum of two and a maximum of 10 years; faced with this, the accused rejected the bargaining, exercising his right to trial, at the end of which he was sentenced to life imprisonment; upon appeal, the punishment attributed due to the non- establishment of the agreement was declared constitutional.[113] In other words, "the Supreme Court thus gave its imprimatur to a bizarre system of justice in which the crime of uttering a forged $88 check is 'worth' five years and in which the crime of standing trial is 'worth' imprisonment for life.",[114] a description that unquestionably characterises a nightmare for a continental perspective of justice.[115]

In *Brady v. United States* (from 1970) the accused had already been charged with aggravated kidnapping, which, according to the law at the time, could carry the death penalty, but only if convicted by a jury. In other words, bargaining could have avoided this consequence if life imprisonment without trial had been accepted, which was consented to by the accused. Later, this legislation was declared unconstitutional, so that several death row inmates were able to overturn their situation in court; thus, in the case herein described, the accused appealed to annul the coercively bargained conviction, which was not accepted by the Supreme Court, as the consensus was

prison or punishment, would quickly resort to this type of benevolent confession, which would be serious. Moreover, it must be considered that anyone who confessed under these conditions would in reality be wanting much more to shorten the interrogation and hide something than to confess" (Eymerich 1993, p. 127, free translation).

[111] Tedesco (2005), p. 312.

[112] For a description of various contemporary real cases of innocents convicted through guilt recognitions in bargains, see: Dervan and Edkins (2012), pp. 2–5, 16–17 and 25.

[113] Albergaria (2007), p. 61; Diego Díez (1999), p. 115.

[114] Alschuler (1979), p. 242.

[115] Pizzi and Montagna (2004), p. 442.

supposedly "voluntary, intelligent and supervised by a defence lawyer".[116] Thus, the law exerted an unconstitutional influence, but accused individuals who succumbed to such pressure were not considered, as, incomprehensibly, only accused individuals who resisted the illegitimate coercion could question their convictions.[117]

The coercive power of the bargain proposal in criminal proceedings is highlighted by numerous scholars[118] due to the abusive intensification of criminal sanctions for refusing to agree,[119] which is commonly referred to as the "trial price",[120]" trial penalty"[121] or "sanction scissors".[122] As previously discussed, **John Langbein** points out similarities, albeit with a difference in intensity, between the intimidation exerted by medieval torture and that undertaken by contemporary negotiation mechanisms, which involve threats of harsher punishments if the right to trial is exercised.[123] Thus, the "intrinsic injustice of the system" is affirmed, as accused individuals who refuse to agree are considered "inconvenient and disruptive, and end up being punished more heavily", which may result in the conviction of innocent individuals.[124]

Thus, the argument that no one is compelled to self-incriminate, due to the right not to produce evidence against oneself, becomes a dead letter if there is the promise of a reward with a reduction of the criminal sanction and, *contrario sensu,* a worsening of the situation for those who do not.[125] Therefore, the requirement of voluntariness in accepting the bargain is fallacious,[126] as the mechanisms operate by means of threats, which render any free choice of defence impossible.[127] This demonstrates a problem that is certainly, intensified by the Brazilian social inequality landscape, which is already permeated by deficiencies in criminal legal assistance.[128] Moreover, the excuse that the accused's position in the criminal prosecution is

---

[116] Dervan and Edkins (2012), pp. 12–13; Alschuler (1975b), pp. 48–50; Alschuler (2009), pp. 678–679.

[117] Alschuler (1975b), p. 51.

[118] Albergaria (2007), p. 116; Anitua (2010a), p. 146; Shecaira (2002), p. 323.

[119] According to Candace McCoy (2005), p. 23, the punishments imposed after refusing the bargain can be up to nine times greater, compared to the one agreed upon earlier. On this, see item Sect. 4.1.6 of this work.

[120] McCoy (2005), p. 21.

[121] Lippke (2011), pp. 10–23.

[122] Schünemann (2013b), p. 308.

[123] Langbein (1978), pp. 12–13.

[124] Dias and Andrade (1987), p. 486.

[125] "To say that no one is obliged to testify against themselves, but that if they do, they will be rewarded with a reduction in sentence, means, indirectly, to worsen the situation of those who exercise the right not to confess and thus enshrines a form of coercion to self-incrimination" (Córdoba 2005, p. 244, free translation).

[126] Lippke (2011), p. 1799.

[127] Langbein (1992), p. 121; Anitua (2005b), p. 21.

[128] Prado (2006b), p. 224.

intrinsically coercive and uncomfortable[129] remains weakened and characterised as a "reduction to absurdity", since the coercion imposed by the threat of more severe punishment if the agreement is refused is illegitimate and illegal, whereas conducting an investigation or prosecution is legitimate and legal[130] provided that the minimum requirements, such as good cause, are present.[131]

Similarly, some argue that conducting the trial with all its guarantees also leads to the potential conviction of innocent people, which would demonstrate a situation identical to the bargain.[132] However, the rational reduction of risks respecting due process is undeniable.[133] Finally, the thesis that counselling the accused cures any defect and enables a rational and voluntary choice[134] is also unsustainable, as the relationships between these actors potentially become dysfunctional and illegitimate, rendering adequate representation impossible.[135]

Furthermore, **Santiago Vegezzi** exposes the hypocrisy of the argument according to which the accused benefits from a reduced sentence: there is no improvement in the situation of the accused who accepts the bargain, but rather a shifting of responsibility in the criminal prosecution, as the agreement is an expression of the State's inefficiency in providing adequate legal service, which is counterbalanced by the coercion of the accused to waive the right to trial.[136] In other words, "given the impossibility—generalised by State inefficiency—of convicting the prisoner immediately after arrest, one decides to 'negotiate' with them, exploiting the inequality of conditions that have existed since the very start".[137]

---

[129] "The position of someone who is on the verge of being accused, or is already responding to an accusation, is never comfortable, however, this does not invalidate the choice of the consensual route as a defensive strategy" (Leite 2013, p. 215, free translation). Furthermore, the argument that such criticisms are directed at the US plea bargaining model, and thus, do not adapt to the Brazilian reality (idem, ibidem), has already been dismissed earlier in this work (see the introductory considerations in item Sect. 4.1), since the essence of these mechanisms is shared (and hence most of the aporias herein described arise), in addition to the international trends towards expanding spaces for consensus bringing these models closer, imposing a comprehensive critical analysis.

[130] Langbein (1978), p. 13.

[131] Moura (2001), pp. 224–261; Lopes Jr. (2012), pp. 379–383.

[132] Thus, Josh Bowers (2008), p. 3, absurdly claims that the conviction of an innocent by means of bargaining would be a good thing, as it would determine a less severe criminal sanction than the one potentially imposed after the trial.

[133] Diego Díez (1999), p. 53.

[134] In this sense: Easterbrook (1983), p. 311.

[135] On this, see items Sects. 4.1.2 and 4.1.6 of this book.

[136] "The existence of the bargain puts the accused in a situation of conflict that can be resolved through negotiation. This does not mean that the situation has improved, and that, based on the provision of negotiation mechanisms, the accused individuals have a better possibility of resolution, but rather, they must pay for the inefficiency of the State to prosecute them properly with the coerced waiver of their constitutional guarantees" (Vegezzi 2005, p. 349, free translation).

[137] Vegezzi (2005), p. 349.

In this vein, the slowness of the Judiciary certainly serves as a tool to intensify the pressure to accept the agreement,[138] which is even greater in cases where pre-trial detention is ordered,[139] a typical scenario in the dysfunctional Brazilian criminal justice system.[140]

Although empirical evidence of the significant number of innocent people convicted based on the recognition of guilt in bargains is difficult to demonstrate,[141] two studies are paradigmatic in revealing this perverse phenomenon. In a study based on statistics presented by US courts, **Michael Finkelstein** has shown an "implicit innocence rate", whereby the higher the percentage of convictions obtained through bargaining, the lower the overall acquittal rate. In other words, it can be argued that some of the recognitions of guilt were made by defendants who would have been acquitted in a potential trial, following the average acquittal rate prior to the introduction of negotiated mechanisms.[142] Thus, the author concludes that a significant number of bargains (on average 1/3 of the agreements) occurred in cases that would not have resulted in convictions in a trial conducted according to due process rules.[143]

With similar conclusions, but adopting a different methodology, an empirical study published in 2013 was conducted jointly by Law and Psychology professors In summary, voluntary tests were carried out for a supposed study of logics among university students. During the test, a student was accused of cheating for having copied someone else's answer in an individual assignment). It was known, however, that he had done nothing of the sort. In response, the supervisor offered the alleged accused two options: admitting guilt and not receiving the reward for the voluntary completion of the exam, or requesting that the case be referred to the university's ethics board, which, in case of conviction, would warn the student and impose a sanction of attending ethics classes for a semester.[144] Out of the 39 known innocent students, 22 accepted the plea bargain proposal, that is, 56% of the accused, who certainly had not committed the falsely imputed act, admitted guilt in exchange for a

---

[138] According to Albert Alschuler (1976), pp. 1080–1081, the criminal prosecution, aiming at the implementation of the bargain, benefits from the lack of swiftness of the proceeding, while, thus, the anguish of uncertainty in the accused intensifies, that is, prosecutors "sell" the immediate certainty of the legal consequences of the trial in the life of the accused.

[139] Albergaria (2007), p. 139; Redlich et al. (2010), p. 88; Bibas (2003), pp. 2492–2493. In an empirical study developed in lower courts, which try less serious cases, Malcolm Feeley (1997), pp. 185–198 revealed that a significant number of accused individuals accept to acknowledge their guilt to avoid possible detention and end the process quickly.

[140] Regarding the imposition of precautionary measures to coerce the accused to accept the criminal settlement in the model of Brazilian Small Claims Courts, Geraldo Prado (2006c), pp. 24–25, points out this possibility with the provision of art. 69, single paragraph, which authorises the immediate removal of the accused in situations of domestic violence.

[141] Alschuler (1981), pp. 713–714.

[142] Finkelstein (1975), pp. 295–308. In criticism of the methodology adopted by Finkelstein, but asserting that the plea results in a much higher risk of convicting innocent individuals: Alschuler (1979), pp. 230–231.

[143] Finkelstein (1975), pp. 309–310. For a Brazilian perspective, referring to Finkelstein's study: Naves (1995), p. 248.

[144] For a detailed view of the adopted methodology, see: Dervan and Edkins (2012), pp. 28–33.

less severe sanction.[145] This scenario is even more concerning in relation to bargains made with accused individuals with some kind of mental limitation, given that, according to empirical research also conducted in the United States, a third of the participants admitted that they falsely admitted their guilt at least once in their life.[146]

Thus, as previously exposed,[147] the requirement of voluntariness for the admissibility of bargaining was emptied by decisions of the US Supreme Court.[148] Coercions to the accused are often accepted by the Judiciary, as the recognition of the illegality of a bargain is rare, or practically impossible.[149]

Indeed, the bargaining mechanism allows for convictions that would be unfeasible in a trial in accordance with due criminal process.[150] Given this scenario, legal scholars describe the growing use of consensual mechanisms in cases with weak evidentiary basis, in which doubt would prevent the imposition of a criminal sanction: these are the "half-loaf" negotiations,[151] terminology that may be illustrated with the saying "a bird in the hand is worth two in the bush", that is, in the prosecutors' view, a reduced punishment is better than alleged impunity.[152] There is also an increase in benefits offered to the accused in direct proportion to the weakness of the prosecution's case.[153] In other words, the supposedly asserted logic of bargaining—to avoid the Judiciary's work in cases of evident conviction—is completely reversed, as the greater the doubt, the greater the coercion exerted on the accused to waive the trial by admitting guilt.[154] Thus, there is a complete distortion of the conception about the necessity of the trial, as its importance should be highly valued when the prosecution's evidentiary support is weak.[155]

The argument used predominantly by the US Judiciary is so fallacious that it has been used, in a completely distorted manner, to justify the admissibility of an agreement in which the accused maintained his innocence until the very end, although he also consented to the application of the criminal sanction.[156] This is the case of *North Carolina v. Alford,* in which the Supreme Court held that the accused, given the existing evidence, could choose to accept the bargain (and not only in cases of

---

[145] Dervan and Edkins (2012), p. 34.

[146] Redlich et al. (2010), p. 88.

[147] On this, see Sect. 2.2.3.1 of this work.

[148] Alschuler (1976), p. 1.115.

[149] Albert Alschuler (1975a), p. 1.195, cites several cases in which, even when there was an evident mistake by the counsel in inadequately informing their client about the terms of the plea, the agreement was not invalidated by the court.

[150] Finkelstein (1975), p. 309.

[151] Lippke (2011), p. 191.

[152] Alschuler (1979), p. 234; Fine (1987), p. 618.

[153] Heumann (1981), p. 72.

[154] Lippke (2011), p. 202.

[155] Alschuler (1968), p. 64.

[156] Bibas (2003), p. 14.

nolo contendere),[157] even without admitting guilt, as long as it was in his best interest and provided that the judge found a "strong factual basis" for the charges.[158]

Criticising this possibility, some claim its fictional nature as an "Alice in Wonderland mechanism", as it supposedly undermines public confidence in criminal justice.[159] Ironically, **Albert Alschuler** calls this hypothesis a plea of "guilty-but-not-guilty",[160] which certainly represents "one of the most symptomatic aspects of the degradation of a criminal procedure system obsessed with efficiency".[161] In any case, since this decision, bargains accepted by accused individuals who claim innocence has been called "*Alford pleas* ".[162]

Given the above, the premise that legitimises the justification of consensual mechanisms by most of their counsels and that underpinned the decisions of the US Supreme Court for the constitutionality of plea bargaining completely loses its support: negotiation mechanisms are not applied only to those defendants who would have been convicted anyway in a potential trial.[163] In other words, the "issue of the innocent" is no exception, but perennial in the power relations involved in negotiations in criminal justice.[164] Therefore, as pointed out by **Albert Alschuler**, "observers who deny that plea bargaining is likely to result in conviction of the innocent are usually exceptionally naive or exceptionally cynical".[165]

---

[157] This refers to a mechanism in which the accused accepts the criminal sanction without admitting guilt and without civil consequences, but it is only admitted in minor offences and with restrictions in certain US states. On this, see the introduction to Sect. 2.2 of this book.

[158] Hessick and Saujani (2002), p. 198.

[159] Fine (1987), p. 621.

[160] Alschuler (1975a), p. 1294. The author, a staunch critic of plea bargaining in general terms, however, defends the possibility of agreements even in the face of a claim of innocence, as there would be no reason to deny the reduction of the criminal sanction to the accused who is aware of the inherent risks of the trial (Alschuler 1975a, pp. 1.296–1.298).

[161] Albergaria (2007), p. 95.

[162] Leite (2013), p. 79.

[163] Dervan and Edkins (2012), p. 48. In this regard, also: Finkelstein (1975), pp. 310–311.

[164] Dervan and Edkins (2012), p. 4.

[165] Alschuler (1981), p. 715.

4.1.4 The Authoritarian Procedural Setback: Strengthening of Confession, Relativisation of the Rules of Exclusion of Illegal Evidence, Obfuscation of Publicity, and Disappearance of the Adversarial Principle Due to the Prevalence of the Pre-Trial Investigation

In addition to the criticisms outlined (and also fostered by them), the introduction of negotiation mechanisms in criminal justice inevitably leads to the intensification of the authoritarian traits in key aspects of criminal procedure.[166] This violates constructions painstakingly structured by scholars based on the historical development of criminal procedural dogma, fundamentally by weakening the accused's rights as a subject facing State punitive prosecution.[167] Thus, with the acceptance of agreements between prosecution and defence for the recognition of the accused's guilt, the resurgence of confession as the queen of evidence and the only foundation capable of supporting a conviction is revealed; rules for excluding illicit evidence are relativised, while there is no control over the motivation behind the prosecutor's decision to bargain; the obfuscation of publicity, as negotiations inevitably encourage the concealment of fundamental issues of criminal persecution; and the disappearance of the adversarial principle due to the pre-eminence of the pre-trial investigation, since the conviction of the public prosecutor and the establishment of the terms of the agreement are based on what is produced in pre-trial inquiries.

First, it is important to emphasise the illegitimate "overvaluation of the incriminating confession",[168] caused by the bargain, since its procedure authorises the issuance of a conviction sentence based fundamentally (and, as a rule, exclusively) on the recognition of guilt by the accused in exchange for the supposed benefit promised by the prosecutor, in a scenario aggravated by illegitimate coercions and pressures, as previously described.[169] Therefore, we return to an authoritarian model of tariffed evidence with the consecration of confession as the "queen of evidence",[170] a "*probatio probatissima*",[171] typical of the Inquisition's procedural system,[172]

---

[166] Giacomolli (2006a), pp. 116–118.

[167] "[...] with the plea bargaining one of the greatest evolutionary achievements of the reformed criminal procedure in Europe is annihilated: the position of the accused as a subject of law. After all, plea bargaining generally occurs without the presence of the accused, who, in this sense, ends up being completely mediated by his counsel" (Schünemann 2013a, p. 253).

[168] Rodríguez García (1997), pp. 104–105 (free translation). Also in this sense: Casara (2011), p. 152.

[169] Albergaria (2007), p. 116.

[170] Langbein (1978), p. 14.

[171] Córdoba (2005), p. 245; Anitua (2005b), p. 16.

[172] "Before the Inquisition Court, the accused's confession is enough to convict them. The crime of heresy is conceived in the brain and hidden in the soul: therefore, it is evident that nothing proves more than the accused's confession" (Eymerich 1993, p. 138). On this, see: Coutinho (2001), pp. 26–27.

which even allows comparisons between contemporary bargaining and medieval tortures,[173] within the appropriate proportions of the intensity of coercion.[174]

There is a clear "return to the past" here, invalidating the democratic imposition of the need for solid and lawful evidence to undermine the presumption of innocence.[175] The aesthetics of confession[176] that is consolidated through psychic economy[177] and that permeates the reward mechanisms, leads to the sedimentation of the recognition of guilt as irrefutable evidence for conviction, which leads to a procedural discourse in which the adversarial principle and the defence are completely rendered impossible by the hallucinatory power of evidence (the unquestionable confession).[178]

Therefore, legitimising a bargaining mechanism ultimately undermines the entire construction of procedural rules as limiting the establishment of guilt in criminal justice.[179] Judges and prosecutors are authorised to prejudge the "necessity" of a trial to prove the act and its authorship, which, of course, falls outside the legitimate scope of criminal adjudication.

Furthermore, in a system permeated by the bargaining mechanism, it is impossible to control the legality of the evidence,[180] since the public prosecutor's deliberation on the relevance and content of the proposal is exempt from jurisdictional limitations, allowing any element to be considered in forming the decision, including

---

[173] Langbein (1978), pp. 12–19; Tedesco (2005), pp. 317–319; Alschuler (1983), p. 972.

[174] As pointed out by Geraldo Prado (2006b), p. 143, one cannot compare the models of consensual resolution of today with the brutal practices of the inquisition. It is thought that, in intensity, the medieval tortures stand out from the current scenario of pressures and coercions, which is based on the threat of more severe criminal sanction in case of the exercise of the right to trial. However, there is a certain similarity in the construction of a system in which confession becomes conclusive proof, usually obtained through intimidation of the accused, albeit in a modernly accepted guise.

[175] Giacomolli (2006a), p. 116; Lopes Jr. (2012), p. 646.

[176] "With this transformation, a kind of discursive advantage is gained over any kind of defence or justification that the accused may make. The fact, a mere historical reminiscence, diluted in a mnemonic device, liquefies in the documentation, always watched and kept secret, out of the reach of the accused. What is more, by possessing the body of the accused, the extortion of the confession, by interrogation, establishes the judge in a knowledge that is beyond the fact. From this point on that it becomes possible to know the full truth, the delinquent, their intentions, reasons, motives, in short, their lives" (Gloeckner and Amaral 2013, p. 338, free translation).

[177] "This psychic economy also allows the accused, through the interference it produces in the product sedimented in the proceeding, and according to the psychic capture it exerts on the inquisitor to induce them to error, whether when whistleblowing on accomplices, be they community members or fictitious entities. As a repentant, cooperative individual, their services rendered may earn them a lighter sentence. The fact is that cooperation would primarily allow the unearthing of truths hitherto unknowable" (Gloeckner 2013, p. 152, free translation).

[178] "They say that what is evident dispenses with proof. A simulacrum of self-referentiality, the pretension of a self-centred justification, evidence corresponds to a too hasty satisfaction in the face of mere plausibility indicators. In some way, evidence instigates a disdain for the adversarial principle" (Martins 2011, p. 3, free translation).

[179] McCoy (2005), p. 19.

[180] Alschuler (1968), p. 79; Weigend (2021).

illicit evidence or biased preferences, for example.[181] Moreover, according to US caselaw, the execution of the bargain remedies any previous defects in the criminal prosecution, so that the accused is unable to argue any nullity preceding the moment of the agreement in the event of an appeal.[182] In this scenario, without any limitation to illegally produced evidence or procedural violations, the arbitrary action of State power during pre-trial investigations or at the beginning of the trial is encouraged.[183]

Regarding the obfuscation of publicity, the possibility of agreements between prosecution and defence inevitably encourages informal negotiations,[184] which harks back to situations of secret trials, without the presence of the accused.[185] According to **Albert Alschuler**, the bargaining procedure takes place behind closed doors, without even respecting the most rudimentary rules.[186]

Finally, this entire scenario points to the strengthening of pre-trial investigation, since the implementation and content of the agreement are based on the elements produced in the pre-trial stage of criminal prosecution.[187] Therefore, the production of the evidentiary basis that will determine the accused's conviction occurs during the investigation, led by the Public Prosecutor's Office, aiming to "gather enough arsenal to convince the suspect to accept a penalty in advance without a trial".[188] **Bernd Schünemann** calls this phenomenon the "apotheosis of the inquiry", which reveals an "inversion of all the values upon which all continental European procedural practice is based".[189] Indeed, this represents an "overflow of the function of the investigation stage",[190] which is compounded by the violation of defence possibilities and the obstruction of the adversarial proceeding resulting from the primacy of unilaterally produced acts without due judicial review.[191]

---

[181] Hessick and Saujani (2002), p. 196.

[182] Albergaria (2007), p. 105; Rodríguez García (1997), p. 51.

[183] Alschuler (1968), p. 82. Also in this sense: Alschuler (1981), p. 713.

[184] Heumann (1981), p. 69; Malan (2010). On the importance of publicity and its violations caused by bargaining, see: Anitua (2010b), pp. 155–157.

[185] Bovino (2005), p. 72.

[186] Alschuler (1975a), p. 1270. Similarly: Turner (2009), p. 1.

[187] Schünemann (2013a), p. 238; Bovino (2005), p. 84.

[188] Borges (2013), p. 165.

[189] Schünemann (2004), p. 186.

[190] Fernandes (2005), p. 307.

[191] Giacomolli (2006a), p. 117.

4.1.5 *The Imbalance of the Scales Between Procedural Actors: Prosecutor as the One Who Accuses and the One Who Judges. Is There Equality Between the Parties in the Bargain?*

In addition to the criticisms raised so far, the establishment of a negotiation model of criminal justice leads to the overvaluation of the accuser's role, which is reinforced by the already described widespread distortion of the roles of the actors in the criminal-legal field.[192] The role performed by the prosecutor in the trial acquires unique relevance due to the variety of aspects developed by them,[193] significantly expanding the characterisation of the Public Prosecutor's Office as an instance of crime control,[194] by informalising the State's response to crime.[195] Thus, the establishment of a "hypocritical justice system" is highlighted,[196] with the punitive power being exercised fundamentally based on the accuser's decision by usurping the judge's decision-making functions.[197] This is the scenario described by **Milton Heumann**, who, based on empirical research in US justice system, highlights the widespread assertion by prosecutors in interviews about the relative insignificance of judges and the regularity of the ir activities being carried out by the accuser.[198]

Therefore, this violates the separation of the prosecuting and the judging powers,[199] fundamental to the adequacy of the adversarial system, while the concentration of these responsibilities in the figure of the prosecutor is characterised,[200] which ultimately subverts fundamental principles of criminal procedure.[201] This accurately

[192] On this, see item Sect. 4.1.2 of this work.

[193] Diego Díez (1999), p. 74.

[194] Dias and Andrade (1987), p. 471.

[195] Albrecht (2010), pp. 308–309. According to the author: "We can affirm, based on the analysis of procedural executions and personnel development in the Criminal Justice System, that there is a clear global trend: criminal jurisdiction is largely displaced by the procedural solutions of the Public Prosecutor's Office" (Albrecht 2010, p. 308, free translation).

[196] Rodríguez García (1997), p. 42. It is even pointed out a similarity to the medieval inquisitive system, in which there was a concentration of functions in the role of the inquisitor (Langbein 1978, pp. 17–18).

[197] "Indeed, in cases in which the discretion to investigate or not, to suspend or not the investigative procedure, is left in the hands of the prosecuting body; at the moment when the decision is ratified by the judicial body, without the possibility of examining the formal and substantive requirements, the Public Prosecutor's Office takes on the typical functions of the adjudicating body" (Giacomolli 2006a, p. 103, free translation).

[198] Heumann (1981), p. 94.

[199] Albergaria (2007), pp. 110–115.

[200] Anitua (2010b), p. 150.

[201] Dias and Andrade (1987), p. 484; Anitua (2010b), pp. 158–159. On the inquisitive consequences of bargaining, in opposition to the theses that negotiated justice is an inevitable reflection of the accusatory model of party action and judicial passivity, see: Vasconcellos (2015).

describes an "invasion of the judge's reserve"[202] which is no longer exclusively subject to the law, but to the supposed will of the parties.[203] The decision regarding the accused's guilt is made by the prosecutor (based on elements produced in the pre-trial investigation),[204] violating the principles of *nulla poena, nulla culpa sine iudicio* and *nullum iudicium sine accusatio ne*,[205] which has characterised the phenomenon described by legal literature as the consecration of the Public Prosecutor's Office as "a judge at the doors of the court".[206] There is a clear trend toward increasing the importance of the prosecutor's functions in the US legal history,[207] which peaked with the "triumph of plea bargaining ", as described by George Fisher.[208]

However, some question this criticism, asserting that, in fact, it represents a "change in the role of the judge", since they would exercise the function of monitoring the legality of the agreement established.[209] According to **Scarance Fernandes**, in the negotiation model commonly adopted in countries of continental origin, the judge takes on a "triple role": to examine the merits to test the possibility of acquittal or extinction of punishability; to analyse the legal qualification of the fact; and to ascertain the voluntariness and intelligence of the accused's acceptance.[210] This attempt to mitigate the aforementioned aporia of the bargain (usurpation of decision-making powers by the prosecutor) fails to eliminate its clear practical configuration, while, in addition to the previously described weakening of review through judicial approval (which is carried out formally and automatically),[211] albeit duly limited, the power of the ministerial representative exceeds any legitimate space, since the decision about the pertinence of the case, the guilt of the accused, and the criminal sanction to be imposed is fundamentally determined by the prosecutor's opinion.

Thus, the already existing inequality between prosecution and defence, pervasive in criminal procedure,[212] is intensely exacerbated in a system guided by the bargain-

---

[202] Teixeira (2000), pp. 67–69.

[203] "This means an unequivocal incursion of the Public Prosecutor's Office into an area that should be dominated by the Court, which erroneously limits itself to ratifying the result of the agreement between accused and prosecutor. Not without reason, scholars assert that the prosecutor is the judge at the doors of the court" (Lopes Jr., 2002, p. 120, free translation).

[204] Langbein (1992), p. 124; Lynch (2012), p. 296.

[205] Duarte and Marques (2008), p. 71.

[206] Dias and Andrade (1987), p. 484.

[207] Dervan (2011b), pp. 244–246.

[208] Fisher (2003), pp. 13–39.

[209] Leite (2013), p. 42. In this sense, the Italian Constitutional Court dismissed the unconstitutionality of the negotiated mechanism due to the violation of the principle of the judge's sole subjection to the law under the (inconsistent) argument that the review of the agreement between the parties is carried out at the time of ratification (Diego Díez 1999, pp. 159–161, free translation).

[210] Fernandes (2005), p. 258. However, the author admits the inevitable expansion of the powers of the Public Prosecutor's Office in systems characterised by alternative rites (Fernandes 2005, p. 264, free translation).

[211] Alschuler (1976), pp. 1062–1064. On this, see item Sect. 2.2.3 of this work.

[212] On equality in criminal proceedings and its relationship with the adversarial principle and the separation of the functions of accusing and judging, see: Costa (2001b), pp. 89–139.

ing mechanism.[213] By taking on the judging role, the public prosecutor completely undermines any possibility of equality and equality of arms between the parties in criminal justice.[214] The situation becomes absurd: faced with the ineffectiveness of the State, which proves incapable of producing sufficient lawful evidence to dispel the presumption of innocence of the accused, the public prosecutor offers benefits to enable a consensual conviction, which "completely explodes the inequality of conditions in which the accused finds himself from the beginning of the prosecution".[215] In other words, "plea bargaining does not constitute an authentic negotiation between two parties on the same level. There is no equality of arms in this secret procedure, which is more inquisitorial than adversarial".[216] Such a scenario, of course, is intensely problematic in the criminal justice landscape,[217] characterised by social inequalities and prosecution selectivity, which will lead to the strengthening of the perverse effects of the bargain.[218]

Therefore, the fundamental premise of negotiation mechanisms, which underpins their legitimacy as an agreement between free and equal parties,[219] is fallacious and illusory given the practical consequences bargaining in the criminal justice system,[220] especially exacerbated by the prosecutor usurpating decision-making functions by the prosecutor.[221] There is a war of and for powers between the actors in the legal-criminal field,[222] which inevitably ends up harming the weakest and most vulnerable party in the punitive prosecution scenario: the accused.[223]

---

[213] "Within an authoritarian procedural structure as is the nature of criminal proceedings, the accused is necessarily in a position of inferiority in relation to the judicial actors, whose social role places them in a position of superiority. In this context, the freedom to negotiate is more illusory than real. Far from contributing to the equality of the parties, negotiated proceedings reinforce inequality, since the contract is also a privileged instrument of domination of the strong ones over the weak ones"' (Rodrigues 1998, p. 240, free translation).

[214] "Thus, it also mortally violates the essential core of the guarantee of equality of arms, by hypertrophying the powers of the accuser: the latter, in practice, replaces judge and jury, concentrating the powers to formulate the accusation, judge the cause and establish the penalty" (Malan 2010, p. 3, free translation). On the equality of arms in criminal procedure, see: Vieira (2014), pp. 163–236.

[215] Vegezzi (2005), p. 349.

[216] Costa (2001a), p. 47.

[217] Prado (2006b), pp. 83 and 224.

[218] According to Eduardo Costa (2011a, free translation), p. 46, the bargain is "a proceeding that, moreover, extraordinarily aggravates social (as well as ethnic) inequalities not only because of its casuistry, but also because the negotiation (better said, the capitulation) will generally be accepted by those who have few or no economic resources, since the defence in court represents, in addition to a high risk, a huge financial burden. This is the stark reality of plea bargaining".

[219] Langer (2005), pp. 128–133.

[220] "In a structural context of this type, freedom of negotiation is more illusory than real. Far from contributing to the equality of the parties, negotiated proceedings may reinforce their inequalities [...]" Tulkens (2005), p. 713). In this sense, also: Rodrigues (1998), p. 240.

[221] Heumann (1981), p. 118.

[222] Giacomolli (2006a), p. 114.

[223] "The issue of the swfitness of justice is, therefore, omnipresent in the debate on negotiated justice. It is the paradigm of justice proclaimed by an impartial third party and guarantor of the rights

4.1.6 The Disappearance of the Trial and of the Defence: Questioning the Waivability of These Rights. From the Criticism of the Illusion of Autonomy to the Unveiling of Punishment for Non- waiver

As previously outlined, the bargaining system distorts the roles played by actors in the criminal justice field, distorting their procedural relationships and their spheres of action. However, the point of greatest tension concerns the obstruction of the right to defence, as consensual mechanisms distance the accused from their typical position of resistance to the State's punitive intent.[224] In this regard, one can point to a contemporary trend of reducing the space for exercising the right to defence.[225] In a system governed by the possibility of bargaining, there is a complete distortion of the practice of defence, which is caused, fundamentally, by the corruption of the relationship between the accused and their legal counsel in the face of negotiations and the supposed advantages of a potential guilt admission agreement.[226] It is pointed out that the very essence of bargaining calls for inadequate defensive assistance,[227] for, as **Albert Alschuler** states, "the plea bargaining system is an inherently irrational method of administering justice and necessarily destructive of sound attorney-client relationships".[228]

In this vein, it is asserted that this archetype inevitably tempts the legal counsel in a direction contrary to the interests of the accused,[229] so that even well-intentioned and prepared professionals end up adopting stances contrary to the procedural action that is most beneficial to the accused.[230] The counselling to the accused will

---

of the weakest that is put into question, but at the expense of the weakest. The problems of managing the criminal system require technical and operational solutions, not changing the rules of the game. It reflects a unique degradation of the Rule of Law that practical considerations place demands on the level of law enforcement" (Rodrigues 1998, p. 241, free translation).

224 Diego Diez (1999), p. 50.

225 "It is necessary to point out the notable trend, revealed in recent years, to compress the space of the right to defence in criminal proceedings. Sometimes the right to defence is replaced by procedural behaviours of the accused, to which legal efficacy is attributed at the level of the resolution of the main issue—the so-called consensus solutions –, sometimes this space is simply reduced, under the pretext of controlling the serious forms of criminality that are currently manifesting themselves" (Prado 2006a, p. 120, free translation). On the right to defence in criminal proceedings, see: Saad (2004), pp. 207–241.

226 "Finally, the bargain eliminates all possible content of the right to defence, a circumstance that in itself allows fundamentally questioning the 'certainty' necessary for the Court to sentence a conviction […]" (Bovino 2005, p. 80, free translation).

227 Hessick and Saujani (2002), p. 189. This is also the description made by Milton Heumann based on empirical research with interviews with lawyers: Heumann (1981), p. 190.

228 Alschuler (1975a), p. 1180.

229 Hessick and Saujani (2002), p. 219.

230 Alschuler (1975a), p. 1180.

often be given by someone interested in their admission of guilt,[231] whether for economic or political benefits, or even for a naive excuse for fears of the risks of trial.[232]

This scenario becomes evident when the existence of professionals who have never conducted a defence before a US jury is uncovered.[233] In other words, there is a practical pathologisation of the legal counsel's role, which can lead to undue pressures for the acceptance of the agreement[234] or even dishonest attitudes[235] or, still, aiming at interests unrelated to the specific case in question.[236] On the other hand, "well-intentioned" legal counsels are weakened by the fear of claiming the rights of the accused in the trial and ending up causing a more severe criminal sanction due to the non-acceptance of the agreement.[237] The bargaining model, therefore, encourages dishonest legal counsels at the same time it fosters impulses and pressures on the honest ones.[238]

In this scenario, the legal counsel moves away from their primary role, as their main function becomes the duty to predict the final outcome of a potential trial by communicating to the client their chances of acquittal, which is calculated under the shadow of illegitimate pressures exerted by threats of more severe sanctioning in case of non-recognition of guilt.[239] Therefore, a "schizophrenic relationship" is characterised,[240] in which the legal counsel starts from an initial presumption of guilt, which generally entails a suggestion to accept the bargain and, in the event of refusal, adopts a defensive position that clearly does not adequately meet the minimum level of trust required in the client-counsel relationship.[241]

---

[231] Hessick and Saujani (2002), p. 207.

[232] Hessick and Saujani (2002), pp. 219–220.

[233] Fine (1987), p. 624.

[234] Rodríguez García (1997), p. 59; Alschuler (1975a), pp. 1191–1192.

[235] According to Regina Rauxloh (2011), pp. 312–313, in Germany, it is common for the accused to lack information about a potential waiver of the right to appeal the conviction, which is often not provided by the appointed counsel.

[236] For instance, there are cases in which the legal counsel suggests accepting the bargain aiming at favours from the public prosecutor in other cases he sponsors (Alschuler 1975a, p. 1215).

[237] "Legal counsels, fearful that their advice against accepting the simplified route, with the loss of the offered advantages, may harm them in the event of a conviction, tends to guide their clients to agree, protecting themselves from potential discredit regarding their knowledge and professional skills. [...] A vicious and dangerous circle is created in which legal counsels and defendants agree due to the fear of a negative outcome and not because of a secure evaluation of the possibility of conviction" (Fernandes 2005, p. 267). Also in this sense, emphasising that, in case of doubt, legal counsels tend to encourage the agreement: Albergaria (2007), p. 41.

[238] "The legal counsel, fearful that their advice against accepting the simplified route, with the loss of the offered advantages, may harm them if there is a conviction, tends to guide their client to agree, protecting himself from potential discredit regarding his knowledge and professional skills. [...] A vicious and dangerous circle is created where the lawyer and the defendant agree due to the fear of a negative outcome and not because of a secure evaluation of the possibility of conviction" (Fernandes 2005, p. 267, free translation). Also in this sense, emphasising that, in case of doubt, the lawyer tends to encourage the agreement: Albergaria (2007), p. 41.

[239] Alschuler (1975a), pp. 1198–1205.

[240] Alschuler (2009), p. 680.

[241] Alschuler (1975a), pp. 1311–1312.

Thus, another supposedly legitimising premise of negotiated justice—the adequate assistance of the legal counsel to ensure the free and informed decision of the accused—proves to be fallacious and inadequate in light of the practical implementation of bargaining in the criminal legal field, as all actors, including legal counsels, succumb to bureaucratic pressures and conflicts of interest that characterise this model.[242] Therefore, "private defence attorneys, public defenders, and appointed attorneys are all subject to bureaucratic pressures and conflicts of interest that seem unavoidable in any regime grounded on the guilty plea" and "the difficulty of providing effective representation within the guilty-plea system may reflect the intolerable nature of the system itself.".[243]

Furthermore, this demonstrates a presumption of guilt,[244] in complete violation of the essential and democratic presumption of innocence,[245] shared even by the defence counsel, who, due to their improper need to consider the client's situation at the initial stage of criminal prosecution, in a situation permeated by pressures and coercion from the bureaucratic system, ends up encouraging the acceptance of the bargain, consolidating a stance similar to a general premise that all their clients are guilty in practice.[246] This scenario is exacerbated in a context of precarious public defence provided to accused individuals in need, which is typical in both the United States and Brazil.[247] All of this inevitably leads to spaces for discretion, arbitrariness and prejudices, in which the defensive attitude is based on illegitimate and discriminatory criteria.[248] In this sense, based on empirical studies, **Vanessa Edkins** states that the accused's race can directly determine the stance of their counsel regarding the recommendation about the acceptance of the bargain, as her study shows that black accused individuals receive three times more suggestions to recognise their guilt.[249]

On the other hand, in addition to the complete distortion and obstruction to the exercise of the right to defence caused by the systematic typical of a negotiable criminal justice system, attention should be also paid to essential matters regarding its waiverability. Among US scholars, there is a debate between the inalienability of rights and the contractual autonomy of the parties in freedom[250]: authors who defend the possibility of negotiating rights in exchange for benefits oppose to those who point out the unconstitutionality of the exchange involving the accused's freedom,[251]

---

[242] Bibas (2003), p. 2478.

[243] Alschuler 1986, p. 149; Hessick, Saujani (2002), pp. 219–220.

[244] Alschuler (1975a), p. 1313.

[245] Heumann (1981), pp. 58–61.

[246] As already shown, the presumption of innocence is the cornerstone of criminal procedure, and for a detailed analysis, refer to: Moraes (2010), pp. 173–261; Lopes Jr. (2012), pp. 235–239.

[247] Hessick and Saujani (2002), p. 211.

[248] Regarding the American situation, see: Turner (2009), p. 512.

[249] Albergaria (2007), pp. 124–125; Rauxloh (2011), p. 308; Dias and Andrade (1987), p. 491.

[250] Alschuler (1981), p. 698.

[251] Jenia Turner (2009), pp. 35–36, describes certain rights, such as the right to appeal and to a speedy trial, which cannot be waived according to the positions of certain US courts.

although it is generally accepted without major objections to the logic that if a person holds a right, it can be waived.[252] However, in debates guided by thinkers of continental origin, this problem becomes complex: on the one hand, the possibility of ending the proceeding without evidence production is challenged (since the effects of guilt recognition, usually determined according to the contours of the confession mechanism, do not entail such a consequence, while there is no mechanism similar to the US guilty plea), and, on the other hand, the waivability of the right to defence is qualified.[253]

Aside from the already unveiled illusion of the accused's freedom to consent to the bargain,[254] some argue that the acceptance of the agreement represents the exercise of the right to defence.[255] However, it is believed that this claim cannot be upheld, since, according to **Alberto Bovino**, this requires at least a stance of minimal resistance.[256] Even though there are arguments asserting that no fundamental right is waived in the bargain, it is clear that the recognition of guilt in a negotiated agreement entails the removal of the right to evidence, to defence, to the presumption of innocence, to the adversarial proceeding, among others.[257] However, it is not to say that there is a prohibition on the accused's confession,[258] but rather to question the possibility of conviction without the production of incriminating evidence and the consequent dismissal of the proceeding with the imposition of a criminal penalty.

---

[252] Fisher (2003), p. 91.

[253] Vegezzi (2005), p. 362.

[254] Rosimeire Leite (2013), pp. 34–35, argues that, instead of restricting the accused's actions with the non-waiver of the right to defence, attention should be paid to the implementation of the protection of minimum guarantees for the implementation of the bargain, thus renewing the belief in contractual freedom and the sufficiency of lawyer's assistance to compensate for any deficiencies. However, as already shown (see items Sects. 4.1.3 and 4.1.6), such assertions are fallacious in the face of the dysfunctions caused by the implementation of a negotiation system, which makes the accused's free decision and adequate legal counsel assistance unfeasible.

[255] "From this perspective, the waiver would not only be a restriction, but also a form of exercising the fundamental right, in which the holder opts to authorise limitation with the intention of obtaining advantages that would otherwise not be achieved" (Leite 2013, p. 31, free translation).

[256] "In summary, to defend oneself means, in simple terms, to present some degree of resistance to the persecutory activity. Consequently, the full admission of guilt for the fact described in the indictment, its legal qualification and the established criminal sanction, that is, the 'conformity' required by art. 431 *bis*, inc. 2, of the CPP of the Nation of Argentina, cannot be considered a defensive measure" (Bovino 2005, p. 83, free translation).

[257] Fairen Guillen (1970), p. 261.

[258] "No accused has ever been prohibited from confessing, and this would make no sense, as it would violate the freedom of action peculiar to the human being. Nor in lands accustomed to torture is confession encouraged as a means of demonstrating something. From a purely formal point of view, nothing would prevent the Public Prosecutor's Office from taking advantage of the confession, as a source of evidence, to deepen its research and introduce evidence obtained due to the source. What is happening now is that from this subtle distinction, promoted by the indication of a result of the accused's procedural activity as a means of proof, instead of their own statements, it is intended to circumvent constitutional prohibitions and transform the accused into a witness" (Prado 2006a, p. 10, free translation).

On the one hand, **Fairén Guillén** argues that, in abstract, the right to defence is unwaivable, but it can be waived in specific cases provided that the conditions authorising the negotiation mechanism are present, regulated in the respective legal system in accordance with constitutional provisions.[259] However, **Geraldo Prado**, seemingly revisiting premises stated in previous works,[260] argues for the need to analyse the waivability of the said right in the light of the landscape of social inequality (typical of the Brazilian penal system),[261] which inevitably and directly influences the impossibility of effective personal autonomy of the accused to make the free decision to waive the right to trial and defence,[262] so as to determine its concrete unwaivability.[263]

Thus, before any possible debates about the availability of the accused's rights in the framework of negotiated justice, the aforementioned coercion inherent in the relationships established amid the possibility of bargaining in criminal proceedings ultimately renders any autonomy of will unfeasible, eliminating the free decision-making that is a prerequisite for any waiver.[264] Therefore, the fundamental aporia of the consensual mechanism, which makes any space for negotiation and renunciation in freedom impossible, concerns the supposed reward offered in exchange for the recognition of guilt,[265] which inevitably distorts the procedural relationships and the premises of criminal procedure.[266] In other words, it is argued that freedom cannot

259 Fairen Guillen (1970), p. 267.

260 Prado (2006b), pp. 124–125.

261 "Such is, however, the strength of the discourse of consensus and the magical power of the idea of freedom that even the critics of the delegitimised penal system of our lands end up involved, in one way or another, by the seductive efficacy of this libertarian discourse and, despite exposing the political use of criminal law (and now the informalised criminal procedure), they admit a state of absolute human freedom by which the individual, subject of rights, would have the natural right to deprive themselves of their own lives" (Prado 2006b, p. 186, free translation).

262 Prado (2006b), p. 224.

263 "The non-waiving of a fundamental right by an individual is the logical antecedent of its unavailability and, within the legal field, it invalidates, contradicting the Constitution, any act tending to the abdication of individual rights" (Prado 2006b, p. 189, free translation). In this sense, reinforcing this position: Prado 2012, p. 54–55. Also asserting the non- waiving, Alberto Bovino (2005), p. 69, highlights a comparison with the peaceful impossibility of an accused to, no matter how evident their responsibility, voluntarily go to prison in order to serve a sentence without it being declared in a definitive condemnatory sentence; similarly, the accused cannot agree to serve a criminal sanction before a valid sentence.

264 "[...] every waiver or consent, to be so qualified, needs total freedom of decision, which is, by essence, non-existent in the negotiation system" (Díaz Cantón 2005, p. 252, free translation).

265 "In other words, the problem is not in the confession, but in the offering of something in exchange for it" (Tedesco 2005, p. 329, free translation).

266 "[...] Thus, if this right were waivabele, this abdication should be free and voluntary. However, in this case, the State uses the negotiation mechanism as an element of coercion to prevent the free exercise of the right, causing invalid waivers that are invalid because they have been obtained through coercive measures carried out by public officials" (Bovino 2005, p. 77, free translation).

be considered a commodity for negotiation between the accused and the State,[267] under penalty of characterising criminal justice as a space for fostering "perverse barter".[268]

Furthermore, it should be noted that, far beyond a settled question between the options of waiving or not procedural rights, the accused is offered the possibility of an illusory choice, whereas any refusal to bargain, with the exercise of the right to the trial, ends up resulting in a more severe criminal penalty for the accused in the possible subsequent conviction.[269] In other words, the offer of a supposed benefit (which, often, proves to be illusory in practice)[270] in exchange for the recognition of guilt for the agreement, does not consist in a reward for those who accept this proposal, but rather in a punishment (and a clearly intimidating one) to accused individuals who exercise the right to trial.[271] According to **Gabriel Anitua**, "what underlies the supposed reduction of the penalty as a 'reward' for the accused's collaboration, is, in truth, an effective threat to request a more severe sanction in case of exercise of rights and there is a conviction".[272] Although the US Supreme Court has declared the admissibility of the "risk of a more severe criminal sanction", which results in a "difficult decision for the accused", this argument proves fallacious in practice in the face of the accused's perspective before the risk (or, depending on the level of punitiveness of the respective criminal justice system, almost certainty) of the more severe conviction.[273]

---

[267] "The waiver of the preliminary stage hearing and judgement, widely practiced in the US criminal procedure behind the facade of the jury trial procedure, cannot, in a Rule of Law, be sold cheap as chips." (Schünemann 2013a, p. 260, free translation).

[268] "The criminal settlement, in fact, finds no other foundation than that of a perverse barter. In the unequal confrontation with the prosecution, what can the accused or indicted give in exchange for the reduction of the sentence but his own declaration of guilt or the so-called co-defendant, although unfounded, of other accused?" (Ferrajoli, 2014, p. 691, free translation).

[269] "The negotiating fury of the accusation can lead to bureaucratic perversion, in which the passive party not willing to 'agree' sees the criminal proceeding become a complex and bureaucratic war. Everything is more difficult for those who are not willing to 'do business'"(Lopes Jr. 2002, p. 121, free translation).

[270] Gifford (1983), p. 56.

[271] "Thus, it has been pointed out that it is not legitimate to reward a confession with the mitigation of the sentence, since this derives, indirectly, from an aggravation of the punishment for those who exercise the right to silence, or, in this case, to submit to trial. Thus, the advantage comes to have, as a counterpart, a threat that constitutes a form of pressure for confession" (Tedesco 2005, p. 316).

[272] Anitua (2005a), pp. 148–149.

[273] Alkon (2010), pp. 394–395.

These are the so-called "sanction scissors",[274] empirically explained in specific studies[275] and unquestionably present in decisions of the US Supreme Court, such as the already described in *Bordenkircher v. Hayes* (in which the defendant was accused of issuing a false cheque and had to choose between accepting a bargain with a five-year prison sentence or exercising the right to trial and risking a life sentence for recidivism)[276] or in *Brady v. United States* (in which the accused had to choose between consenting to a life sentence or the uncertainty of a trial that could lead to a death sentence),[277] both cases admitted as lawful and constitutional.

Therefore, in light of this, it is clear that the bargaining entails a waiver of the right to defence, distancing the accused from their primary position in criminal justice[278] through consent given in a scenario of undue pressures and coercion, that is, violating fundamental guarantees for limitating/legitimising punitive prosecution in a Democratic Rule of Law.[279] Negotiated justice ultimately undermines the very notion of due process, as the argument that criminal sanctions would be imposed in response to motivated jurisdiction is fundamentally fallacious[280]: consensual agreements between prosecution and defence result in the waiver of the trial as a tool for law enforcement and containment of arbitrariness.[281] This is a phenomenon described by US scholars as the "vanishing trials",[282] which elucidates the paradox that, in legal systems characterised by the exponential expansion of the number of

---

[274] "As confirmed by the experiences I have carried out, the accused's denials at the hearing are no longer taken seriously by the judge, any possibility of acquittal is destroyed, and the penalty applied ends up being influenced by the so-called sanction scissors (*Sanktionsschere*), that is, a more severe penalty is imposed, so that the previous threat of this penalty does not seem, afterwards, a frivolous bluff of a poker game. With this, the supposedly mitigated penalty gradually becomes the standard penalty, so that the agreement, which supposedly grants a penalty discount to the accused, transforms before their eyes into a misleading advertisement" (Schünemann 2013b, p. 308, free translation).

[275] Dervan and Edkins (2012), p. 15.

[276] Lippke (2011), p. 11.

[277] Alschuler (1975b), pp. 48–50.

[278] "The hallmark of the defence in criminal procedure lies precisely in participating in the proceeding, pursuing the protection of an interest that needs to be the opposite of that initially assigned to the prosecution, under penalty of the proceeding becoming an instrument of political manipulation of people and situations" (Prado 2006b, p. 121, free translation).

[279] Bovino (2005), p. 70; Anitua (2005a), p. 145.

[280] "There is certainly a prosecution, but there is no evidence, nor defence and, in this way, there is no valid sentence" (Bovino 2005, p. 90).

[281] "[...] when reforms are directed solely at expanding negotiation mechanisms, and this is certainly what can happen when starting from differences between minor and major offences, the waiver ends up affecting the very case, a guarantee that we should not forget it was hard-won throughout the years" (Armenta Deu 2012a, p. 284).

[282] Galanter (2004); Armenta Deu (2012b), pp. 164–166; Burns (2009), pp. 1–7. According to Gabriel Anitua (2005a), p. 155, "by relying on these joint wills, it will be possible to omit the oral and public reception of evidence, and the formulation of the parties' conclusions on their merits. In other words, the trial will be omitted".

laws, there is a significant reduction in the number of trials.[283] In other words, it completely undermines the pillars of constitutional instrumentality,[284] "ultimately banishing the most important of all: the right to a fair trial".[285]

4.2 The Reality That Questions the "Revolution": Empirical Criticisms of Bargaining. A Study of the Introduction of Spaces for Consensus in Brazilian Criminal Justice and Their Potential to Enhance Violations of Fundamental Rights

Having described the criticisms of the negotiated justice model in broad terms, especially in light of the trends towards expanding its spaces of applicability in criminal proceedings, the aim now is to demonstrate the practical implementation of these aporias in the current Brazilian scenario, in the Small Claims Courts. Although the applicability of the mechanisms of criminal settlement and conditional suspension of the criminal prosecution is limited to less serious cases and their regulation presents differences in relation to the US plea bargaining (which is the main object of some of the studies cited),[286] it is noted that the practical implementation of negotiated justice in Brazil entails violations of the assumptions of criminal proceedings in a similar way to that described above, that is, the listed criticisms are currently present in Brazil. In this sense, given the general characteristics of Brazilian criminal prosecution (especially its selectivity and inequality), the negative consequences of bargaining inevitably stand out, which would certainly be exacerbated with a potential expansion of spaces for consensus.

Initially, it is relevant to describe the legal scholars' stance that determined the reception of Law 9.099/1995 at the time of its enactment. This law was euphorically hailed by some scholars, being described as "a true revolution in the Brazilian criminal procedural system"[287] and "undoubtedly the most promising way of the much-awaited debureaucratisation of criminal justice".[288] Thus, it was pointed out that "the new statute was received without reservations and became the repository of expectations for the transformation of an obsolete, selective and stigmatising criminal justice system".[289]

---

[283] Galanter 2006, p. 33.

[284] Gloeckner (2013), pp. 28–31.

[285] Lopes Jr. (2002), pp. 118–119.

[286] Regarding the theoretical applicability of the criticisms developed earlier, refer to the initial considerations of topic Sect. 4.1.

[287] Grinover et al. (2005), p. 41. Also: Fernandes et al. (1999), p. 12.

[288] Fernandes et al. (1999), p. 49; Gomes (2012), p. 487. Also affirming the revolutionary character of the criminal settlement mechanism, although recognising areas of legislative inconsistency that should be filled by scholarship, see: Bitencourt (1997), pp. 103–107.

[289] Prado (2006a), p. 1.

However, in addition to the possible objection to such "euphoric language" discourses, which—as revealed by **Geraldo Prado**—prevent potential criticisms of their content based on arguments of authority,[290] studies reveal that the effective implementation of the Small Claims Courts and the processing of minor offensive infractions challenge the aforementioned "revolution" (usually perceived in close relation with supposed irrefutably positive effects of informalising and accelerating of criminal justice), weakening such praises based on three aspects: (1) even though it presents alleged purposes of rationalisation and reduction of the incidence of punitive power, the enactment of Law 9.099/1995 led to the resurgence of cases previously not criminally protected, thus causing the expansion of social control through criminal law; (2) the sociological arguments that legitimise the procedure of the Small Claims Courts, fundamentally based on ideas of greater proximity and conciliation between perpetrator and victim (aiming at a resolution of the conflict in a consensual and peaceful manner), are not implemented in practice, as there is no value given to the dialogue between the parties, since the legal actors guide their actions aiming at obtaining the case closure as quickly as possible (by means of its dismissal or the immediate imposition of the criminal sanction); and, (3) the implementation of the negotiation mechanisms of Law 9.099/1995 (especially of the criminal settlement, but also of the conditional suspension of the criminal prosecution) is permeated by constant violations of the rights and fundamental guarantees of the accused, completely distorting the functions of the criminal trial. For this, empirical studies based on data collected in Small Claims Courts carried out in different throughout Brazil and published at an academic level will be used.[291]

Firstly (1), some scholars revealed certain intriguing reflections brought by Law 9.099/1995 and its negotiation mechanisms.[292] According to **Maria Lúcia Karam**, "in Brazil, not long after the creation of the Small Claims Courts, this 'functional economy' was already perceived in the enlargement of the penal system".[293] Therefore, it is argued that, unlike the official discourse that justified the reform due to the resulting decriminalisation to reduce demand in criminal justice,[294] the inno-

[290] "In the cited example, if we agree with the fact that Law n. 9.099/95 introduced advances and produced a revolution, those who disagree with this point of view may be labelled as outdated and supporters of regression, considering the direct and indirect sense (denotation and connotation, respectively) attributable to the terms 'advance' and 'revolution'!" (Prado 2006a, p. 7, free translation).

[291] Particularly referring to: Almeida (2014); Fernandes et al. (1999); Pinheiro (2007); Anziliero (2008); Fullin (2011).

[292] "The concept of a minor offence, in its perverse logic, invoked the already forgotten trivial offences, which, due to cost, effectiveness and proportionality between the offence and the penalty, were not worthy of being prosecuted. However, by obscuring the concept of punishment, a kind of reinstatement of these same offences was operated, recreating their processing, which is now more flexible, since the offence will no longer be punished with a deprivation of liberty. And thus, guarantees become superfluous, erecting a clear administrative character to the criminal field, by means of consensus" (Gloeckner 2009, p. 302, free translation).

[293] Karam (2004), p. 38.

[294] Grinover et al. (2005), pp. 47–49.

vation resulted in an expansion of the field of social control through punitive power, completely distorting the alleged purposes of its drafting.[295] This ideological inversion became evident when, in the first years of enforcement of the new regulation, the conversion of the criminal settlement into a deprivation of liberty in case of non-compliance was widely accepted; in other words, the mechanism that was supposed to reduce the number of imprisonments ended up aggravating the situation.[296]

In an empirical study on the informalisation of the justice system, **Rodrigo de Azevedo** presents data on the establishment of the Small Claims Courts in Porto Alegre and from the period immediately after the enactment of Law 9.099/1995. According to the graphs, one may conclude that, in addition to not reducing the caseload in the Common Criminal Courts, the reform led to a large number of cases to be tried in the Small Claims Courts.[297] In other words, the new mechanisms were used in a scope of offences that were not previously prosecuted by criminal justice.[298] Moreover, Azevedo highlights the types of conflicts observed in the hearings: "(...) it was found that most minor offences stem from situations of conflict between neighbours (41%), between spouses (17%), between relatives (10%), or in relationships between consumer and merchant (10%)".[299] Therefore, the expectation concerning this reform was not met, since there was no significant reduction in the procedural movement in the Small Claims Courts.[300]

---

[295] "In conclusion, this is what happens with the Small Claims Courts, as the model is not only unfit to instrumentalise them [...] but fulfils different functions from those declared (insofar as it expands the action of social control, bringing into the system conflicts that were out of its reach), that is, the reproduction of the selective functioning of the criminal system" (Santos 2002, p. 70).

[296] Prado (2006a), p. 18. Subsequently, such conversion was prohibited by the Brazilian Superior Courts.

[297] Azevedo (2000), pp. 134–136; Kant de Lima (2003), p. 40.

[298] Azevedo (2000), p. 136. In this sense, some argue that, although it caused the expansion of the incidence of Criminal Law, such expansion is positive by judicialising these conflicts, which, previously, were discussed informally in society (or in Police Stations), which allowed greater risks of selectivity and arbitrariness. However, it is thought that such judicialisation did not necessarily have to be done through the criminal sphere of Law, which should be subsidiary in the intervention of social relations. In other words, the cases currently resolved in the JECs (for example, minor disputes between neighbours) could be protected in the scope of civil liability. As pointed out by the author, from the early years, the conflicts protected in the Small Claims Courts were between neighbours, spouses, relatives or in relationships between consumer and merchant or employer and employee (Azevedo 2000, p. 157). On this data, in a more recent study: Anziliero (2008), pp. 183–184. Also affirming the positive contribution of the judicialisation of the selectivity previously carried out at police stations: Leite (2013), p. 280.

[299] Azevedo (2000), p. 157.

[300] "With the implementation of the Small Claims Courts, a significant reduction in the procedural movement in the Common Criminal Courts was expected, which could focus on more serious offences. The analysis of the procedural movement verified in the judicial district of Porto Alegre in the 2 years before and after the implementation of the Courts does not confirm this expectation" (Azevedo 2000, p. 134, free translation).

Although an empirical study carried out in São Paulo also claims a "strong and positive impact of the law on the justice system in São Paulo",[301] as a rule, the statistics described by scholars confirm the conclusions of **Rodrigo de Azevedo**, for instance, in an analysis of the situation in Brasília,[302] in which he asserted: "the creation of the Small Claims Court, as a bifurcation of the Brazilian penal system, led to the expansion of formal penal control which began to intervene in criminality, which was previously outside the formal control system".[303] Thus, it can be stated that the declared objectives of the new legislation (decriminalisation, rationalisation and reduction of the caseload in common courts) diverged from the actual consequences in practice.[304]

Therefore, in line with the critique previously developed regarding the symbiotic relationship of reciprocal legitimisation between bargaining and the phenomenon of the expansion of Criminal Law (Sect. 3.1.1), one may conclude that the introduction of spaces for consensus in Brazilian criminal justice, through the mechanisms of criminal settlement and conditional suspension of the criminal prosecution, although applicable in cases limited by the legal text, resulted in the expansion of the State punitive control in social relations.[305] The innovative legislation brought about effects distinct from those apparently intended, so that the implemented reform ended up being distorted.[306] And, similarly, it can be anticipated that any further expansion of spaces for consensus in the Brazilian criminal procedural system, which is also motivated by efficiency-driven intentions to reduce the caseload in the courts, will bring about counterproductive effects, causing illegitimate inflation of social control through the State punitive power.[307] This was clearly shown in the Ecuadorian example described by **Jorge Paladines** when revealing that the Flagrancy Management Units, created in Quito and Guayaquil in 2012, although

[301] Fernandes et al. (1999), p. 27.

[302] Pinheiro (2010), pp. 97–115.

[303] Pinheiro (2010), p. 95.

[304] "Thus, being permeable to the needs of structuring strategies for a more efficient penal response, and, to "At the same time, less perceptibly, the operational code represented by normative production quenches social control, by enacting a law that enables its expansion, also allied to the perception, within the realm of public opinion, as well as specialised scholarship of positive-dogmatism, of a formula seen as a true 'lifeline' for the institutional bankruptcy that the penal system has been experiencing" (Miranda 2004, p. 234).

[305] "Hence our criticism of negotiated justice and Small Claims Courts, true expressions of the law and order movement, insofar as they contribute to the trivialisation of criminal law, fostering pan-penalisation and repressive symbolism" (Lopes Jr. 2002, p. 110).

[306] "Therefore, by placing in the creation and implementation of the Special Criminal Court the expectation of retraction of traditional penal intervention, as a prerequisite for the acquisition of efficiency in dealing with serious issues, the official discourse is mistaken. In reality, the JEC expands the penal system by controlling crimes that remained on the margins of the formal system, therefore not occupying the traditional system" (Pinheiro 2010, p. 97).

[307] Anitua (2005a), pp. 137–160.

ostensibly justified for greater control of the legality of detentions, became "judicial machines to promote immediate convictions".[308]

Furthermore (2), the second argument questioning the latent effects of negotiated justice within the Brazilian legal-criminal field concerns the assertion that, contrary to the intended valorisation of dialogue and conciliation for conflict resolution,[309] in practice, there is a distancing from such aspirations, as legal actors guide their actions aiming to close the case as quickly as possible (either through its dismissal or the immediate imposition of criminal sanctions), that is, little attention is paid to the effective consensual resolution of the conflict by means of dialogue.[310] In the empirical studies herein cited, there are several references to the total inoperability of the fast-tracked procedure for the realisation of the declared intention of the Small Claims Courts.[311] According to statistics described by **Dineia Anziliero**, more than half of those involved (victims and accused) stated that there was not enough clarification and dialogue about the incident at the pre-trial hearing.[312] In this sense, it is worth noting that the generalised stance of the actors in the criminal system of the JECs is guided by the search for the quickest possible case closure, initially encouraging the victim to desist and then pressuring the accused to accept the criminal settlement, without any intention of consensually resolving the conflict by means of dialogue.[313] There is a consolidation of a logic that prioritises the dismissal of circumstantial terms to avoid prosecuting the case further.[314]

Therefore, negotiation mechanisms are instruments of expansion of punitive power, which are implemented with the aim of imposing a swift and unquestionable

---

[308] "The Flagrancy Units did not generally promote a discussion about the rights of the accused, but a debate about the election of forms of punitive social control that did not limit the process of imprisonment, leading us to the greatest growth of incarceration in the republican history of the country. Therefore, one must constantly ask whether in reality this management model generated less impunity or, on the other hand, increased it at the expense of the victims of the flagrancy factory" (Paladines 2013, p. 161, free translation).

[309] Almeida (2014), p. 23.

[310] "[...] the preliminary hearing appears as an opportunity for punitive negotiation with the offender, much more than an opportunity for the promotion of dialogue between the parties or the mediation of the conflict" (Fullin 2011, p. 49, free translation).

[311] "In this aspect, it contradicts the legal-criminal discourse, in which the Small Claims Court corresponds to the consensual model of criminal justice, to affirm that this court does not present itself as a space for conciliation. It is confirmed, in the operation of the Small Claims Court of Brasília, the symbolic function of the penal system that, when working with the logic of archiving, does not present itself as a space for conflict resolution" (Pinheiro 2010, p. 101, free translation).

[312] Anziliero (2008), pp. 150–155.

[313] "In other words, it is this way of dealing with conflict with aversion that authorises its repression. Therefore, the strategies of the operators sometimes achieved the renunciation of jurisdictional provision (by the victim), sometimes the acceptance of the measure imposed in the criminal settlement (by those jurisdictionally accused as offenders), which meant, in either case, the return of the conflict to society" (Almeida 2014, p. 83, free translation).

[314] In this sense, Fabiana Pinheiro reveals that "it is observed that most of the procedures are stillborn, as they reach the judicial sphere with the retraction or renunciation presented by the victim in the police sphere" (Pinheiro 2010, p. 100, free translation).

punishment, so that the actors involved remain instrumentalised by this intention. In other words, any space for effective dialogue dedicated to resolving the conflict aiming at the interests of the parties (offender and victim) are diminished (or even excluded),[315] resulting in a proceeding in which the only active voice is the accusatory claim, which, by means of coercion, overpowers any defensive resistance.[316]

Finally (3), empirical findings confirm the occurrence of the problems previously described in general criticisms of bargaining and negotiated justice (topic 3.1). Thus, by pointing out that the implementation of the consensual mechanisms of Law 9.099/1995 (particularly the criminal settlement) leads to constant violations of the accused's fundamental rights and guarantees, the unavoidable aporias of the negotiation model are revealed, which, indeed, were expressed in a much more aggravated way in a scenario of potential expansion of spaces for consensus.

The first fundamental point in which the criticism of consensual mechanisms in the Brazilian reality is clearly perceived concerns the coercion inherent in the proposal of a criminal settlement, which makes it impossible for the accused to supposedly freely accept it and deeply intensifies the risks of convicting the innocent (see item Sect. 4.1.3).[317] As explained by **Vera de Almeida**, in several of the hearings observed during the empirical research in the Small Claims Courts of Rio de Janeiro, argumentative pressure was exerted on the accused to encourage agreement, as there are routine advisements in a threatening tone that the best option would be to accept the criminal settlement[318] and the assertion that the author of the act would "suffer a greater penalty" in case of refusal.[319] Thus, there is no rational and free choice by the accused, since "in other terms, never uttered by legal actors, but tacitly suggested, the options are: punishment by alternative measure or punishment by trial".[320]

---

[315] Almeida (2014), p. 96.

[316] "Given this context, the criminal settlement, an institution inserted in our criminal procedural system with the purpose of promoting dialogue between the parties and being an informal procedure, is adapting to the force - and thus moving away from the original model -, to the specific purpose of a markedly inquisitorial procedural model and hence only resulting in the objective of subjecting the accused to punishment, as happens in the other facets of this system. The gap observed between doctrinal and legal discourses and the practices of operators is probably a reflection of a legal culture founded on the predominant punitive function of criminal law [...]" (Almeida 2014, p. 225, free translation).

[317] "Thus, the mere threat of the process has become the main 'bargaining chip' to convince the person suspected of committing the criminal act to accept the penalty - even if it is not institutional - without the inherent mechanism of due legal process, legally guaranteed from the democratic Constitution of 1998" (Shecaira 2002, p. 323, free translation).

[318] The author describes a situation in which, after hearing a request for a new hearing, the conciliator stated that "this would be conducted by the prosecutor, and that this operator 'was not soft, no' and that he 'would hardly not take into account the testimony of the police'. She then added the following 'advice': 'In my opinion, I think it's better for you to accept the criminal settlement, after all, it won't be recorded on your criminal record'. Although appearing to be advice, these words were pronounced in a tone that bordered on threat, with the conciliator raising the volume of her voice as she spoke" (Almeida 2014, p. 102, free translation).

[319] Almeida (2014), p. 151.

[320] Fullin (2011), p. 148.

Therefore, in addition to the intimidation caused by the threat of registering in criminal records of a potential conviction, the very implementation of the trial consists of an unnecessary burden and risk with the purpose of determining the accused's choice for its non-implementation.[321] Besides the weakening of voluntariness, there is also a routine lack of information to the accused about the consequences of the agreement and their procedural situation, that is, there is a widespread violation of another requirement of the bargain, namely, the information/intelligence of the accused's decision (Sect. 2.2.3).[322]

Furthermore, the imposition of the criminal sanctions occurs without any adequate motivation,[323] both in its quantification in the proposal offered by the public prosecutor, and in its evidentiary legitimacy to justify State punitive intervention.[324] In fact, the prosecutor's position is fundamentally determined by the information contained in the circumstantial term produced by the police authority, that is, an element of pre-trial investigation that, besides being illegitimate for the justification of a conviction, is generally poorly drafted.[325] Here, the practical implementation of the previously described criticism about the authoritarian procedural setback caused by the negotiation mechanisms is highlighted, with the violation of the possibilities of defence and the obstruction of the adversarial proceeding resulting from the primacy of unilaterally produced acts without due judicial review (Sect. 4.1.4) is perceived.

---

[321] "This statement, reproduced at various other times, attests that the criminal record was used as a threat and, the judicial procedure sounded to the ears of the jurisdictional as something that scared, this when the jurisdictional activity was not also considered unnecessary, costly and uncertain. That is, the acceptance of the criminal settlement did not result from a manifestation of spontaneous or voluntary will, but rather contaminated by these ideas" (Almeida 2014, p. 112, free translation). In this sense, it is worth citing the research carried out by Malcolm Feeley (1997), pp. 199–243, in the *Lower Criminal Courts* of the 1990s, in which it was concluded that the accused accepted to acknowledge their guilt and the immediate imposition of a punishment due to the damages caused by the process itself and its inherent uncertainties.

[322] Almeida (2014), pp. 99–103.

[323] Exposing the problem, Geraldo Prado (2006b), p. 142, asks: "The question that remains unanswered is simple: after all, is the jurisdictional protection, full or limited, provided in a procedure that is more concentrated - and informal - than the very fast track? Or, in another way, does the granting of the removal from the home, for example, or the imposition of a criminal penalty violate the principle of due legal process, as they are determined in a procedure whose only database are the superficial information contained in the circumstantial term?".

[324] "This argument is proven by the last interview transcribed above, in which the operator admits that even when there is no evidence, he offers the criminal settlement. The inversion of the rites assumed by him (first offers the criminal settlement, then seeks the evidence) demonstrates that the statements already presented about the inquisitorial nature of the criminal settlement and the inversion of the presumption of innocence, which transform the institute - of decriminalising origin - into punishment/penalty" (Almeida 2014, p. 158, free translation).

[325] Fullin (2011), pp. 50–51.

Regarding the distortion of the presumption of innocence, it is clear that the version of the facts described by the victim is often valued,[326] which, along with the primacy of the circumstantial term as forming the conviction of the accuser, completely violates the stance of doubt regarding the accused's guilt.[327] As previously stated (Sect. 4.1), the negotiation mechanisms completely invert the fundamental logic of the democratic criminal procedure, which is perceived in the Small Claims Courts from the shifting of the burden of proof to the accused and the settled preconceived perception that their innocence is untenable.[328]

The establishment of spaces for consensus in Brazilian criminal justice today also unveils the fallacy of the argument used by the US caselaw (Sect. 2.2.3), and reproduced in Brazil[329]: that the assistance of a legal counsel ensures legality and respect for the rights of the accused when bargaining. As explained (Sect. 4.1.6), in a scenario guided by negotiations about the guilt of the accused, the distortion of the relationship between client and legal counsel is inevitable, which completely undermines the effective respect for the right to a full defence and the informed decision of the accused. The described empirical research confirms this assertion, as, in addition to the conclusion of several agreements without the presence of a legal counsel (in violation of Law 9.099/1995),[330] numerous counsels adopt a position in favour of accepting the criminal settlement, either due to personal and relational interests

[326] "It is worth saying, once again this statement reproduced the idea that the allegation of the supposed author of the fact 'would not have weight' or that 'would have weight inferior to that of the victim', in the face of the valuation of the circumstantial term. It is observed, therefore, that the operators emphasised the version of the victims, endowing them with prejudices in their favour, resulting, consequently, in the devaluation of the statements of the supposed authors of the criminal facts. Thus, if the victim's statement was endowed with truthfulness, the accused's was presumed to be untruthful" (Almeida 2014, p. 104, free translation).

[327] "Thus, if the strategies seen in the hearing demonstrate barriers to the constitution of an interaction space that promotes less punishment-centred outcomes for the author of the fact, there are still Another element that also seems to contribute to clouding the possibility of dialogue between the parties that could lead to a resolution outside of the criminal settlement. This is, as already pointed out, the presumption of guilt that hangs over the person who is seen as the perpetrator of the offence, without evidence being presented and debated in court" (Fullin 2011, p. 133, free translation).

[328] "The field research described so far is showing that in the practices of the operators, the sense of presumption of guilt of the defendant prevails, even in the initial phase of the procedure. The certainty that the defendant will not be able to 'prove' their innocence is often mentioned by these operators and, at times, such discourse was directed directly at the offenders themselves. This discourse reveals, on the other hand, that the procedure takes on inquisitorial contours, given the impossibility of the accused providing evidence of their innocence. The proof of innocence, in this case, gives way to the truth constructed unilaterally by the prosecution, which suggests the presumption of guilt of the accused" (Almeida 2014, p. 113, free translation).

[329] "A strong argument against this movement was that a penalty could not be applied without a trial. However, it is responded that there would be no prejudice to the right of defence, as in the pre-trial agreement the suspect would be assisted by a lawyer" (Fernandes et al. 1999, p. 12, free translation).

[330] Azevedo (2000), p. 169; Almeida (2014), pp. 100–103.

with the accuser or for fear of the risks of the trial.[331] In this regard, **Vera de Almeida** concludes that "even professionals who advocate for the individual constitutional guarantees of the accused are contaminated with the negative representation of the criminal settlement, as an instrument of penalty".[332]

Furthermore, it is observed in the Small Claims Courts the strengthening of the accusing body, which, as previously stated (Sect. 4.1.5), takes on decision-making functions by determining the guilt of the accused and the contours of the punishment in the dynamics of negotiations.[333] As a result, the myth of equality of the parties becomes even more unacceptable and completely distances the necessary jurisdiction for the imposition of a criminal sanction in a Democratic Rule of Law, since, as described by **Vera de Almeida**, the presence of the judge at the hearing is exceptional and their ratifying act is an artificial and inoperative control.[334]

Finally, it is essential to empirically confirm that the possibility of negotiations between the actors of the legal-criminal field leads to a complete distortion of their primary functions, for, in pursuit of their private interests unrelated to the concrete case and due to their perverse relations of mutual cooperation, they encourage (or, rather, pressure and coerce) bargains for the early imposition of criminal sanctions based on the consented recognition of guilt of the accused (Sect. 4.1.2).[335] The description of the Small Claims Courts reality highlighted that what determines the action of legal operators is the pursuit of power,[336] guided by attention to their own

---

[331] Fullin (2011), pp. 92–95.

[332] Almeida (2014), p. 156.

[333] Fullin (2011), p. 117. According to Vera de Almeida (2014), p. 180, "the observation of the field has been showing that the application of this institute is developed in an isolated, exclusive and unlimited way by those who have the power to say when and if it will be applied and also who will be affected and in what way. This solitary operator of the criminal settlement is the prosecutor. Their power to define and classify the penal responses contained in the criminal settlement is a tautological power, insofar as - thanks to a knowledge (intimate and not universalised) that recognises even their own power -, their definitions will guide their decisions", (free translation).

[334] "[...] throughout the entire period of visiting the courts, it was not possible to find an example of a judicial decision rejecting the proposals offered by the prosecutors. As the ratifying sentences, in turn, practically transcribed the terms of these proposals, it is possible to affirm that from the beginning to the end of this procedure the defendants were unaware of the reasons and grounds that justified the punishments imposed" (Almeida 2014, p. 89, free translation).

[335] "However, even though they maintain distinctions, in all the courts the control of the time of the hearing emerges as an always present element, favouring curious alliances between certain legal actors. In addition to managerial purposes, these alliances reveal aspects of the meanings of punishment in informality, a question that will be highlighted later, but which requires, first and foremost, a clarification about the way in which, similar to a scenario, the actors and the rules of procedure of the preliminary hearings present themselves to the spectator" (Fullin 2011, p. 78, free translation).

[336] "Once again, the feeling remained that what dominates the actions of these "However, even though they maintain distinctions, in all the courts the control of the time of the hearing emerges as an always present element, favouring curious alliances between certain legal actors. In addition to managerial purposes, these alliances reveal aspects of the meanings of punishment in informality, a question that will be highlighted later, but which requires, first and foremost, a clarification about the way in which, similar to a scenario, the actors and the rules of procedure of the prelimi-

interests, which ends up highlighting a shared objective, as asserted by **Carmen Fullin**: "far from acting in opposing forces, legal counsel and prosecutor, intermediated by the judge, aim at the same objective: to shorten the time of the hearing without failing to obtain the acceptance of the criminal settlement, consensually seen in that circumstance as the best way out for everyone".[337]

Therefore, one may conclude that, although limited to less serious cases, the spaces for consensus introduced by Law 9.099/1995 result in violations of fundamental rights, amplifying distortions to the assumptions of criminal procedure. Thus, especially considering the typical circumstances of criminal justice (guided by selectivity and inequality in the implementation of State punitive power), any expansions of the negotiation mechanisms are extremely prone to aggravate these problems and, therefore, should be rejected in the Brazilian legal-criminal field. In this sense, the cited studies affirm that criminal settlement (and, thus, also the bargain in a broad sense) actually serve s to expand the incidence of State punitive power[338]; in other words, even in the current Brazilian scenario, negotiated justice is an instrument of penalisation by means of the total emptying of the right to trial in a proceeding with every guarantee.[339]

Regarding the non-prosecution agreement, included in the Brazilian Code of Criminal Procedure in 2019, empirical research suggests a trend of weakening judicial review. According to the legislation (art. 28-A, CPP), the ANPP must go through judicial ratification, at which point "the judge must verify its voluntariness, by hearing the person under investigation in the presence of their legal counsel, and its legality" (§ 4°), conducting, for this purpose, a public and oral hearing. Furthermore, "if the judge considers the conditions set out in the non-prosecution agreement to be inappropriate, insufficient or abusive, they shall return the case to the Public Prosecutor's Office for the proposal to be reformulated, with the consent of the accused and their counsel" (§ 5).

---

nary hearings present themselves to the spectator" (Fullin 2011, p. 78). operators is the dispute for the power to decide, for the power to apply the law, which resulted in different treatments, even when the criminal facts were identical, resulting in repeated offences to equality and legal security of the defendants" (Almeida 2014, p. 142, free translation).

[337] Fullin (2011), p. 96.

[338] "[...] despite Brazilian doctrine considering the criminal settlement as an agreement between the prosecutor and the defendant, in practice it ends up being recognised as an instrument of application of a prior punishment, even if it means the application of a lesser penalty than that which the judicial procedure may entail. That is, the criminal settlement, in these cases, corresponds to an instrument of penalisation" (Almeida 2014, p. 151). In a way similar: Fullin (2011), p. 154, free translation.

[339] "[...] the rejection of the criminal settlement was not understood by the operators as a right of the jurisdiction, as a possibility that opens up for the other party to offer their counterproposal, as occurs in a dialogic relationship. Thus, unlike the category that our theorists formulate, the criminal settlement must be imposed and accepted without any contestation and at any cost [...]" (Almeida 2014, p. 151, free translation).

Besides adopting fairly open terms, these provisions have been applied in practice in different ways.[340] For instance, there is data that already indicates the failure to hold a hearing to review the agreement, despite this being a legal requirement, and a certain weakness of review over voluntariness in judicial practice,[341] in addition to disparities between clauses established in the agreements.[342] Based on a study about the judge's understanding of the review to be done in the approval of the ANPP, "there is a trend towards weakening this review", which might be attributed, "especially, to the non-conduct of hearings, to the lack of concern in ensuring adequate information to guarantee the voluntariness of the person charged and to the insufficient review over the factual basis for the approval of the criminal settlement".[343] Furthermore, when a hearing is conducted, there is not an effective verification of voluntariness and the proper understanding of the person about the agreement.[344]

Therefore, the facts indicate that judicial review must be strengthened for the effective protection of the rights of those involved and for the legitimisation of negotiated justice in the Brazilian criminal procedure. For several reasons, an innocent person may accept a criminal agreement, or even, although guilty, consent to illegal, abusive or disproportionate conditions. The argument that, if there is abuse, the accused should refuse the agreement and defend themselves in the proceeding is reductionist, since, in this case, the person will be subject to the risk of an unjust conviction. Be it for rational or passionate reasons, there may be agreements with illegitimate clauses imposed by the prosecution, which must be subject to judicial review so as to verify voluntariness, effective legal counselling, the factual basis, and the proportionality of the agreement.

References

Albergaria PS (2007) Plea Bargaining. Aproximação à justiça negociada nos E.U.A. Almedina, Coimbra

Albrecht PA (2010) Criminologia. Uma fundamentação para o direito penal. Lumen Juris, Rio de Janeiro

Alkon C (2010) Plea bargaining as a legal transplant: a good idea for troubled criminal justice systems? Transnatl Law Contemp Probl 19:355–418

Almeida VR (2014) Transação penal e penas alternativas. Uma pesquisa empírica nos Juizados Especiais Criminais do Rio de Janeiro. Lumen Juris, Rio de Janeiro

Alschuler AW (1968) The prosecutor's role in plea bargaining. Univ Chic Law Rev 36:50–112

[340] National Council of Justice. *Strengthening paths for penal alternatives*: a national survey of the application of the non-prosecution agreement in Brazil. Available at: http://cnj.jus.br/wp-content/uploads/2023/09/lancamento-levantamento-anpp-1.pdf.

[341] Vasconcellos and Paz (2024).

[342] Santiago et al. (2024).

[343] Vasconcellos and Paz (2025).

[344] Vasconcellos and Paz (2024).

Alschuler AW (1975a) The defense attorney's role in plea bargaining. Yale Law J 84(6):1179–1314
Alschuler AW (1975b) The supreme court, the defense attorney, and the guilty plea. Univ Colo Law Rev 47:1–71
Alschuler AW (1976) The trial judge's role in plea bargaining, part I. Columbia Law Rev 76(7):1059–1154
Alschuler AW (1979) Plea bargaining and its history. Law Soc Rev 13:211–245
Alschuler AW (1981) The changing plea bargaining debate. Calif Law Rev 69:652–730
Alschuler AW (1983) Implementing the criminal defendant's right to trial: alternatives to the plea bargaining system. Univ Chicago Law Rev 50(3):931–1050
Alschuler AW (1986) Personal failure, institutional failure, and the sixth amendment. N Y Univ Rev Law Soc Change 14:149–156
Alschuler AW (2009) Plea bargaining and the death penalty. DePaul Law Rev 58:671–680
Andrés Ibañez P (1997) Por um ministério público dentro da legalidade. Rev Minist Publico Lisboa 18(70):9–41
Anitua GI (2005a) El juicio penal abreviado como una de las reformas penales de inspiración estadunidense que posibilitan la expansión punitiva. In: Maier JBJ, Bovino A (comps) El procedimiento abreviado. Del Puerto, Buenos Aires
Anitua GI (2005b) La importación de mecanismos consensuales del proceso estadounidense en las reformas procesales iberoamericanas. Rev Gen Der Procesal 6:1–23
Anitua GI (2010a) El principio de legalidad y el principio de oportunidad: interrogantes y aporías en los sistemas anglosajones y continentales. In: Anitua GI (ed) Ensayos sobre enjuiciamiento penal. Del Puerto, Buenos Aires
Anitua GI (2010b) En defensa del juicio. Comentarios sobre el juicio penal abreviado y el "arrepentido". In: Anitua GI (ed) Ensayos sobre enjuiciamiento penal. Del Puerto, Buenos Aires
Anziliero DL (2008) Descaminhos da informalização da justiça penal no Brasil: entusiasmo e crise nos Juizados Especiais Criminais. Dissertation, Pontifícia Universidade Católica do Rio Grande do Sul, Porto Alegre
Armenta Deu T (2012a) Lecciones de derecho procesal penal, 6th edn. Marcial Pons, Madrid
Armenta Deu T (2012b) Sistemas procesales penales. La justicia penal en Europa y América. Marcial Pons, Madrid
Azevedo RG (2000) Informalização da justiça e controle social. IBCCrim, São Paulo
Badaró GH (2019) Epistemologia judiciária e prova penal. RT, São Paulo
Barros MA (2013) A busca da verdade no processo penal. 4th ed. RT, São Paulo
Beck U (1998) La sociedad del riesgo. Hacia una nouva modernidad. Paidós, Barcelona
Bibas S (2003) Harmonizing substantive-criminal-law values and criminal procedure: the case of Alford and nolo contendere pleas. Cornell Law Rev 88(6):1–74
Bibas S (2004) Plea bargaining outside the shadow of trial. Harv Law Rev 117(8):2463–2547
Binder AM (2005) Legalidad y oportunidad. In: Baigún D et al (eds) Estudios sobre justicia penal: homenaje al profesor Julio B. J. Maier. Del Puerto, Buenos Aires
Bitencourt CR (1997) Juizados Especiais Criminais e alternativas à pena de prisão. Lei n. 9.099, de 26.9.95. 3 ed. Livraria do Advogado, Porto Alegre
Borges CMR (2013) Um olhar para além dos sistemas processuais penais. Rev Bras Ciênc Crim 104(21):147–171
Bottino T (2014) Habeas corpus nos tribunais superiores: pontos para reflexão e debate. Bol IBCCrim 262(22):2–4
Bourdieu P (1989) O poder simbólico. Bertrand, Rio de Janeiro
Bovino A (2005) Principios políticos del procedimiento penal. Del Puerto, Buenos Aires
Bowers J (2008) Punishing the innocent. Univ Penn Law Rev 156:1–55
Burns RP (2009) The death of the American trial. University of Chicago Press, Chicago
Campos MS (2010) Crime e Congresso Nacional. Uma análise da Política Criminal aprovada de 1989 a 2006. IBCCrim, São Paulo
Carvalho S (2010) Antimanual de criminologia, 3rd edn. Lumen Juris, Rio de Janeiro

Casara RRR (2011) O acordo para aplicação da pena: novas considerações acerca da verdade e do consenso no processo penal brasileiro. In: Coutinho JMM, Carvalho LGG (eds) O novo processo penal à luz da Constituição. Análise crítica do Projeto de Lei n. 156/2009, do Senado Federal, vol 2. Lumen Juris, Rio de Janeiro
Choukr FH (2002) Processo penal de emergência. Lumen Juris, Rio de Janeiro
Córdoba GE (2005) El juicio abreviado en el Código Procesal Penal de la Nación. In: Maier JBJ, Bovino A (comps) El procedimiento abreviado. Del Puerto, Buenos Aires
Costa EM (2001a) Princípio da oportunidade: muitos vícios, poucas virtudes. Rev Ministério Público Lisboa 22(85):37–49
Costa PBFM (2001b) Igualdade no direito processual penal brasileiro. RT, São Paulo
Coutinho JM (2001) Introdução aos princípios gerais do direito processual penal brasileiro. Rev Estudos Criminais 1:26–51
Coutinho JM (2002) Efetividade do processo penal e golpe de cena: um problema às reformas processuais no Brasil. Bol Fac Direito Univ Coimbra 78:687–697
D'Avila FB (2009) Ofensividade em Direito Penal. Escritos sobre a teoria do crime como ofensa a bens jurídicos. Livraria do Advogado, Porto Alegre
Dervan LE (2011a) Overcriminalization 2.0: the symbiotic relationship between plea bargaining and overcriminalization. J Law Econ Policy 7(4):645–655
Dervan LE (2011b) The surprising lessons from plea bargaining in the shadow of terror. Ga State Univ Law Rev 27(2):239–298
Dervan LE, Edkins V (2012) The innocent defendant's dilemma: an innovative empirical study of plea bargaining's innocence problem. J Crim Law Criminol 103(1):1–48
Díaz Cantón F (2005) Juicio abreviado vs. Estado de derecho. In: Maier JBJ, Bovino A (eds) El procedimiento abreviado. Del Puerto, Buenos Aires
Dias JF, Andrade MC (1987) Criminologia: o homem delinquente e a sociedade criminógena. Ed Coimbra, Coimbra
Diego Díez LA d (1999) Justicia criminal consensuada. Algunos modelos del derecho comparado en los EE. UU., Italia y Portugal. Tirant lo Blanch, Valencia
Dieter MS (2013) Política criminal atuarial. A criminologia do fim da história. Revan, Rio de Janeiro
Duarte HG, Marques LAM (2008) Justiça consensual e tutela dos direitos individuais. PHRONESIS: Revista do Curso de Direito da FEAD, 4:65–74
Easterbrook FH (1983) Criminal procedure as a market system. J Leg Stud 12:289–332
Eymerich N (1993) Manual dos inquisidores. Fundação Universidade de Brasília, Brasília
Fairen Guillen V (1970) La disponibilidad del derecho a la defensa en el sistema procesal acusatorio español (La conformidad del acusado). Rev Fac Derecho Mex 77–78:125–164
Feeley MM (1992) The process is the punishment. Handling cases in a lower criminal court. Russell Sage, New York
Feeley MM (1997) Legal complexity and the transformation of the criminal process: the origins of plea bargaining. Isr Law Rev 31:183–222
Fernandes AS (2005) Teoria geral do procedimento e o procedimento no processo penal. RT, São Paulo
Fernandes AS (2008) Reflexões sobre as noções de eficiência e de garantismo no processo penal. In: Fernandes AS, Almeida JRG, Moraes MZ (eds) Sigilo no processo penal. Eficiência e garantismo. Ed RT, São Paulo
Fernandes AS, Penteado JC, Barros MA (1999) Reflexos da Lei dos Juizados Especiais na justiça criminal paulista. Rev Forense 95(347):11–28
Ferrajoli L (2014) Direito e razão. Teoria do garantismo penal, 4th edn. RT, São Paulo
Ferreira MAG (2013) A presunção da inocência e a construção da verdade. Contrastes e confrontos em perspectiva comparada (Brasil e Canadá). Lumen Juris, Rio de Janeiro
Fine RA (1987) Plea bargaining: an unnecessary evil. Marquette Law Rev 70(4):615–632
Finkelstein MO (1975) A statistical analysis of guilty plea practices in the federal courts. Harv Law Rev 89(2):293–315

Fisher G (2003) Plea bargaining's triumph. A history of plea bargaining in America. Stanford University Press, Stanford
Fullin CS (2011) Quando o negócio é punir: uma análise etnográfica dos Juizados Especiais Criminais e suas sanções. Tese (Doutorado em Antropologia), Faculdade de Filosofia, Letras e Ciências Humanas, Universidade de São Paulo, São Paulo
Galanter M (2004) The vanishing trial: an examination of trial and related matters in federal and states courts. J Empir Legal Stud 1(3):459–570
Galanter M (2006) A world without trials? J Disp Resol 2006(1):7–33
Galícia CR (2013) Direitos processuais penais fundamentais: um jogo de conveniência? Bol IBRASPP 3(5):16–18
Garapon A, Papadopoulos I (2008) Julgar nos Estados Unidos e na França: cultura jurídica francesa e common law em uma perspectiva comparada. Lumen Juris, Rio de Janeiro
Garland D (2001) Culture of control. Crime and social order in contemporary society. University of Chicago Press, Chicago
Giacomolli NJ (2006a) Legalidade, oportunidade e consenso no processo penal na perspectiva das garantias constitucionais. Livraria do Advogado, Porto Alegre
Giacomolli NJ (2006b) O devido processo penal. Abordagem conforme a Constituição Federal e o Pacto de São José da Costa Rica. Atlas, São Paulo
Gifford DG (1983) Meaningful reform of plea bargaining: the control of prosecutorial discretion. Univ Ill Law Rev 1983(1):37–98
Grinover AP, Fernandes AS, Gomes Filho AM, Gomes LF (2005) Juizados Especiais Criminais. Comentários à Lei 9.099, de 26.09.1995. 5 ed. RT, São Paulo
Glassner B (2009) The culture of fear. Basic Books, Nova Iorque
Gloeckner RJ (2009) Risco e processo penal. Uma análise a partir dos direitos fundamentais do acusado. JusPodivm, Salvador
Gloeckner RJ (2013) Nulidades no processo penal. Introdução principiológica à teoria do ato processual irregular. JusPodivm, Salvador
Gloeckner RJ, Amaral AJ (2013) Criminologia e(m) crítica. Champagnat, Curitiba
Gomes LF (2012) Introdução às bases criminológicas da Lei 9.099/95 – Lei dos Juizados Especiais Criminais. In: García-Pablos de Molina A, Gomes LF (coords) Criminologia, 8th edn. Ed. RT, São Paulo
Guedes GP (2014) O direito a não produzir prova contra si mesmo: aproximações entre os cases da Corte Interamericana de Direitos Humanos e do Supremo Tribunal Federal. Pontifícia Universidade Católica do Rio Grande do Sul, Porto Alegre, Dissertação
Hessick A, Saujani R (2002) Plea bargaining and convicting the innocent: the role of the prosecutor, the defense counsel, and the judge. Brigham Young Univ J Public Law 16:189–242
Heumann M (1981) Plea bargaining. The experiences of prosecutors, judges, and defense attorneys. The University of Chicago Press, Chicago
Husak D (2008) Overcriminalization. The limites of the criminal law. Oxford University Press, Oxford
Jakobs G (2010) Direito penal do cidadão e direito penal do inimigo. In: Callegari A, Giacomolli N (org.) Direito penal do inimigo. Livraria do Advogado, Porto Alegre
Kant de Lima R, Amorim MS, Burgos MB (2003) A administração da violência cotidiana no Brasil: a experiência dos Juizados Especiais Criminais. In: Amorim MS, Kant de Lima R, Burgos MB (org.) Juizados Especiais Criminais, sistema judicial e sociedade no Brasil. Ensaios interdisciplinares. Intertexto, Niterói
Karam ML (2004) Juizados Especiais Criminais. A concretização antecipada do poder de punir. RT, São Paulo
Karam ML (2009) Recuperar o desejo da liberdade e conter o poder punitivo. Lumen Juris, Rio de Janeiro
Khaled JRSH (2013) A busca da verdade no processo penal: para além da ambição inquisitorial. Atlas, São Paulo
Langbein JH (1978) Torture and plea bargaining. Univ Chicago Law Rev 46(1):3–22

Langbein JH (1992) On the myth of written constitutions: the disappearance of criminal jury trial. Harv J Law Public Policy 15(1):119–127

Langer M (2005) La dicotomía acusatorio-inquisitivo y la importación de mecanismos procesales de la tradición jurídica anglosajona. Algunas reflexiones a partir del procedimiento abreviado. In: Maier JBJ, Bovino A (eds) El procedimiento abreviado. Del Puerto, Buenos Aires

Leite RV (2013) Justiça consensual e efetividade do processo penal. Del Rey, Belo Horizonte

Lippke RL (2011) The ethics of plea bargaining. Oxford University Press, Oxford

Lopes A Jr (2002) Justiça negociada: utilitarismo processual e eficiência antigarantista. In: Carvalho S, Wunderlich A (eds) Diálogos sobre a Justiça Dialogal. Teses e antíteses sobre os processos de informalização e privatização da Justiça Penal. Lumen Juris, Rio de Janeiro

Lopes JA (2012) Direito processual penal, 9th edn. Saraiva, São Paulo

Lynch G (2012) Frye and Lafler: no big deal. Yale Law J Online 122:39–43

Machado MRA (2005) Sociedade do risco e direito penal. Uma avaliação das novas tendências político-criminais. IBCCrim

Malan DR (2006) Processo penal do inimigo. Rev Bras Ciênc Crim 59:223–259. São Paulo, mar.-abr

Malan DR (2010) Sobre a condenação sem julgamento prevista no projeto de reforma do CPP (PLS n° 156/09). Bol IBCCrim 17(207):2–3, São Paulo, fev

Martínez S (1999) Confesión en el juicio abreviado. Cuad Doctr Jurispr Penal 5(9B):373–398. Buenos Aires, out

Martins RC (2011) O ponto cego do direito. The brazilian lessons, 2nd edn. Lumen Juris, Rio de Janeiro

Martins Pinto F (2012) Introdução crítica ao processo penal. Del Rey, Belo Horizonte

Martins RC (2013) A hora dos cadáveres adiados. Corrupção, expectativa e processo penal. Atlas, São Paulo

McCoy C (2005) Plea bargaining as coercion: the trial penalty and plea bargaining reform. Crim Law Q 50:1–41

Miranda ALV (2004) Transação penal, controle social e globalização. Sage, Porto Alegre

Moraes MZ (2010) Presunção de inocência no processo penal brasileiro: análise de sua estrutura normativa para a elaboração legislativa e para a decisão judicial. Lumen Juris, Rio de Janeiro

Moura MTA (2001) Justa causa para a ação penal: doutrina e jurisprudência. RT, São Paulo

Naves LF (1995) Plea bargaining: a transação penal nos Estados Unidos da América. Rev Fund Esc Super Minist Publico Dist Fed Territ 5(3):219–260. Brasília

Paladines JV (2013) Fábrica flagrancia: la gestión procesal de la detención en Ecuador. In: Machado BA (coord.) Justiça criminal e democracia. Marcial Pons, São Paulo

Pastana DR (2003) Cultura do medo. IBCCrim, São Paulo

Pinheiro FA (2007) Juizado Especial Criminal: do modelo consensual à radicalização da função simbólica do sistema penal. Dissertação (Mestrado em Direito), Faculdade de Direito, Universidade Federal de Santa Catarina, Florianópolis

Pinheiro FA (2010) Juizado Especial Criminal: do discurso jurídico penal à operacionalidade do sistema penal. Sistema Penal & Violência, v. 2, n. 2, p. 90-103, Porto Alegre, jul.-dez.

Pizzi WT, Montagna M (2004) The battle to establish an adversarial trial system in Italy. Mich J Int Law 25:429–466

Prado G (2006a) Da delação premiada: aspectos de direito processual. Boletim IBCCrim 159:10–12. São Paulo, fev

Prado G (2006b) Sistema acusatório. A conformidade constitucional das leis processuais penais, 4th edn. Lumen Juris, São Paulo

Prado G (2006c) Transação penal. 2nd ed. Lumen Juris, Rio de Janeiro

Prado G (2012) Campo jurídico e capital científico: o acordo sobre a pena e o modelo acusatório no Brasil – a transformação de um conceito. In: Prado G, Martins RC, Carvalho LGG (eds) Decisão judicial. A cultura jurídica brasileira na transição para a democracia. Marcial Pons, São Paulo

Queijo ME (2012) O direito de não produzir prova contra si mesmo, 2nd edn. Saraiva, São Paulo

Rauxloh RE (2011) Formalization of plea bargaining in Germany: will the new legislation be able to square the circle? Fordham Int Law J 34(2):296–331
Redlich A, Summers A, Hoover S (2010) Self-reported false confessions and false guilty pleas among offenders with mental illness. Law Hum Behav 34:79–90
Rodrigues AM (1998) A celeridade no processo penal: uma visão de direito comparado. Rev Port Cienc Crim 8(2):233–250
Rodríguez García N (1996) A justiça penal e as formas de transação no direito norte-americano: repercussões. Rev Bras Ciênc Crim, n. 13, ano 4, p. 79–92
Rodríguez García N (1997) La justicia penal negociada. Experiencias de derecho comparado. Ediciones Universidad de Salamanca, Salamanca
Rodríguez JL (2005) Procedimiento abreviado en Costa Rica, presunción de inocencia y derecho de abstención de declarar. In: Maier JBJ, Bovino A (eds) El procedimiento abreviado. Del Puerto, Buenos Aires
Rosa AM (2010) Processo penal eficiente? Não, obrigado. In: Rosa AM, Carvalho TF (eds) Processo penal eficiente & ética da vingança. Lumen Juris, Rio de Janeiro
Rosa AM (2014) Guia compacto do processo penal conforme a teoria dos jogos, 2nd edn. Lumen Juris, Rio de Janeiro
Rosa AM, Amaral AJ (2014) Cultura da punição. A ostentação do horror. Lumen Juris, Rio de Janeiro
Rosa AM, Silveira Filho SL (2009) Para um processo penal democrático. Crítica à metástase do sistema de controle social. Lumen Juris, Rio de Janeiro
Saad M (2004) O Direito de Defesa no Inquérito Policial. RT, São Paulo
Saavedra GA (2010) Reificação vs. dignidade. In: Teixeira A, Oliveira E (eds) Correntes contemporâneas do pensamento jurídico. Manole, Barueri
Saavedra GA, Vasconcellos VG (2011) Expansão do Direito Penal e relativização dos fundamentos do Direito Penal. Revista de Estudos Criminais, São Paulo, no 42, pp 123–142
Sánchez-Vera Gómez-Trelles J (2012) Variaciones sobre la presunción de inocencia. Análisis funcional desde el derecho penal. Marcial Pons, Madrid
Santos BMM (2015) Defesa Social—uma visão crítica. Estúdio, São Paulo
Santiago NA, Soares Filho S, Rocha Leitão I (2024) Variações na aplicação dos acordos de não persecução penal em Maracanaú/CE: um estudo de caso sobre a dosimetria da pena de prestação pecuniária. Rev Bras Dir Proc Penal 10:3.
Santos SS (2002) Juizados Especiais Criminais: funções instrumentais e simbólicas. Dissertação, Faculdade de Direito, Universidade Federal de Santa Catarina, Florianópolis
Scalcon RL (2013) Ilícito e Pena. Modelos opostos de fundamentação do direito penal contemporâneo. GZ, Rio de Janeiro
Schünemann B (2004) Cuestiones básicas de la estructura y reforma del procedimiento penal bajo una perspectiva global. Rev Derecho Penal Criminol 25(76):175–197
Schünemann B (2013a) Audiência de instrução e julgamento: modelo inquisitorial ou adversarial? Sobre a estrutura fundamental do processo penal no 3.° milênio. In: Schünemann B, Greco L (eds) Estudos de direito penal, direito processual penal e filosofia do direito. Marcial Pons, São Paulo
Schünemann B (2013b) Um olhar crítico ao modelo processual penal norte-americano. In: Schünemann B, Greco L (eds) Estudos de direito penal, direito processual penal e filosofia do direito. Marcial Pons, São Paulo
Shecaira SS (2002) Controle social punitivo e a experiência brasileira: uma visão crítica da Lei n. 9.099/95. In: Choukr FH, Ambos K (eds) Processo penal e Estado de Direito. Edicamp, Campinas
Silva Sánchez JM (2011) La expansión del derecho penal, 3rd edn. Edisofer, Madrid
Simon J (2007) Governing through crime. How the war on crime transformed American democracy and created a culture of fear. Oxford University Press, Oxford

Tedesco IF (2005) Algunas precisiones en torno al juicio abreviado y al privilegio contra la autoincriminación. In: Maier JBJ, Bovino A (eds) El procedimiento abreviado. Del Puerto, Buenos Aires
Teixeira CA (2000) Princípio da oportunidade. Manifestações em sede processual penal
Tulkens F (2005) Justiça negociada. In: Delmas-Marty M (org) Processos penais da Europa. Lumen Juris, Rio de Janeiro
Turner JI (2009) Plea barganing across borders. Aspen, New York
Vasconcellos VG (2015) Barganha no processo penal e o autoritarismo consensual nos sistemas processuais: a justiça negocial entre a patologização do acusatório e o contragolpe inquisitivo. Rev Trib 953:261–279
Vasconcellos VG, Paz CM (2024) O controle judicial da voluntariedade para homologação do acordo de não persecução penal: pesquisa empírica nas varas criminais de Goiânia/GO. Rev Est Emp Dir 11
Vasconcellos VG, Paz CM (2025) O controle judicial sobre o acordo de não persecução penal: pesquisa empírica sobre a visão de juízes e juízas criminais de Goiânia/GO em 2024 (prelo)
Vegezzi S (2005) Juicio abreviado: su recepción en el orden jurídico argentino. In: Maier JBJ, Bovino A (eds) El procedimiento abreviado. Del Puerto, Buenos Aires
Vieira RS (2014) Paridade de Armas no Processo Penal. Gaz Jurid, Brasília
Wacquant L (2007) Punir os pobres. A nova gestão da miséria nos Estados Unidos, 3rd edn. Revan, Rio de Janeiro
Wacquant L (2011) As prisões da miséria, 2nd edn. Zahar, Rio de Janeiro
Weigend T (2021) Exclusion without trial? Exclusion of evidence and abbreviated procedures. Rev Bras Direito Processual Penal 7(1):247
Wermuth MAD (2011) Medo e direito penal. Reflexos da expansão punitiva na realidade brasileira. Livraria do Advogado, Porto Alegre

Chapter 5
Final Considerations

In light of the scenario outlined based on the critical analysis of the trends toward expanding spaces for consensus within Brazilian criminal procedure, one can state, as a *general conclusion*, that the introduction of bargaining mechanisms in a generalised and uncontrolled manner, authorising the imposition of sanctions without respect for due process rules, should be criticised and rejected within criminal justice, as it increases the risk of unjust penalties lacking the proper verification of facts, which in turn leads to inevitable violations of the premises of criminal procedure by completely distorting its essence: being an instrument of limitation of the State's punitive power.

In a specific manner, considerations regarding the following issues were proposed, and they will be succinctly outlined below: (1) what are the characteristics of negotiated justice and, specifically, of bargaining?; (2) What is its relationship with trends towards simplification and procedural diversification, such as the provision of the principle of opportunity?; (3) what are the consequences of the expansion of spaces for consensus to the premises of democratic criminal procedure?; (4) are agreements between prosecution and defence for the imposition of punitive sanctions based on guilty pleas in exchange for benefits legitimate options for criminal justice in a Democratic Rule of Law?

1 Initially, *negotiated consensual criminal justice* was defined as a model guided by the acceptance (consensus) by both parties—prosecution and defence—of a procedural collaboration agreement with the accused withdrawing from their position of resistance, usually imposing early termination, abbreviation, complete or partial suppression of the proceeding, aiming fundamentally, to facilitate the imposition of a punitive sanction with some percentage of reduction, which characterises the benefit to the accused due to the waiver of the due course of the criminal proceeding

V. G. de. Vasconcellos, *Criminal Agreements and Negotiated Justice*,
https://doi.org/10.1007/978-3-032-16962-4_5

with all the guarantees inherent to it (Sect. 2.1.3).[1] Thus, the *bargain* is a type of consensual justice, a procedural instrument that results in the waiver of the defence through the acceptance (and possible collaboration) of the defendant to the accusation, usually presupposing a confession in exchange for some benefit (usually, mitigation of sentence), negotiated and agreed between the parties or only expected by the accused (Sect. 2.2.1). Thus, its essential elements are the waiver of the defence (which distorts the accused's typical posture of resistance and contestation), the imposition of an anticipated punishment, and the expectation of the accused of receiving some benefit for such consent or avoiding punishment by exercising their rights.

1.1 Based on the example of the US plea bargaining, which serves as the primary reference in terms of negotiated criminal justice, the three admissibility requirements constructed in books and jurisprudentially were pointed out (Sect. 2.2.3): in summary, these are (a) voluntariness, indicating that the agreement is not induced by real or threatened physical violence or by mental coercion that vitiates the will of the accused; (b) intelligence or information, that is, the accused must be aware of their situation before the charges made and the facts described by the accuser, as well as the consequences of their act of accepting the bargain, both in relation to the rights they waive and the punishments that will be imposed on them, in addition to the collateral effects; and, (c) adequacy, that is, the need for a factual basis that supports the recognition of guilt by the accused.

1.2 However, the premises underpinning the legitimacy of negotiated justice—asserting that such a mechanism is an agreement between parties in an equal situation, carried out voluntarily and with full knowledge—are fragile, since, as shown: (a) the equality between the parties is illusory, for, in addition to the inherent disparity in the criminal proceeding, in a bargaining system there is the undue usurpation of decision-making functions by the prosecutor, exceeding their powers and their possibilities of coercion to the accused through threats of more severe criminal sanctions in case of refusal to the agreement (Sect. 4.1.5); (b) the accused's freedom to carry out the bargain or exercise the right to trial is superficial, as the coercibility of the proposal is inherent to its system, with the potential for convictions of innocent people and unjust sanctions (items Sects. 4.1.3 and 4.1.6); and, (c) the assistance by a legal counsel, who would inform the accused of their procedural situation and the consequences of the bargain (and which, thus, would legitimise the bargaining model), becomes potentially ineffective considering the distortion of the relationship between client and legal counsel in a scenario of negotiations and bureaucratic pressures towards the swift execution of agreements for the imposition of consented criminal sanctions (Sect. 4.1.2).

[1] The references pointed out in parentheses refer to the chapters and topics developed earlier in the work, which analyse in depth the conclusions here condensed, and, therefore, the reader is referred for further grounds.

1.3 The justifications pointed out in support of agreements within criminal procedure, typically associated with the reasons for their emergence, are primarily founded on a supposed practical necessity, due to the overload of criminal justice by the increasing quantity and complexity of the cases under judgement (Sect. 2.2.2). However, the advent of this mechanism is not directly related to the growth of procedural demand, since its use is also generalised in jurisdictions with a moderate workload. Therefore, one can conclude that the bargain originated and spread from the actions of that criminal justice actors, due to the full adherence to their personal conveniences, which, undoubtedly, deviate from the agenda of legitimate interests of criminal justice in a Democratic Rule of Law (Sect. 4.1.2).

1.4 Negotiated justice is currently articulated within the Brazilian legal-criminal field through the mechanisms of criminal settlement and of the conditional suspension of the criminal prosecution—specifically within the Small Claims Courts, regulated by Law 9.099/1995—of the turn state's evidence, which, although provided for in various statutes, had its procedural aspects defined by Law 12.850/2013, and of the non-prosecution agreement (NPA). The former are mechanisms of restricted applicability to minor offences (characterised, respectively, with a maximum abstract penalty of up to 2 years and a minimum equal to or less than 1 year), which, even though euphemistically treated by part of legal literature as non-punitive alternatives, represent the anticipated materialisation of penal power based on the accused's waiver of defence (Sect. 3.1). On the other hand, the turn state's evidence (or, in other words, cooperation agreement) which is of growing importance within the Brazilian scenario, represents a mechanism essentially built on the incentive to the accused's confession with the expectation of benefit/reward to their procedural condition, usually from the reduction of their future punishment, aiming at facilitating the State's persecutory activity, distinguishing itself from bargain due to the inherent incrimination of third parties (Sect. 3.2). The NPA was included in the Criminal Procedure Code by Law 13.964/19, significantly expanding the scope of negotiations for medium-severity offences, but still in a system similar to Law 9.099/95, i.e., without the possibility of imprisonment and the continuation of the proceeding in the event of non-compliance (Sect. 3.3).

1.5 The expansion trends of spaces for consensus in Brazilian criminal procedure are exposed by legislative reform projects (PLS 156/09 - PL 8.045/10 and 236/12, respectively, new Codes of Criminal Procedure and Penal), which present provisions that expand the possibilities of agreements between prosecution and defence for obtaining a guilty plea. Both proposals show deficiencies in the regulations of the said provisions: the former proposes a "fast track" for crimes with a maximum penalty of up to eight years, and the latter provides for the "bargain" mechanism, without any limitation by the severity of the offence. Given this scenario, improvements to such regulations were suggested in an attempt to reduce damage. Still, the opposition to these changes was maintained, which supported the rejection of the propositions (Sect. 3.4).

2 Negotiation mechanisms permeate a broad international trend in criminal matters towards procedural acceleration and diversification, which aims to speed up the resolution of cases or the introduction of alternative options to the need to carry out the ordinary proceeding concerning all the rules of due process. In this sense, the scenario of foreign legal systems points to a strong inclination towards the provision of exceptions to the principle of compulsoriness of public criminal action, from the existence of spaces for opportunity. Thus, "bargain" was defined as an expression of consensual justice, which takes place through the non-promotion or the non-full maintenance of the State's claim, since there is a consented reduction of punishment; i.e., this mechanism is used with the provision of opportunity spaces for the public prosecutor (Sects. 2.1.3 and 2.2.1).

2.1 After unveiling of the conceptual imprecision of the definitions widely used by legal scholars concerning the principles of (procedural) legality, compulsoriness and opportunity, new meanings were proposed, aiming to enable an effective critical debate. To this end, the dysfunctionality of the term "legality" was unveiled, even when defined as "procedural legality", as its meaning is inevitably attached to the idea of substantive law of the need for regulation by law (Sect. 2.1.1). Thus, the terms "compulsoriness" and "non-compulsoriness/opportunity" are suggested, which can be implemented in a scenario of respect for legality or of broad discretion. Given the above, one can define: (a) *principle of legality* as the obligation that guides the stance and decisions of State actors of criminal justice and, therefore, from the legal provisions, the impositions and limitations provided for in the law for their acting; (b) *compulsoriness of public criminal action* determines the prosecution of all facts of which public authorities become aware and that are classified as punishable acts according to the current legal system, without the possibility of exemption from this duty by utilitarian criterion or related to the minor severity of the criminal act, even if provided for by law; and, (c) *opportunity (or non compulsoriness)* authorises the non-filing of the indictment or the suspension of the criminal prosecution according to the option of the State prosecutor authority (usually with the consent of the defence) based on utilitarian, criminal-political, economic criteria etc., which can be provided for in law, in a scenario of legality, or not, in a panorama of discretion (Sect. 2.1.2).

3 In assessing the legitimacy of the expansion trends towards the spaces for consensus, it is important to note that the bargain and the negotiation mechanisms in a broad sense inevitably lead to violations of the rules of due criminal procedure as a requirement for a criminal conviction, since they hinder the exercise of defence, distort the roles of the actors in the legal-criminal field, exponentially increase the likelihood of convictions of innocents, result in illegitimate punishments for the exercise of the right to a lawsuit, distort the presumption of innocence and the adversary proceeding, among other criticisms (Sect. 4.1). Furthermore, as exposed, their justifications present questionable legitimacy in justifying a supposed systemic need for negotiations between prosecution and defence, which, in fact, hides a symbiotic functional use that allows the undue expansion of State control through punitive power in a scenario of expansion of Criminal Law (Sect. 4.1.1).

3.1 Based on six critical topics (Chap. 4), the foundation was laid for the conclusion that the expansion of spaces for consensus, through mechanisms similar to bargaining, leads to violations of the premises of criminal procedure and, therefore, shall be avoided: (a) *Expansion of Criminal Law and the obstacle of due process*, in which the procedural commodification caused by the authorisation of agreements between the parties and the consequent qualification of fundamental guarantees, both phenomena intrinsically related to the use of criminal procedure as a swift means of anticipated implementation of punitive power in response to the demands of an uncontrolled expansion of State criminal intervention; (b) *Bargains, relations and concessions,* in which the distortion of the roles of the actors in the criminal system was presented due to the primacy of their personal interests based on the power of bargaining; (c) *The issue of the innocent individual and the coercibility of the proposal,* which clarified the inherent pressure to the possibility of bargaining, which, as shown by the cited empirical research, results in the confession of innocents for fear of more severe punishments in case they exercise their right to trial; (d) *The authoritarian procedural setback,* in which a violation of fundamental procedural precepts was demonstrated, such as the return to the tariffed system of evidence with primacy of confession and the consequent integral obstruction of the exercise of defence and right to be heard; (e) *The imbalance in the scales of procedural actors*—in which one of the fundamental premises of the bargain, the equality between the negotiating parties—was weakened, in addition to exposing the undue usurpation of decision-making functions by the prosecution due to their pivotal role in determining the guilt and penalty of the accused; and, (f) *The disappearance of the trial and of the defence*, in which the possibility of renouncing the right to defence and the supposed autonomy of will for the implementation of the pact was put into question, asserting that the bargain goes beyond the denial of defence, being characterised as a *non- proceeding.*

3.2 Due to its power of intimidation, fundamentally determined by the aggravation of punishment in the event of refusal to the agreement, bargaining leads to an exponential increase in the risk of conviction of innocents and of unfair sanctions, as shown in the empirical studies cited. Thus, the premise that legitimises the justification of consensual mechanisms by the majority of its advocates and that founded the decisions of the US Supreme Court for the constitutionality of the plea bargaining is left without foundation: negotiation mechanisms are not applied only to those accused who would be convicted anyway in any eventual full trial, that is, the problem of the innocent individual is not exceptional, but perennial in the power relations that involve negotiations in criminal justice (items Sects. 4.1.3 and 4.1.6). In this sense, the empirical research carried out in the Small Claims Courts and regarding the non-prosecution agreement described exposes that the practical implementation of the negotiation mechanisms in Brazil deeply increases the risk of violations of fundamental rights (item Sect. 4.2).

4 Given the above, one concludes that the generalisation of agreements between prosecution and defence for the imposition of criminal sanction from the recognition of guilt in exchange for benefits is not an appropriate and legitimate option for the criminal justice of a Democratic Rule of Law. Therefore, the expansion of negotiated justice should be criticised, in order to avoid generalisation and lack of effective control over criminal negotiations. Suppose agreements are included in procedural systems. In that case the regulation should be limited, so that the proceeding should be kept as the rule for the imposition of criminal sanctions. In this context, the following minimum parameters should be adopted:

4.1 the strengthening of the exercise of the right to defence, especially through effective assistance by a technical defender, full access to case files, and eventual consolidation of defence investigation mechanisms, considering that the State's response to the case shall essentially be based on what is produced during the pre-procedural stage;

4.2 the limitation to the discretion of the prosecuting body in negotiations (concerning the suitability and conditions), through criteria established by legislation and in the Public Ministry's own regulations, in addition to the strengthening of internal ministerial control for review and standardisation;

4.3 respect for strict legality in defining the agreed clauses, that is, they should only be admitted if authorised by law and in accordance with constitutional and conventional dictates;

4.4 the consolidation of effective judicial review in the agreement approval stage, particularly concerning the necessary factual-evidentiary basis and any abusive clauses;

4.5 the protection of the right against self-incrimination to delineate the boundaries of utilising confession in the event of termination or when sharing information with other cases;

4.6 attention to due process, to the right to be heard, and to transparency in consolidating the negotiation procedure in all its stages, both in negotiations and in any eventual termination.

The manufacturer's authorised representative in the EU is Springer Nature Customer Service Centre GmbH, Europaplatz 3, 69115 Heidelberg, Germany. If you have any concerns regarding our products, please contact ProductSafety@springernature.com

Printed and bound by CPI Group (UK) Ltd, Croydon, CR0 4YY
05/10/2026
02228046-0003